OCR DESIGN & TECHNOLOGY·FOR·GCSE

Official Publisher Partnership

FOOD TECHNOLOGY

BARBARA DINICOLI

MERYL SIMPSON

VAL FEHNERS

EDITOR: BOB WHITE

HODDER
EDUCATION
AN HACHETTE UK COMPANY

Orders: please contact Bookpoint Ltd, 130 Milton Park, Abingdon, Oxon
OX14 4SB. Telephone: +44 (0)1235 827720. Fax: +44 (0)1235 400454.
Lines are open from 9.00am to 5.00pm, Monday to Saturday, with a 24-
hour message-answering service. You can also order through our website
www.hoddereducation.co.uk

If you have any comments to make about this, or any of our other titles,
please send them to educationenquiries@hodder.co.uk

British Library Cataloguing in Publication Data
A catalogue record for this title is available from the British Library

ISBN: 978 0 340 981 979

First Edition Published 2009
Impression number   10 9 8 7 6 5 4 3 2
Year   2012 2011 2010 2009

Copyright © 2009 Barbara DiNicoli, Meryl Simpson and Val Fehners

Hachette UK's policy is to use papers that are natural, renewable and
recyclable products and made from wood grown in sustainable forests.
The logging and manufacturing processes are expected to conform to the
environmental regulations of the country of origin.

Cover photo © Thinkstock/Corbis
Typeset by Fakenham Photosetting Ltd, Fakenham, Norfolk
Printed in Italy for Hodder Education, an Hachette UK Company, 338 Euston
Road, London NW1 3BH

CONTENTS

ACKNOWLEDGEMENTS

The authors would like to thank the following: Nisbets Next Day Catering Equipment; GCSE students at the Dronfield Henry Fanshawe school; Abel and Co for the organic vegetable box; Robert Latimer of Latimer's Shellfish delicatessen, Whiburn; St Mary's RC High School Technology Department, Chesterfield; Alice Brashaw and Marc Boardman of St Mary's High School, Chesterfiled; Sheff's Special; The Simpson family for photographs; Brian Simpson for his support and patience; Katherine Swords for help with photography; Samantha Johnson, Rebecca Jagger, Lauar Kelly, Nicole Radley, Emma-Jane Heaton, David Mitchell, Sarah Bierton and Natalie Bradwell for providing examples of their work; Judith Price and Stuart Thompson at the Technology Department of Dronfield Henry Fanshawe school; Paul DiNicoli for his support and Philippa DiNicoli for her help with ICT work.

The authors and publishers would like to thank the following for use of photographs and illustrations in this volume:

Figure 1.1 © Ekaterina Monakhova/iStockphoto.com; Figure 1.7 © Gregor Lajh/iStockphoto.co; Figure 2.2 © digitalskillet/iStockphoto.com; Figure 2.13 originally published in Delia Clarke and Betty Herbert; *Food Facts* (Nelson Thornes; 1986) and reproduced by kind permission of the author; Figure 2.15 © Phil Date/ iStockphoto.com; Figure 2.16 © Crown copyright material is reproduced with the permission of the Controller of HMSO and Queen's Printer for Scotland; Figure 2.19 Maximilian Stock Ltd/Photolibrary Group; Figure 2.21 © Majoros Laszlo/ iStockphoto.com; Figure 2.22 www.purestockX.com; Figure 2.27 © Claudia Dewald/iStockphoto.com; Figure 2.32 ©Stockbyte/Photolibrary.com; Figure 2.33 © iofoto/iStockphoto.com; Figure 2.34 Digital Vision; Figure 2.37 Food Collection; Figure 2.38 © Tomas Bercic/iStockphoto.com; Figure 2.42 © The Fairtrade Foundation; Figure 2.43 printed with kind permission of Traidcraft; Figure 2.44 printed with kind permission of Traidcraft; Figure 2.45 © The Soil Association; Figure 2.47 © Ferran Traite/iStockphoto.com; Figure 2.49 © Carme Balcells/ iStockphoto.com; Figure 2.50 © László Rákoskerti/iStockphoto.com; Figure 2.51 Courtesy of Coeliac UK; Figure 2.52 © diego cervo/iStockphoto.com; Figure 2.53 © Tova Teitelbaum/iStockphoto.com; Figure 2.55 © Joe Biafore/iStockphoto.com; Figure 2.57 © Mikhail Kokhanchikov/iStockphoto.com; Figure 2.59 © Tom Marvin/iStockphoto.com; Figure 3.5 © MP – Fotolia.com; Figure 3.9 © Jack Puccio/iStockphoto.com; photos in Table 3.3 (from left to right) © Claudia Hung/iStockphoto.com, © purplevine – Fotolia.com, © muddy – Fotolia.com; Figure 3.15 © Igor Dutina/iStockphoto.com; Figure 4.2 © JMD – Fotolia.com; Figure 4.3a © Jovan Nikolic/iStockphoto.com; Figure 4.3b Ingram; photos in Table 5.1 (from left to right) © Kelpfish – Fotolia.com, Ingram, © Steve Lovegrove – Fotolia.com; Figure 5.1 © Studioshots/Alamy, Figure 5.4 © Jason

Lugo/iStockphoto.com; photos in Table 5.3 all Panasonic UK; photos in Table 5.6 (from left to right) © William Berry – Fotolia.com, © Elena Elisseeva – Fotolia.com, © Robert Linton/iStockphoto.com; Figure 5.8 www.purestockX.com; Figure 5.9 © Monkey Business – Fotolia.com; Figure 5.11 © Julián Rovagnati – Fotolia.com; Figure 5.13 © Lee Pettet/iStockphoto.com; Figure 5.14 © Alexey Stiop/iStockphoto.com; Figure 5.145 © petforsberg/Alamy; Figure 5.16 © Igor Dutina – Fotolia.com; Figure 5.18 (from left to right) © Olivier Blondeau/iStockphoto.com, © Yanik Chauvin/iStockphoto.com, © Jill Chen/iStockphoto.com, © Marcus Clackson/iStockphoto.com, © Elena Elisseeva –Fotolia.com, © ALEAIMAGE/ iStockphoto.com, © Monkey Business – Fotolia.com; Figure 5.20 reproduced by kind permission of OCR; tablespoon in Figure 6.1 © Irochka – Fotolia.com; vegetable knife in Figure 6.2 © KVaSS – Fotolia.com; rotary grater in Figure 6.2 © Aleksandr Ugorenkov – Fotolia.com; rotary whisk in Figure 6.3 © Agatha Brown – Fotolia.com; blender on page 150 © Alexandra Draghici/iStockphoto.com; food processor on page 150 © Natalia Bratslavsky/iStockphoto.com; bacteria in Figure 7.1 © Henrik Jonsson/ iStockphoto.com; moulds in Figure 7.1 © Mike Wiggins/iStockphoto.com; Figure 7.2 © Darko Radanovic/iStockphoto.com; Figure 7.3 © Stuart Pitkin/iStockphoto.com; Figure 7.4 © Chris Dascher/iStockphoto.com; Figure 7.5 © Sebastian Kaulitzki/iStockphoto.com; Figure 7.7 www.purestockX.com; Figure 7.8 Ingram; Figure 7.9a © Tomasz Trojanowski – Fotolia.com; Figure 7. 9b © Kelly Cline/iStockphoto.com; Figure 7.13 © Dušan Zidar/iStockphoto.com; Figure 7.14a © Ernesto Solla Domínguez/iStockphoto.com; Figure 7.15 © Vallentin Vassileff/ iStockphoto.com; Figure 7.16 © broker – Fotolia.com; photos in Table 7.5 (from top) ©

Rafa Irusta/iStockphoto.com, © Kelly Cline/iStockphoto.com, © Kelly Cline/iStockphoto.com, © Rob Bouwman – Fotolia.com, © Kelly Cline/iStockphoto.com; Figure 8.3 © gerenme/iStockphoto.com; Figure 8.6 www.purestockx.com; Figure 8.9 © Peter Scholey /Alamy; 8.10 © Dr. Heinz Linke/iStockphoto.com; 8.11 © Jonathan Heger/iStockphoto.com; 8.12 © Kronick/iStockphoto.com; 8.13 © webphotographeer/iStockphoto.com; photo in Table 8.7 © Colin Underhill /Alamy; Figure 8.15 © David J. Green /Alamy; Figure 8.16 © Shaun Finch – Coyote-Photography.co.uk/ Alamy; Figure 9.3 © Dr. Heinz Linke/iStockphoto.com; Figure 9.5 © Dr. Heinz Linke/iStockphoto.com; 9.6 © Steven Miric/iStockphoto.com; 9.7 © Dr. Heinz Linke /iStockphoto.com; 9.8 Ingram; 9.9 © Bulent Ince/iStockphoto.com; Figure 10. 4© mediablitzimages (UK) Limited/Alamy; 10.05 © dieter Spears/iStockphoto.com; Figure 11.1 Digital Vision/Photolibrary Group; Figure 11.2 © Ieva Geneviciene – Fotolia.com; Figure 11.4 © Jill Chen/iStockphoto.com; Figure 11.5 © Mark Evans/iStockphoto.com; Figure 13.3 © Olivier Blondeau/ iStockphoto.com; Figure 13.6 Ingram; Figure 13.8 © Gary Unwin – Fotolia.com; Figure 13.10 © Dawn Hudson – Fotolia.com; Figure 13.11 © Fairtrade Foundation; Figure 13.12 printed with kind permission of Traidcraft; Figure 15.1 © vm/iStockphoto.com

All other photos in this volume taken by the authors.

Illustrations by Art Construction.

Every effort has been made to trace and acknowledge ownership of copyright. The publishers will be happy to make arrangements with any copyright owners that it has not been possible to contact.

HOW TO GET THE MOST OUT OF THIS BOOK

Welcome to OCR Design and Technology for GCSE Food Technology (specification numbers J302 and J042).

The book has been designed to support you throughout your GCSE course. It provides clear and precise guidance for each of the four units that make up the full course qualification, along with detailed information about the subject content of the course. It will be an extremely effective resource in helping you prepare for both controlled assessment and examined units.

The book has been written and developed by a team of writers who have considerable specialist knowledge of the subject area and are all very experienced teachers.

The book:
- *is student focused. The aim of the book is to help you achieve the best possible results from your study of GCSE Food Technology*
- *gives clear guidance of exactly what is expected of you in both controlled assessment and examined units*
- *contains examiner tips and guidance to help improve your performance in both Controlled Assessment and examined units*
- *provides detailed information relating to the subject content and designing*
- *is designed to help you locate information quickly*
- *is focused on the OCR specification for GCSE Food Technology*
- *has relevance and value to other GCSE Food Technology courses.*

The book outlines the knowledge, skills and understanding required to be successful within GCSE Food Technology. It is designed to give you a 'body of knowledge' which can be used to develop your own knowledge and understanding during the course and support you when undertaking both controlled assessment and examined units.

Chapters 1–11 form the 'body of knowledge'. Chapters 12–15 give specific guidance about each of the units that make up the GCSE course.

Unit A521 Introduction to Designing and Making

Chapter 12 gives detailed information about the structure of the controlled assessment unit and the rules relating to the controlled assessment task you will undertake. It clearly explains what you need to do section by section and includes examiner tips to help improve your performance. Specific reference is made to the assessment criteria and an explanation is provided as to how the criteria will be applied to your product. Examples of students' work are used within the text to reinforce the requirements of each section.

Unit A522 Sustainable Design

This chapter provides detailed information relating to this unit. It gives a clear explanation of the structure of the examination and gives further information relating to the key aspects of sustainability in relation to GCSE Food Technology. The chapter examines:

- what we mean by the 6R's in relation to food products
- the social issues governing the trends in food consumption
- the moral issues concerning food production
- the impact of cultural issues on food products
- how to select ingredients/materials that are both suitable and sustainable
- current issues affecting the design of new products.

Unit A523 Making Quality Products

Chapter 14 follows a similar format to Chapter 12. It explains the requirements of the unit section by section and includes examiner tips to guide you through the controlled assessment task.

Unit A524 Technical Aspects of Designing and Making

Chapter 15 is designed to help you prepare for the written examination. It clearly describes the format of the examination paper and gives examples of questions. Examiner tips are given to help you identify the type of question and the approach you should take in completing your answer.

Icons used in this book

Introduction boxes provide a short overview of the topics under discussion in the section.

KEY POINTS

- Key Points boxes list key aspects of a topic.

KEY TERMS

Key Terms boxes provide definitions of the technical terms used in the section.

EXAMINER'S TIPS

Examiner's Tips boxes give tips on how to improve performance in both the Controlled Assessment and examined units.

LEARNING OUTCOMES

Learning Outcomes boxes highlight the knowledge and understanding you should have developed by the end of the section.

ACTIVITY

Activity boxes suggest interesting tasks to support, enhance and extend learning opportunities.

CASE STUDY

Case study boxes provide examples of how real-life businesses use the knowledge and skills discussed.

QUESTIONS

Questions boxes provide practice questions to test key areas of the content of the specification.

CHAPTER 1

DESIGN PROCESS

1.1 DEVELOPING AND WRITING A DESIGN BRIEF

By the end of this section you should have developed a knowledge and understanding of how to:

- provide a detailed description of a design need
- consider food trends, consumer preference, dietary needs, media influence and sustainability
- identify the users and the market for the intended product
- develop a design brief.

*When a new product is developed, the first step is to identify a **need**. By carrying out initial research, the product type and user group can be identified and a **design brief** can be written.*

Identification of a need

Your first step is to identify a **need**. Products should be developed according to what people want. These people become your **user group** or your **intended target market**. For example, some food products are developed specifically for people on a special diet, such as weight watchers, others for people living on their own in the form of single-portion products, others for a specific age group, such as children.

Figure 1.1 Identify your intended target market

Consideration of food trends, consumer preference, dietary needs, media influence and sustainability

Consumers change their ideas about the products they want to buy as they are influenced by a changing economic, technological and social environment. In order for you to be successful you must identify changing consumer needs and new trends and develop products to meet these. This can be done by adapting an existing product or by developing a completely new and original product.

There are many different issues affecting people's choice of food. For example:

Current dietary trends – low in fat, sugar and salt, high in fibre.

Social issues – cost remains the top priority for some people, particularly those on low incomes. Other people may have more money to spend on food products. Consequently there has been an increase in the number of luxury products available.

Environmental issues – using locally grown ingredients, using recycled materials for packaging.

Ethical issues – deciding whether to use genetically modified foods, organic foods.

Cultural issues – religious beliefs prevent some people eating certain products.

Media influence – advertising is very powerful in encouraging consumers to try new products. Products may be associated with a particular image or specific characteristic, for example a healthy food product.

Initial research

Any information you collect and present should be relevant. There are two kinds of research material which you should use:

Primary research material is your own information which you have obtained from interviews, questionnaires and observations.

Secondary research material is information which has been collected by other people, for instance from books or newspapers.

You can carry out your initial research to identify a need by:

- reading newspapers or magazines or looking on the internet
- looking at existing products and thinking how they can be extended into a range of products
- carrying out questionnaires and/or interviews
- observing market trends by watching television advertisements, looking at products in supermarkets, etc.
- considering national concerns, e.g. 5 a day campaign.

Figure 1.2 Researching information from newspapers

When you collect information from **secondary sources, such as newspapers, the internet or magazines,** the information should be summarised concisely in your own words.

Questionnaire and interviews

A questionnaire and/or interview should be designed so that it helps you to extract specific information from people about the **qualities** they would like to see in a new product. When you design your questionnaire, start with an **introduction**. This will allow the public to:

- focus on the theme of the questionnaire/interview so that thoughts are clear
- feel involved from the start so a more satisfactory response is given
- understand the purpose of the questionnaire/interview.

The questions need to be clear and easy to understand and answer. It should be easy for you to **collate** the results using graphs, tables, tally charts, pie charts, etc. before **analysing** the results and coming to your **conclusions**.

The questionnaire/interview must not be too

Figure 1.3 Carrying out a questionnaire

long or people will become irritated and often will not think about their response but will just give the first response that comes into their thoughts.

Different types of questions can be used:

1. **Closed** – can be a very quick way of finding out specific information. They provide a yes/no type response or offer a limited choice of answers, e.g.

   Do you like the flavour of chocolate?
   Yes ☐   No ☐

2. **Multichoice** – offers a range of responses for the respondents to choose from, e.g.

   Which flavour do you prefer?
   Chocolate ☐   Lemon ☐   Coffee ☐
   Ginger ☐

3. **Ordered choice** – sometimes it is useful for the respondent to rank a set of options by numbering them in order from 1 to the maximum number you are interested in, e.g.

   Place in order of preference the following flavourings (indicate by numbering from 1–4 in order where 1 is the most preferred).
   Chocolate ☐   Lemon ☐   Coffee ☐
   Ginger ☐

4. **Open-ended questions** can produce a wide variety of responses that take a long time to interpret and put into categories. However, these may give some interesting results which could provide valuable information relating to moving the design forward or a new idea. They are useful for finding out about attitudes and opinions, e.g.

   What do you like about
   ....?

   What flavour would you like the biscuit to be and why?

Designing the correct questions can be time consuming. Questions should always be *checked* before you use the questionnaire. Make sure that each question will lead to a useful answer, for instance, do you really need to know a person's age/gender?

ICT can be used to design the questionnaire, analyse and compare data, and present results.

QUESTIONS

Initial research is carried out to identify a need and to find out the qualities people require in a new product.

1. List two methods that can be used to carry out research.

2. Why is it important to carry out this initial research?

3. How can findings from research be recorded? Give two ways.

The purpose of the design brief

Once you have identified the product type and user group, a **design brief** can be written. This is a short statement that outlines the problem to be solved. For example: design and make a low-in-sugar, chilled dessert that is suitable for a family.

ACTIVITY

1. Research information on a current food trend. Use newspapers, magazines or the internet.
   - Summarise the information you

find to identify a need (product type and user group).
- Write a design brief that outlines the problem to be solved.

2. Find a label from a food product. Suggest a target group for the product and give a reason for your answer. Why is it important for a manufacturer to know the target group?

KEY POINTS

- Lifestyles and technology are changing our food choices.
- Research findings should be analysed and used.
- A design brief is a short statement outlining the design problem to be solved.

KEY TERMS

USER GROUP or **INTENDED TARGET GROUP** – the person or group of people who will use the product
BRIEF – a clear statement of design intention
RESEARCH – the use of a variety of sources to find relevant information

1.2 DRAWING UP A DESIGN SPECIFICATION

LEARNING OUTCOMES

By the end of this section you should have developed a knowledge and understanding of how to:

- analyse a design brief
- carry out further research to help in the design and development of a new food product
- evaluate existing products to determine their suitability for the intended user
- develop a design specification.

The design brief needs to be analysed to allow other areas of research to be identified. By carrying out further research and evaluating existing products you will be able to develop a design specification for a new product.

Analysing a design brief

Once you decide on your design brief, you need to **analyse** it carefully. Contained within the brief will be certain key words – it is important that you identify these. You need to pick out the key words and any other points which you think are important to the brief. This is called **analysing the brief**.

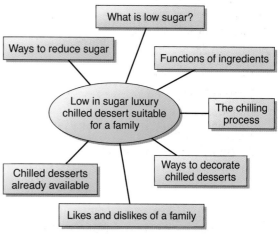

Figure 1.4 Example of the analysis of a design brief. A spider diagram has been used to show how you can pick out the key words and other relevant points that need to be researched from the brief

Name of product	Low in sugar with less than 5 g/100 g	Aimed at 11–19 year olds	Sold chilled	4+ portions	Attractive	Colourful	Tasty	Good portion size

Table 1.1 Table showing identified needs for a chilled dessert for 11–19 year olds

Further research

By analysing the brief you will be able to identify further research you will need to undertake to help you in the design and development of a new food product.

You need to think carefully about the amount of research you do and how you will present it.

Remember that:

- projects have to be completed within a certain number of hours
- research is only part of the process
- information can be presented in a number of ways, such as text, diagrams, charts or bulleted lists
- information should be presented clearly and concisely in your own words
- information should be relevant to your design brief.

Identifying complex associations linking principles of good design with technological knowledge

Collecting, analysing and applying relevant data allows you to show an understanding of technological knowledge when designing and developing food products. For example, through research, the different ways of reducing fat content can be identified. This knowledge can then be applied during the designing and development of a successful food product.

Evaluation of existing products

Evaluation of existing products allows you to see what products are already available and to identify how these products meet identified needs, i.e. the qualities identified from the analysis of results from your questionnaire/interview. You could taste some products and carry out **sensory analysis** so you can evaluate how existing products meet identified sensory qualities e.g. texture, taste and appearance. Sensory analysis is part of product analysis. Carrying out this type of research may also give you some ideas when designing food products. The products you choose to evaluate should be relevant to your brief.

ACTIVITY

Create a table like the one in Table 1.1 on page 5 which shows the qualities (identified needs) that a student found through analysis of a questionnaire for a chilled dessert which is to be aimed at 11–19 year olds.

- Choose three chilled desserts and evaluate them against the identified needs.
- Write a conclusion from your findings.
- Choose one of the desserts and evaluate in detail against the identified needs.

Developing a design specification

Once you have carried out all your research, a design specification for a new product can be written. It is usually written as a series of bullet points or a numbered list. It may be divided into what are essential criteria and what are the desirable criteria for the product.

A design specification is important because it clearly states the general details (criteria) of the product that is to be developed. It is also a checklist for evaluation throughout the development of the new product.

How to produce a design specification

First you must look back at your design brief and your analysis. You need to make a list of the main points identified when you analysed your brief. You should look back over your research, particularly the analysis of your questionnaire/interviews.

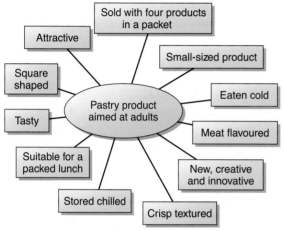

Figure 1.5 Example of a design specification for a pastry product aimed at adults

Look at the example design specification in Figure 1.5. Note that the student has not stated a type of pastry or product, leaving plenty of opportunity for a wide range of practical skills.

QUESTION

Explain why a design specification is important when developing new products.

ACTIVITY

Design a questionnaire to find out the qualities teenagers would like to see in a new snack product.
- Ask ten teenagers to complete the questionnaire and draw conclusions from the results. Using your conclusions, develop a design specification.

KEY POINTS

- **Analysing the brief** means identifying the key words and any other points which are important to the brief
- **A design specification** clearly states the general criteria for the product to be developed.

1.3 GENERATING, RECORDING AND MODELLING IDEAS

LEARNING OUTCOMES

By the end of this section you should have developed a knowledge and understanding of how to:

- generate, record and model design ideas, understanding the relevance of function and aesthetics
- carry out sensory analysis including rating/ranking and how to record results in appropriate ways (star profiles and charts)
- evaluate design ideas against a design specification.

Generating, recording and modelling of design ideas will allow a number of products to be adapted and trialled. Through sensory analysis testing, qualities can be monitored and improvements identified. Evaluating ideas against the criteria in your design specification will inform you how each idea has met the specification.

Where can I find ideas?

- Recipe books
- Analysis of research information
- Existing products
- Websites.

The design ideas you choose to trial should allow you to demonstrate a range of practical skills appropriate to your brief, for example, peeling, chopping, grating, meat preparation, shaping, rolling, sauce making (roux, blended, all in one), kneading, cake and pastry making, piping. You could list the ideas you find to give you time to think and make decisions as to which products you will trial.

You must always ensure that the design ideas you choose to trial are fully explained. You can do this by:

- listing ingredients
- describing the modifications/adaptations to each recipe, such as different shape, flavour, texture, ingredients, assembly, presentation/finishing techniques
- giving reasons for modifications/ adaptations
- carrying out nutritional analysis
- modelling ideas, which means making your designed practical ideas
- using sensory analysis to evaluate the ideas
- suggesting any improvements to the products
- evaluating products against each of the criteria in the design specification.

How can I communicate my design ideas?

- Word-processed documents
- Annotated sketches
- Mood boards

Figure 1.6 Demonstrating practical skills appropriate to your brief

Figure 1.7 Communicating design ideas through photographs

- Analysing nutritional computer printouts
- Sensory analysis charts
- Photographs of your practical products.

Modifying/adapting recipes to meet the needs of the user group

Ingredients can be substituted to alter recipes and proportions can be varied to alter the nutritional content of a product. The shape, finishing techniques and the way the product is assembled can also be changed.

Assembling means fitting together the different parts of a food product, for instance meat sauce, pasta sheets, cheese sauce and grated cheese when making a lasagne.

When changes are made, the colour, flavour, texture and nutritional value of the finished product will be altered (see Table 1.2).

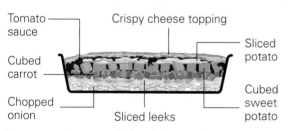

Figure 1.8 Annotated sketch for a spicy vegetable layer pie

Tomato sauce
Crispy cheese topping
Cubed carrot
Sliced potato
Chopped onion
Sliced leeks
Cubed sweet potato

QUESTIONS

1. List three ways of communicating thoughts when generating ideas.

2. Suggest four different flavourings that could be added to each of the following products:
   i) shortbread biscuits
   ii) bread.

3. Look at the pizza nutritional printout in Figure 1.9. How much fat per 100g does the pizza contain?

4. What would be the effect of reducing the fat content in the lower-in-sugar cream-filled éclairs in Figure 1.9?

ACTIVITY

Draw an annotated sketch of a layered dessert.

Lower in sugar cream filled éclairs		
Typical Value	Per 100g	Per Serving
Energy	1695 KJ 405 kcal	559 KJ 125 kcal
Protein	5.97 g	1.97 g
Carbohydrate of which sugars	18.4 g 5.18 g	6.07 g 1.52 g
Fat of which saturates	34.6 g 16.4 g	11.4 g 5.41 g
Fibre (NSP)	0.56 g	0.19 g
Sodium	0.27 g	0.09 g

Nutrition Information – Pizza		
	Typical Values	
	per 100g	per Serving 32 g
Energy	1168 kJ 279 kcal	374 kJ 89.3 kcal
Protein	12 g	3.84 g
Carbohydrate	49.2 g	15.7 g
Fat	5.16 g	1.65 g

Figure 1.9 Nutritional printouts for lower-in-sugar éclairs and a lower-in-fat pizza

Reducing fat	Reducing sugar
Result is less moist	Less flavour
Less flavour	Paler colour
Product will stale more rapidly	Poorer keeping
Paler colour	Capacity to rise reduced
Increasing fat	**Increasing sugar**
Result may be greasy	Baked mixtures become s
Flavour may be improved	during baking, then hard on
Darker colour	cooling
	Increased cooking time
	Darker colour

Table 1.2 What happens when the proportions in a recipe are altered?

▶ Sensory analysis

Food is essential for life, but needs to have many qualities if it is to be enjoyed by a wide variety of people. It is important that all food products are carefully and consistently prepared so that the taste, aroma and appearance are of the highest quality.

To enable the qualities to be **monitored** and **recorded** during the designing and making of a new product, sensory analysis tests (the tasting of foods) are carried out. This enables **modifications** (changes) to be made at each stage of the development of the product so that the end result is successful. This prevents money from being wasted. It also allows a food manufacturer to check that the product matches the specification, finds out what the consumer likes/wants and tests the shelf life. Checks can be made throughout production to maintain consistently high standards and the products can be compared with those of competitors.

Sensory analysis tests

Sensory analysis is used to gather information on food products to establish their most important characteristics. There are several types of test – these meet British Standard BS5929.

a) Preference or acceptance tests – these tests would be used to evaluate 'product acceptability' by finding out the opinions, likes and dislikes of the consumer. There are two types of preference tests that can be used: **hedonic ratings tests** and **paired preference tests**.

Hedonic ratings test – testers give their opinion of one or more samples of food from 'extreme like' to 'extreme dislike' (see Table 1.3).

Paired preference test – testers are given two samples of food and have to indicate which sample they prefer, for instance tuna fishcakes or salmon fishcakes.

Sample	1. Dislike Very Much	2. Dislike	3. Neither Like nor Dislike	4. Like	5. Like Very Much	Comments
X						
XX						
XX						
XXXX						
XXX						

Table 1.3 Hedonistic ratings test

Discriminatory testing – these tests are used to see whether people can tell the difference between two samples, for instance when an ingredient or quantity of ingredient is changed and when manufacturers are copying another brand, for example two brands of cheese and onion crisps or a vegeburger and a beefburger. These are **objective** tests. You will find several types of discriminatory tests.

Paired comparison – a pair of coded samples is given for the comparison of a specific characteristic, such as sweetness, crunchiness, smoothness. A minimum of 20 tastes will give a useful result.

Triangle test – Three samples are given to the tester. Two samples are the same and the tester is asked to identify the 'odd one out'. This test is useful if you have made small changes to a product, for instance made a lasagne low in fat **or** used more economical ingredients.

b) Grading tests – these test for the degree of intensity of a specific sensory property, such as sweetness. Food samples are ranked in order to show consumer preference. You would use these tests to:

- select a small number of samples from a large sample to enable a more precise test to be carried out
- find out consumer preferences
- obtain rapid results.

Examples of grading tests are: **ranking, rating** and **profiling**.

Ranking test – used to sort a **variety** of foods into order (e.g. different-flavoured crisps made by one manufacturer). A set of coded samples is presented to the tester. The tester has to rank the samples in order of either:

- a specific attribute, e.g. sweetness, saltiness
- a preference on a hedonic scale or ranking.

Taste the samples and put them in the order you like best		
Sample code	Order	Comments
⑩		
〉		
☛		
⇔		

Table 1.4

Ranking test with descriptor – used to place a **variety of one type** of food into order (e.g. the flavour of cream of tomato soups processed by different methods).

| Ranking according to flavour ||
Sample code	Creaminess choice
⑩	2nd
❯	1st
☞	4th
⬭	3rd

Table 1.5 Ranking test with descriptor

Rating test using a descriptor – used to show how much tasters like or dislike **several aspects** of one product (e.g. flavour, colour, nutrition of a cold dessert) or **one aspect** of several products (e.g. crispness of a range of pizza bases) (see Table 1.6).

Star profile – used to **describe** the appearance, taste and texture of a food product. It can also be used to record the suitability of other aspects of the product (such as packaging). A **descriptor** is identified at the end of each line. The descriptor used will depend on the product being tested. When the food is tasted, the taster assesses the identified areas and marks the star

diagram as required. The marks on each point are joined together to identify them clearly (see Figure 1.10).

Profiling tests – this is also called sensory profiling. Sensory profiling is used to obtain a detailed, descriptive evaluation of the differences between products and to find out how much of each difference there is.

A sensory profile of each product is developed which may include the characteristics of texture (mouthfeel), flavour, aroma, appearance and sound. These may be assessed together.

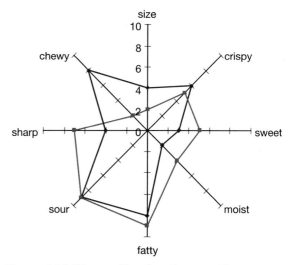

Figure 1.10 Star profile of a citrus cookie

Tasting words	Votes by tasting panel (1 = poor, 2 = average, 3 = good, 4 = v good, 5 = excellent)					Total	Average
Flavour	4	4	5	3	4	20	4
Thickness	1	1	2	1	2	7	1.4
Colour	3	4	1	5	2	15	3
Smoothness	3	2	1	2	3	11	2.2

Table 1.6 Rating test using a descriptor

During sensory profiling testing:

- trained assessors are used because of the complexity of the tests
- a set of coded samples is presented to six or more trained assessors
- each assessor has to rate the intensity of each descriptor on a scale of 1 to 5 (1 is the lowest, 5 is the highest)
- results from each assessor are added up and the average rating for each descriptor is worked out
- a visual profile is created by plotting the results on a spider or star diagram.

Carrying out sensory analysis

It is important to use correct procedures when carrying out sensory analysis testing:

- Set up a quiet area where people will not be disturbed (do not allow testers to communicate with each other).
- Give the testers a drink of lemon-flavoured water or a piece of apple to clear the palate.
- Use small quantities of food on plain and identical sized plates/dishes.
- Use coloured lighting.
- Use same garnish or decoration.
- Try not to give too many samples at once.
- Serve at the correct temperature for the product that is being tested.
- Use clean spoons or forks each time. Do NOT allow people to put dirty spoons into your dish.
- Use codes for the products to prevent the testers being influenced by the name of the product (this is known as testing blind).
- Have any charts ready before you begin testing.
- Make sure the testers know how to fill in the charts you are using.

	Tester 1	Tester 2	Tester 3	Tester 4	Tester 5	Average
Meaty	3	3	3	3	4	3.2
Square	4	4	4	4	4	4
Tasty	3	3	3	3	3	3
Attractive	3	3	3	2	3	2.8
Crisp texture	2	2	3	2	3	2.4
Small	1	2	3	2	4	2.4

Key

Poor = 1 Good = 2 Very Good = 3 Excellent = 4

Improvements

Taster 1 – make slightly larger so more filling can be added

Taster 2 – glaze the pasties so they are golden brown

Taster 3 – add herbs to give a little more flavour

Taster 4 – make the pasties larger

Taster 5 – add another vegetable for extra taste

Table 1.7 A rating chart for pasties and the suggested improvements from five tasters

When you carry out sensory analysis of your product this will involve you:

- looking at the product
- smelling the product
- tasting the product.

You will need to ask your **user group** or your **intended target market** to carry out sensory analysis. The results of sensory analysis testing will help you decide whether the product is acceptable; or if it is not acceptable, the information gained can help you decide how the product can be improved. Results from sensory analysis will also be used as evidence when evaluating the product against the design specification.

▶ Evaluation of design ideas

Evaluation is an ongoing process throughout the designing and making of new food products. Evaluation allows judgements to be made about a product, thereby enabling improvements to be made at each stage. As each design idea is trialled you will need to find out:

1. Whether it appeals to your **user group** or your **intended target market**
2. Whether it meets your design specification
3. Any improvements that need to be made.

Sensory analysis testing, using tasters from your user group, with the results being presented in tables or star diagrams, should inform you whether the design idea is appealing and whether any improvements are required.

Evaluating against each criterion in your design specification will inform you how each design idea meets the specification. Results from nutritional analysis and sensory analysis testing should be used as evidence.

Evaluating each idea against the design specification helps to identify which idea should be taken forward to product development.

 QUESTIONS

1. Explain the difference between a rating and a ranking chart.
2. Give clear instructions on how to carry out sensory analysis testing.
3. Table 1.8 shows the taste test results for a new chicken pasta bake.

Characteristics	Tester 1	Tester 2	Tester 3	Tester 4	Tester 5
Portion size	2	2	1	1	2
Amount of chicken	4	4	3	4	4
Creamy cheese sauce	4	3	4	4	3
Crispiness of topping	1	1	2	1	2
Tomato flavour	4	4	4	4	4
Well seasoned	2	1	1	2	2

Key Poor = 1 Good = 2 Very Good = 3 Excellent = 4

Table 1.8 Taste test results for a new chicken pasta bake

From the results shown identify two characteristics that need improving and explain how this could be done.

QUESTION

Give two reasons why evaluation takes place when trialling design ideas.

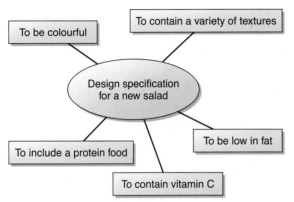

Figure 1.11 Design specification for a new salad

ACTIVITY

Figure 1.11 shows the design specification for a new salad.

Sketch a design idea for the product and explain how the idea meets the specification

KEY POINTS

- Recipes need adapting for design work.
- Sensory analysis testing is used to test the quality of existing products and evaluate design ideas.
- Evaluation is an ongoing process throughout the designing and making of new food products.
- Evaluation enables products to be improved.

KEY TERMS

ANNOTATE – to label a sketch
SENSORY ANALYSIS TESTING – taste/testing of a food product to check its acceptability and to identify improvements
SENSORY DESCRIPTORS – words that describe taste, smell, texture and flavour

1.4 PRODUCT DEVELOPMENT

LEARNING OUTCOMES

By the end of this section you should have developed a knowledge and understanding of how to:

- decide on the final design proposal
- understand how products are developed including costing and taking account of users' views
- understand the relevance of function and aesthetics (sensory and functional considerations during the modification of ideas, i.e. taste, texture and appearance)
- carry out sensory analysis during product development.

Once a number of design ideas have been evaluated against the design specification a decision can be made as to which idea should be taken forward to product development. During development the product is refined through trialling, taking account of users' views, until a desired outcome is achieved. At this stage, costing of the product should be considered.

When a number of products have been trialled you have to decide which product to take forward for product development. Looking back to your evaluations of design ideas will help you make a decision.

You need to clearly explain why you have chosen this product and why you have rejected the other ideas. This is sometimes known as the final design proposal.

Development is all about **changing, testing** or **modifying** all or part of a product until a desired outcome is achieved.

Development gives you the opportunity to try out changes. **Evaluation** enables you to make appropriate decisions. Simple notes, charts or diagrams with comments are adequate ways of recording your results.

Ideas for development work

There are many ways that you could develop a product:

- to improve the nutritional content
- to change the flavour
- to alter the texture
- to alter the shape
- to alter the colour
- to improve the final appearance
- to consider the cost of the product.

Some examples of modifications that can be made to a product are:

- the ingredients used
- proportions of ingredients used
- the finishing technique used
- assembling of the product, e.g. layering differently.

The key is that the product must be developed according to the needs of your **user group** or your **intended target market** so their views must be considered as the product develops. When you start product development, you need to look back to when your idea was originally trialled.

You must always ensure your development work is fully explained. You can do this by:

- listing and costing ingredients
- describing the modifications/changes
- giving reasons for modifications/changes
- carrying out nutritional analysis if this is relevant to the brief
- using sensory analysis to evaluate each development
- an evaluation of each development indicating how effective the modifications/changes have been and any further improvements that need to be made.

Costing food products

Costing is an important part of the development process. As you modify/change your product you will be able to see the effect this has on the cost of the product.

QUESTIONS

1. Traditional plain scones are made by using the following ingredients and shaped by using a round fluted cutter:

   200 g self-raising flour
   50 g margarine
   50 g sugar
   1 egg + enough milk to make up to 125 ml of liquid

   Suggest three adaptations you could make to the scones. Give reasons for these adaptations.

2. Below is a recipe for spaghetti bolognese.

   1 small onion
   25 g margarine
   1 small carrot
   225 g minced beef
   tin chopped tomatoes
   1 stock cube
   4 tomatoes
   salt and pepper
   200 g spaghetti

   (a.) Give two ways in which the fat content can be reduced.

   (b.) Give two ways in which the fibre content can be increased.

3. The ingredients used in a spicy burger product are listed below.

   250 g minced lamb
   25 g breadcrumbs
   10 g coriander – fresh
   2 cloves garlic
   75 g finely chopped onion
   3 g ground cumin
   3 g paprika
   10 ml lemon juice
   5 g mild curry powder
   15 g tomato puree
   1 small egg
   salt and pepper

   The rating chart shown in Table 1.9 shows the results from the tasting and testing of the spicy burger product.

	Taster 1	Taster 2	Taster 3
Evenly browned	3	5	5
Round shape	2	2	1
Excellent aroma	5	5	4
Consistent size	5	5	4
Correct level of spiciness	1	2	2
Even texture	2	2	3

   Table 1.9 Results from the tasting and testing of the spicy burger product

   Consider the results shown in the rating chart. Discuss the implications to the product development team of these results.

4. The ingredients below have been taken from a label for chilli con carni.
   Cooked long grain rice, minced Aberdeen angus beef, tomato, kidney beans, onions, green pepper, plum tomato, red pepper, red wine, rapeseed oil, beef stock, tomato puree, garlic puree, coriander, salt, red chilli, margarine, wheat flour, modified maize starch, parsley, cumin, vegetable bouillon, green chilli, paprika, white sugar, oregano, chili powder, bay leaf.

   State two ways in which the cost of the chilli can be reduced.

Changing ingredients to reduce the cost can sometimes be detrimental to the successful making of the product. However, you could reduce the cost by:

- making slightly smaller portions
- changing an expensive ingredient to a cheaper one, e.g. substituting meat with vegetables
- mixing meat with an alternative protein food, e.g. textured vegetable protein
- increasing the carbohydrate content and reducing, for example, the protein content of the product, i.e. to 'eke out' the use of an expensive ingredient
- using flavourings and colourings instead of fresh ingredients such as fresh fruits
- drizzling chocolate/glacé icing instead of spreading on top of a product.

1.5 PRODUCT PLANNING

By the end of this section you should have developed a knowledge and understanding of how to:
- plan for your final product including costing, being able to match materials and components with tools, equipment and processes when deciding how to make the product
- develop a product specification
- plan for the production of products.

When product development has been completed, planning for the final product can take place. This involves making reasoned decisions about the ingredients and equipment used to make the final product, including costing, development of a product specification and producing a plan of action for the making of the final product.

When you have completed your product development work you will be ready to plan for your final product. Your plans will need to show:

- choice of your final ingredients and equipment
- reasons for your choice of ingredients and equipment
- costing of the final ingredients
- nutritional analysis if this is relevant to the brief.

Food materials

Food technology involves converting raw materials into edible food products.

Food products are made by combining ingredients in different proportions and using a range of different techniques. Food materials can be prepared using a variety of processes and equipment.

When you give reasons for the choice of your final ingredients you are really giving the function of each ingredient for your particular product.

- A particular ingredient could give crunchiness to a product or perhaps give a fruity flavour.
- It could increase the fibre or lower the fat content of the product.
- Using yeast in bread making allows the bread to rise.
- Gluten-free flour is used for a celiac as they have an intolerance to gluten.

You are also required to give reasoned decisions for the equipment you will use. This will involve you listing the pieces of equipment and stating the job that each piece will be used for.

▶ Developing a product specification

A product specification does not provide general points like the design specification. Instead, it describes **very specific characteristics** which a product must have, so the product could be produced in identical batches. It is written after the development work is completed.

The product specification will:

- give success criteria when evaluating the final product

- be written when the development work is completed and the final prototype is ready for manufacturing in large quantities
- give exact and precise details of the product so that a replica of the final prototype can be produced.

You will need to look at your design specification and your development work to produce your product specification which should include a labelled sketch of your final product.

Writing a product specification

Your product specification should include:

- the name of the target group that the product is going to be manufactured for, e.g. teenagers
- any nutritional claims or important information for the label, e.g. **lower** in fat. The actual amount of fat content needs to be given per 100 g
- details of any special dietary claims, e.g. vegetarian
- specific descriptions of the ingredients, e.g. **flaked/ground** almonds, **block/soft** margarine, **diced/sliced** carrots
- sensory qualities of the actual final product
- how it is to be assembled, or the shape and size, e.g. **layers** of..., **round** shape
- finishing techniques, e.g. **brushed with** an egg glaze before baking, **garnished** with two slices of tomato and one small sprig of parsley, **decorated with** ...
- portion size, e.g. will serve four people
- preparation and serving details
- actual cost of the product
- storage requirements, e.g. chilled/frozen, etc.

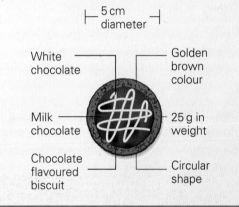

My product must be:
• Suitable for teenagers/adults as this is my target group.
  Chocolate flavoured, as I will add grated milk and plain chocolate to the biscuit base.
• Decorated with white and milk chocolate to create a marbled effect.
• The white chocolate will be spread to within 1 cm of the edge and the milk chocolate will then be drizzled randomly over the top and a skewer
• will be used to drag the drizzled lines into the base chocolate cover.
  Medium sized. I will do this by using 25 g of mixture in each biscuit and making each biscuit 5 cm in diameter.
  Circular shape achieved by rolling mixture into a ball in the hand and
• slightly flattening when on baking tray.
  Attractive, as I will decorate carefully and make sure the biscuit is
• golden brown.
  68 pence for 6 biscuits.
• Crunchy and slight chewy texture achieved by adding crushed Smarties and toffee pieces to the biscuit base.
• Base ingredients consisting of: 100 g margarine, 50 g soft brown sugar, 100 g plain flour, 50 g toffee pieces, 40 g Smarties, 25 g plain chocolate and 25 g milk chocolate.

├─ 5 cm ─┤
   diameter

White chocolate — Golden brown colour

Milk chocolate — 25 g in weight

Chocolate flavoured biscuit — Circular shape

Figure 1.12 A product specification for a biscuit aimed at teenagers

QUESTION

Explain the difference between a design specification and a product specification.

Planning

You will need to plan your making activities. Time management is a very important part of this.

You will be required to:

- plan your work over a number of lessons to show your ability to forward plan (during controlled assessment project 2)
- plan for the making of a practical product to show an effective order of sequences.

The presentation of the plan for a practical product can be in many different forms. A **flowchart** is a diagrammatical way to show a plan of work. A good place to start is to read the original method for the product you are making and then change this to match your new product and add further detail.

A flowchart uses the standard symbols shown in Figure 1.13.

Figure 1.13 Standard flow chart symbols

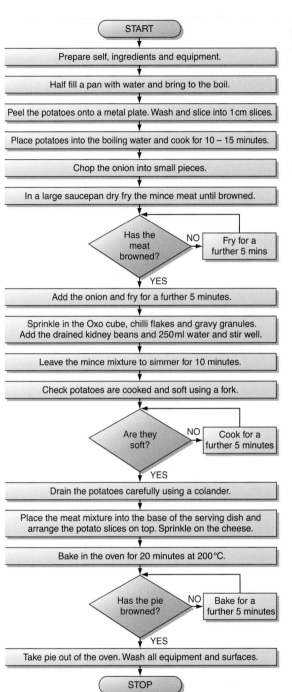

Figure 1.14 Example of a flowchart for a spicy pie

FLOWCHART – a diagram which shows a sequence of events

ACTIVITY

The flowchart in Figure 1.14 for a spicy pie has clear steps which can be followed when making the pie.

For a product that you will be making, design a detailed flowchart for the production of the product.

Alternatively you could present your plan as a chart as shown in Table 1.10.

Health and safety	Process	Quality checks

Table 1.10 Presenting your plan as a chart

1.6 CRITICAL EVALUATION SKILLS

By the end of this section you should have developed a knowledge and understanding of how to:

- critically evaluate products and suggest modifications.

Evaluation is all about making judgements. It is a very important part of designing and making and should be done at all stages so that you can make the right decisions for the next step in the process.

Evaluation takes place:

- *during research – evaluating existing products*
- *whilst generating and trialling ideas – sensory analysis and evaluating ideas against the design specification*
- *during product development, sensory analysis and evaluating the effectiveness of modifications/changes made to the product as it is developed*
- *after production of the final product, sensory analysis and evaluating against the product specification.*

By evaluating throughout the whole process you should be able to make a final product that meets your original design brief.

Evaluation of the final product

The first stage of your evaluation will be to carry out sensory analysis testing with your **user group** or your **intended target market**, for instance a tasting chart or a star profile.

When evaluating your final product your comments need to show:

- how successful you have been in terms of your product specification and your design brief

- suggestions for further modifications.

Comments from your **user group** or your **intended target market** can support your views and they can be given as evidence when you offer conclusions for your work. It is a good idea to ask your testers how the product could be improved as this will help you suggest further modifications.

To achieve a high level you must produce a **critical** evaluation.

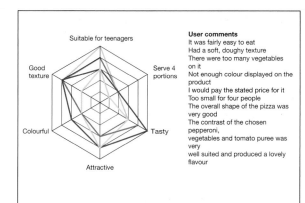

User comments
It was fairly easy to eat
Had a soft, doughy texture
There were too many vegetables on it
Not enough colour displayed on the product
I would pay the stated price for it
Too small for four people
The overall shape of the pizza was very good
The contrast of the chosen pepperoni, vegetables and tomato puree was very well suited and produced a lovely flavour

	Suitable for Teenagers	Serve 4 portions	Tasty	Attractive	Colourful	Good texture
Taster1	4	2	4	3	2	4
Taster2	3	2	5	4	3	3
Taster3	4	1	3	4	2	2
Taster4	5	2	3	3	3	4
Taster5	3	2	5	4	3	4

Figure 1.15 Results for sensory testings of a low-fat pizza

ACTIVITY

Produce a product specification for a product you will be making. Ask three people to carry out sensory analysis testing of the product. Critically evaluate the product against your product specification, giving results from your sensory analysis testing as evidence. Suggest further modifications that could be made to your product, giving reasons for these modifications.

CHAPTER 2

DIET AND NUTRITION

LEARNING OUTCOMES

By the end of this section you should have developed
a knowledge and understanding of the function, deficiencies
and sources in the diet of:

- protein
- fats
- carbohydrates – sugar, starch and fibre
- vitamins – A, B complex, C and D
- minerals – calcium, iron, sodium (salt), fluoride, phosphorus

*Every living thing needs food – it is essential to keep us alive and in good health.
We need food for:*

- *providing the energy we need to survive, to keep us healthy and to help fight disease*
- *growth and repair of body tissues*
- *all bodily functions, which depend upon the energy and trace elements found in the food we eat*
- *stopping us feeling hungry*
- *keeping us happy as we find eating a pleasurable and enjoyable experience.*

❯ Nutrients

Nutrients are substances found in foods. They are divided into two types:

- **The macronutrients – proteins, fats and carbohydrates**. These are needed by the body in relatively large quantities and form the bulk of our diet.
- **The micronutrients – vitamins and minerals.** These are found in food and are vital to health but are required in very small quantities.

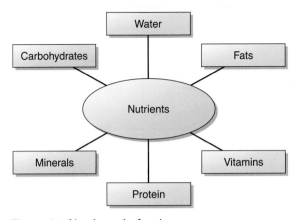

Figure 2.1 Nutrients in food

All foods contain a mix of nutrients. Some foods are higher in some nutrients than others. We should eat a mixture of foods every day.

The government has produced guidelines and advice to encourage the UK population to improve their diet and lifestyle. It has set targets to reduce the numbers of people with diet–related medical conditions such as cancer, coronary heart disease, strokes, diabetes and obesity. Individuals could become healthier by increasing their intake of fruit, vegetables and fibre. Keeping physically active and maintaining a healthy body weight will also help.

Deficiencies or excesses of any particular nutrient could result in a diet–related medical condition, so we need to eat a balance of nutrients every day.

KEY POINTS

- We need a balance of nutrients in our diet every day.
- Foods contain a combination of macro and micronutrients.

2.1 PROTEIN

Protein is one of the macronutrients. It is essential for growth and repair of body tissue and is crucial to the healthy functioning of the body. Protein is made up of complex chains of molecules called amino acids – there are 20 different types of amino acid, each having a specific function in the body.

The functions of protein in the diet are:
- growth, especially in children and pregnant women
- repair of body tissue after illness, accidents and surgery; renewal of cell proteins for people of all ages
- enzymes, vital for metabolism, are composed of proteins
- hormones, which regulate some important bodily functions are also composed of protein
- a secondary source of energy. When the body has used all the amino acids it needs

Figure 2.2 A family eating a meal

for construction, the remainder are 'burnt' for energy.

▶ Why are proteins important?

The human body needs all 20 amino acids for the maintenance of health and growth. Some of these can be made by the body but the others have to be obtained through the food we eat; these are called essential amino acids. There are eight essential amino acids for adults and ten for children.

High biological value

The foods that contain all the essential amino acids are said to have a high biological value (HBV). Most of these come from animal sources (meat, fish, poultry and dairy products) plus the vegetable source, soya. As the vegetarian market grows there is a large range of food products made from soya, such as soya mince, textured vegetable protein (known as TVP) and tofu. Another HBV protein is Quorn® which is the brand name for a food product made from myco-protein.

Low biological value

Vegetable sources of protein include cereals, peas, beans, pulses, nuts and seeds. Because these do not contain all the essential amino acids they are called low biological value (LBV). They can easily be combined in a meal or product to provide all the essential amino acids. This is called food combining or complementary proteins.

Food combining

Vegetarian, vegan or other limited diets rely on combining LBV proteins, for instance beans on toast, dhal and rice, hummus and pitta bread, to form proteins of higher value.

Figure 2.3 All these foods are protein sources of HBV

Figure 2.4 All these foods are protein sources of LBV

Sources of protein in the diet

Animal sources include all meats, such as poultry, offal and game, as well as fish, cheese, milk, eggs and gelatine.

Vegetables sources include soya beans and soya products, pulses, beans, cereal grains and cereal products, nuts and Quorn®.

Protein deficiency

A protein deficiency in the diet causes various problems.

- In children growth slows down or stops.
- There are digestive upsets as enzymes are not produced.
- The liver fails to function normally.
- The muscles become weak and so limbs are thin and the tummy is soft and may look distended.

Kwashiorkor is a protein energy malnutrition disease occurring when a child is weaned from breast milk to a diet low in protein.

QUESTIONS

1. List the functions of protein in the diet.
2. Explain the difference between HBV and LBV proteins.
3. Explain how and why you would combine protein foods to complement each other.

ACTIVITY

Prepare a main course product that combines a range of LBV proteins. Use nutritional software to find out how one portion of the product meets the needs of a teenager.

Plan a meal that will provide 18 g of protein.

KEY POINTS

- Protein is needed for growth and repair of body tissues.
- Protein is made up of amino acids.
- Good sources of high biological value proteins are meat, fish, cheese, eggs, fish and soya.
- Good sources of low biological value protein are pulses, cereals and nuts.

KEY TERMS

AMINO ACIDS – smallest unit of a protein
ESSENTIAL AMINO ACIDS – cannot be made by the body
HIGH BIOLOGICAL VALUE PROTEINS – contain all the essential amino acids
LOW BIOLOGICAL VALUE PROTEINS – do not contain all the essential amino acids
FOOD COMBINING – mixing different low biological value proteins to supply all the essential amino acids

2.2 FATS AND OILS

'Lipids' is a general term for both fats and oils. Oils are fats that are liquid at room temperature. Fat is one of the macronutrients essential to health. All fats and oils have similar chemical structures and functions. All are high in calories. Fat in the diet is important for health and wellbeing.

▶ The functions of fat in the diet

- Fats are used by the body for energy and also form part of the structure of cells.
- Stored under the skin, fat helps insulate the body against the cold.
- Our vital organs, such as kidneys, are protected by a layer of fat.
- Fat is a source of the fat-soluble vitamins A, D, E and K (see vitamins).
- We like to eat fat because it gives foods texture and flavour.
- Fat in our diet helps to promote a feeling of satiety (feeling full after eating).

▶ Sources of fat in the diet

Fats come from both plant and animal sources. There has been a significant increase in the oils and fats available from vegetable sources as consumers and manufacturers look to follow the latest dietary advice.

Plant sources include:

- some fruits, for example avocado pears, olives
- nuts and pulses, for example peanuts, walnuts
- seeds, for example sesame, sunflower and soya.

Animal sources include:

- meat and meat products, such as lard and suet
- dairy products, for example, milk, butter, cheese and cream
- fish, particularly oily fish, for example tuna, salmon and sardines.

▶ The chemistry of fats

Fats are large molecules made up of only the elements carbon, hydrogen and oxygen. They are composed of fatty acids and glycerol. Fatty acids may be saturated or unsaturated.

Saturated fats

Each carbon atom in the fatty acid is combined with two hydrogen atoms. Saturated fats are solid at room temperature and are mainly found in animal foods. Too much saturated fat in the diet has been linked to high blood cholesterol, leading to an increased risk of coronary heart disease, diabetes and obesity.

Cholesterol

Cholesterol has the consistency of soft wax and is produced in the liver and transported round the body in the blood. It has been found that when too much cholesterol is in the blood it is deposited on the walls of the arteries, narrowing them and making them less efficient. Narrowed arteries are one of the major causes of coronary heart disease.

Figure 2.5 Sources of saturated fat in the diet

Unsaturated fats

There are two types of unsaturated fats, polyunsaturated and monounsaturated. Unsaturated fats are usually soft or liquid at room temperature and have a lower melting point.

Monounsaturated fatty acids have one pair of their carbon atoms with only one hydrogen atom attached, so they are capable of taking one more hydrogen atom. They are soft at room temperature but will go solid when placed in the coldest part of the refrigerator. They are found in both animal and vegetable fats. Monounsaturated fatty acids in particular are considered healthier because they can help to lower blood cholesterol, reduce the risk of diabetes and are linked with a lower rate of cancer.

Figure 2.6 Sources of monounsaturated fat in the diet

Polyunsaturated fatty acids have two or more pairs of carbon atoms which are capable of taking up more hydrogen atoms. They are very soft or oily at room temperature. They will not go solid even in the refrigerator.

Figure 2.7 Sources of polyunsaturated fat in the diet

Trans fatty acids are man-made molecules produced when hydrogen is added to vegetable oils. This is called hydrogenation. This process is used to make solid margarines from oil and is used in a variety of manufactured foods. Trans fatty acids behave like saturated fats, raising your levels of cholesterol. Medical research has shown that trans fatty acids are very bad for your cardiovascular system and may increase the risk of breast cancer.

Essential fatty acids (EFAs) cannot be made by the body but are important to the healthy and efficient functioning of the body. It is important to get the right balance of EFAs in our diet. They are essential for regulating body processes, including blood clotting and control of inflammation. Two important ones are:

Omega 3 found in oily fish, seeds, walnut oil, and green leafy vegetables. It helps protect the heart.
Omega 6 found in vegetables, fruits, grains, chicken and seeds. It helps lower cholesterol in the blood.

KEY POINTS

- Fat is a concentrated source of energy
- Excess fat in the diet is stored as body fat
- We are advised to reduce our fat intake to no more than 35 per cent of our total energy intake
- Saturated fats contribute to a high level of cholesterol in the blood.

QUESTIONS

1. Why does the body need fat? Explain why high-fat food products appeal to us.

2. Why should we cut down on the amount of saturated fats that we eat?

3. What is a low-in-fat and a lower-in-fat product? Research this on the internet.

KEY TERMS

ESSENTIAL FATTY ACIDS – small unit of fat that must be supplied in the diet
HYDROGENATION – the process of adding hydrogen to oils to make them into solid fats
LIPID – another name for fat and oils
MONOUNSATURATED FATS – a fat molecule with one hydrogen space
POLYUNSATURATED FATS – a fat molecule with more than one hydrogen space
SATIETY – a feeling of fullness

2.3 CARBOHYDRATES

Carbohydrates are important macronutrients formed from carbon, hydrogen and oxygen. They are mainly used to provide energy and during digestion they are broken down to

ACTIVITY

1. Produce a poster to show 'A guide to the fat in your diet'.

Product name	Regular product	Lower-fat version	How much is the fat reduced per 100 g?

Table 2.1 Supermarket survey to compare fat contents of products

2. Visit your supermarket or supermarket website and conduct a survey of the types of product that have a lower-fat version. Set out your findings in a table like the one in Table 2.1 above.

3. Examine a range of butter, margarines, lard and spreads. Compare the fat content in 100 g of each.

their simplest form, glucose, which can be used for energy. There are three forms: sugar, starch and NSP (fibre).

Functions of carbohydrates

- They provide the body with energy for physical activity.
- They provide the body with energy to maintain bodily functions.
- They provide dietary fibre (non-starch polysaccharide (NSP)) to help digestion.
- They sweeten and flavour foods.

They are divided into sugars and starches also known as simple and complex carbohydrates.

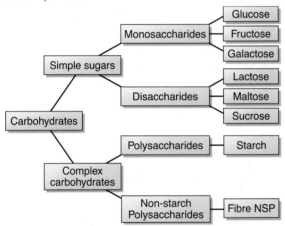

Figure 2.8 **Diagram to show the types of simple and complex carbohydrates**

Simple sugars

There are two main types of simple sugars.

Monosaccharides

Monosaccharides are also known as simple sugars. The simpler the carbohydrate, the more quickly it can be absorbed in the body and the faster energy can be provided.

Glucose is one of these simple sugars and although found in some fruits and vegetables

it is often used by athletes in tablet or powder form to provide a fast-energy boost.

Fructose is similar in structure to glucose and is found naturally in the juices of some fruits and plants but mainly in honey. It can be bought in crystalline form. As it is the sweetest of all sugars it is used by manufacturers to replace sucrose, enabling less sugar to be used to provide the same level of sweetness.

Galactose is formed during digestion of lactose (milk sugar).

Figure 2.9 **Sources of monosaccharides in the diet**

Disaccharides

Disaccharides are double sugars which are made up of two monosaccharides.

Lactose is the disaccharide found in milk, which some people think gives milk its *Glu-Gal* slightly sweet taste.

Maltose, another of the disaccharides, results from the fermentation of cereal grains. Malt is used in some food production and as a *Glu-Glu* dietary supplement.

Sucrose is the most common disaccharide, a white crystalline substance used in homes

Glu-Fru

and industry known as cane sugar. It provides the body with energy but has no other benefits in the diet. It contains no other nutrients. Sucrose comes from sugar beet or sugar cane. We buy it as granulated sugar/ brown sugar/syrup/treacle/castor and icing sugar.

We eat sugar in different forms:

- **intrinsic** sugar found naturally in the cells of fruits and vegetables; it is part of the cells

- **extrinsic** sugars which are those you can see, such as cane sugar, syrup and those added to cakes biscuits, desserts and sweets.

The most common problems relating to sucrose are obesity and tooth decay. Tooth decay is caused when the bacteria in your mouth (plaque) feed on the sucrose to produce an acid. The acid then causes small holes in your teeth (dental caries). Intrinsic sugars are less harmful as they are less likely to lead to tooth decay and are easier for the body to absorb.

Plaque + sucrose = acid
Acid + tooth = decay

Figure 2.10 **Sources of disaccharides**

Polysaccharides

Polysaccharides are complex carbohydrates formed from hundreds of glucose molecules strung together that provide the body with energy and are thus important nutrients. Modern dietary advice recommends that the dietary intake of fibre-rich complex carbohydrates be increased to provide at least 50 per cent of our daily energy needs.

Starches

Starches are found in grain products like bread, rice, cereals and pasta and in some fruits and vegetables. Starches take longer than sugars for the body to digest and so provide a feeling of fullness for longer, helping to avoid over-eating and obesity. All starch comes from plant sources.

Figure 2.11 **Sources of starch in the diet**

Functions of starch in the diet

- broken down slowly into simple sugars by the digestive system to provide energy
- adds bulk to our diet
- proves a feeling of fullness
- excess is converted to fat.

▶ Fibre/NSP

Fibre/NSP (non-starch polysaccharide) is the non-digestible cellulose found in plant foods. It cannot be digested so it passes straight through the digestive system, absorbing moisture and providing bulk. Fibre helps to 'push' other food through the system and helps to 'clean' the walls of the intestine of bacteria. The efficient removal of waste products from the body is vital to health.

Functions of dietary fibre

- holds water and keeps the faeces soft and bulky
- helps prevent various bowel disorders including constipation, bowel cancer, diverticular disease, appendicitis and haemorrhoids (piles)
- can help people to control their body weight because high-fibre foods are filling
- high-fibre diets are linked to lower blood cholesterol.

Too little fibre in the diet can cause constipation and in extreme cases diverticular disease where the lining of the intestine becomes distorted and inflamed.

We should be eating no less than 18 g of fibre a day, although women seem to need more than men. The average person eats only about 12 g a day so that means we should be increasing our intake by 50 per cent.

Sources of fibre in the diet

There are two type of dietary fibre, insoluble and soluble, which have different functions.

Insoluble fibre absorbs water and increases bulk, making the faeces very soft and bulky and easy to pass through the digestive system. Insoluble fibre-rich foods are wholemeal flour, wholegrain breakfast cereals, pasta, brown rice and some fruits and vegetables.

Soluble fibre slows down the digestion and absorption of carbohydrates and so helps to control blood sugar levels which helps stop us feeling hungry. Soluble fibre may also reduce blood cholesterol levels and so may reduce our risk of heart of disease. Good sources of soluble fibre are oats, peas, beans, lentils, most types of fruit and vegetables. Vegetables and fruits also provide more fibre if eaten with their skins on.

Figure 2.12 Sources of fibre in the diet

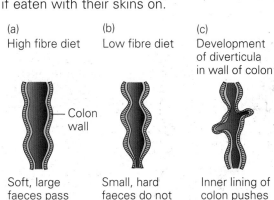

(a) High fibre diet	(b) Low fibre diet	(c) Development of diverticula in wall of colon
Soft, large faeces pass easily through the intestine	Small, hard faeces do not pass easily through colon	Inner lining of colon pushes and distorts colon wall

— Colon wall

Figure 2.13 Diagram to show food waste passing through the digestive system

KEY POINTS

- Sugars and starches release energy into the body.
- Starches are converted to energy more slowly than sugars.
- Sugars contain no other nutrients apart from energy.
- If we eat more carbohydrates than we need for energy, the excess is stored as fat.
- Dietary fibre is a very complex structure and cannot be digested.

QUESTIONS

1. State the function of carbohydrate in the diet.
2. Describe the differences between simple and complex carbohydrates.
3. Although fibre does not provide the body with nutrients, explain why it it important in the diet.
4. Explain the relationship between sugar and tooth decay.

ACTIVITY

1. Design and make a high-carbohydrate main course product for an athlete. Use nutritional software to calculate the percentage of carbohydrate in your product.
2. Collect a range of different breakfast cereal packets. Make a chart to show how much starch, sugar and fibre there is in them. Do you notice a relationship between the amount of sugar and fibre?
3. Choose a traditional recipe and adapt it to increase the fibre content.

KEY TERMS

INTRINSIC SUGAR – contained within the plant cell walls
EXTRINSIC SUGAR –added sucrose to a product
MONOSACCHARIDE – simple sugar
DISACCHARIDE – two monosaccharides combined
POLYSACCHARIDE – complex carbohydrate, either starch or fibre

2.4 VITAMINS

Vitamins are called micronutrients because they are needed in only very small quantities. They all have chemical names but they are usually referred to by letters.

Functions of vitamins in the diet

Vitamins are essential to the body:

- to maintain health
- to help prevent deficiency diseases such as beri beri and rickets
- to regulate the repair of body cells
- to help combat the ageing process
- to help to process carbohydrates and release energy in the body.

There are two main groups of vitamins, fat-soluble and water-soluble. Fat-soluble vitamins A and D are found in the fat in foods. They can be stored in the liver and used by the body when needed. Water-soluble vitamins dissolve in water. They include the B group and C and are not stored in the body, so it is important that foods containing these vitamins are eaten regularly.

Fat-soluble vitamins Chemical name	Function in the body	Good sources	Deficiency	Examples of food source
Vitamin A Retinol Beta carotene is an anti-oxidant vitamin which might protect against cancer	Keeps eyes healthy and improves night vision Helps maintain skin	Retinol is in liver, oily fish, eggs, milk, cheese, butter and margarine Beta carotene is in red, green and orange vegetables and fruits, especially carrots	Long-term deficiency may lead to night blindness Excess may lead to liver and bone damage	
Vitamin D	Works with calcium to build and maintain strong bones and teeth	Dairy products, oily fish, liver, cereals Available by exposure to sunlight	In children it can cause rickets which is a softening of the bones. There is no RNI for vitamin D	

Table 2.2 Fat-soluble vitamins A and D

Water-soluble vitamins B and C

Vitamin B is a group of vitamins all having similar functions. The most important B vitamins are listed in Table 2.3 on page 36.

KEY POINTS

- Vitamins are required in very small amounts.
- Vitamins promote health and help prevent disease.
- They regulate the building and repair of the body.
- They help regulate the chemical reactions which release energy in body cells.

Water-soluble vitamins Chemical name	Function in the body	Good sources	Deficiency	Examples of food source
B_1 Thiamine	Helps the release of energy from nutrients Functioning and normal nervous system	Fortified breakfast cereals, whole grains, meat, eggs, milk, some vegetables	Slows growth and development. Severe deficiency causes beri beri	
B_2 Riboflavin	Normal growth Healthy skin Release of energy	Liver, kidneys, meat, milk, eggs and green vegetables	Poor growth rate Skin and eye problems	
B_3 Niacin	Metabolism growth and energy release Essential for healthy skin and nerves	Meat and poultry, fish, cereals, grains Dairy products Pulses	Deficiency is very rare in UK Pellagra, rough sore skin, weakness and depression	
Folic Acid	Essential for the formation of red blood cells Foetal development	Liver, kidneys Whole grain cereals, pulses, dark green vegetables	Tiredness and anaemia	
Vitamin C Ascorbic acid	Formation of connective tissue Helps wound healing and calcium absorption Blood and blood vessel formation Helps absorb iron	Citrus and soft fruits, oranges, blackcurrants, strawberries Green vegetables, cabbage, new potatoes, peppers	Spotty skin, swollen gums, loose teeth In severe cases scurvy develops	

Table 2.3 Water-soluble vitamins B and C

QUESTIONS

1. Explain why vitamins and minerals are important in the diet.
2. List the water-soluble and the fat-soluble vitamins and their main functions.

ACTIVITY

1. Prepare a salad that would appeal to a teenager to include as many vitamins as possible.
   Make a list of the ingredients and state which vitamins are in the salad.

2. Carry out research about vitamin supplements. Would you recommend someone to take them?

3. Analyse a range of orange drinks to determine the amount of vitamin C in each one. Compare the amount of vitamin C, sugar and the cost of each one.

2.5 MINERALS

Our bodies require mineral elements for a variety of functions. They are micronutrients required in very small quantities. We are going to look at five important minerals: calcium, iron, sodium, phosphorus and fluoride. There are many more and these are called trace elements.

Minerals have four major functions:

- body building (bones and teeth)
- control of body processes, especially the nervous system

- essential part of body fluids and cells
- form part of enzymes and other proteins necessary for the release of energy.

We are going to look at four major minerals and one trace element.

Calcium and iron are the most important minerals needed by the body.

Calcium

Calcium helps form teeth and bones. An adult body contains more than 1 kg of calcium! Calcium is also needed for blood clotting, muscle contraction and enzyme formation. People need differing amounts of calcium each day, depending on their age and sex. Women who are breastfeeding need an increased amount. Young children need a diet high in calcium because their bones are growing rapidly but by about the age of 18 years bones stop growing. We reach peak bone mass at about 30 years when our bones are fully calcified.

If we do not eat sufficient calcium in our diet to maintain blood calcium the body will take calcium from our bones. Osteoporosis is a condition of weakening and thinning of the bones most common in the elderly, especially women.

Vitamin D and phosphorus work together with calcium to help maintain strong bones and teeth.

Iron

Anaemia caused by a lack of iron in the diet is one of the most common nutritional problems worldwide. Women and children are the most at risk. We need iron as it forms haemoglobin, which gives blood its red colour, and it carries oxygen round the body to the cells. Our body can store iron in the liver.

Mineral/ element	Function in the body	Good sources	Deficiency	Examples of food source
Iron	Production of haemoglobin in red blood cells to carry oxygen in the blood	Red meat, kidneys, liver Eggs, bread Green vegetables	Anaemia	
Calcium	Combines with phosphorus to harden bones and teeth Blood clotting Nerve and muscle function Heart regulation	Dairy products Fortified white bread Oily fish Green vegetables Nuts/seeds Citrus fruits	Stunted growth Can cause rickets Osteoporosis	
Phosphorus	Bones and teeth with calcium Muscle function	Dairy products Nuts, meat Fish and foods rich in calcium	People are rarely deficient in this mineral but deficiency causes tiredness and depression	
Sodium	Maintains water balance in the body Nerve transmission	Cheese, bacon, smoked meats, fish, processed foods Table salt	Deficiency is highly unlikely in the UK	
Fluoride	Strengthens teeth against decay	Fish, tea, drinking water, toothpaste	Tooth decay	

Table 2.4 The functions and sources of minerals in the diet

The best sources of iron are liver and kidneys, red meat, oily fish and leafy green vegetables. In the UK breakfast cereals and bread are fortified with iron. Iron obtained from red meat, known as haem iron, is more easily absorbed than that from vegetables. Vegetarians need to ensure that they get an adequate supply of iron from bread, pulses and vegetables. Iron absorption is reduced by the presence of tannins found in tea and coffee and phytates found in unrefined cereals such as bran. Iron absorption is increased by eating non-haem iron-rich foods with foods and drinks containing vitamin C.

QUESTIONS

1. What is the function of calcium in the diet? Why do requirements for this mineral change with age?

2. Suggest a range of meals suitable for a toddler that would include calcium.

3. Give advice to a teenage girl who is a vegetarian on how to get sufficient iron in her diet.

2.6 WATER

Nearly 65 per cent of the human body is made up of water. We need a lot of water every day. If someone becomes very short of water they can die in hours because the blood gets thicker and difficult to pump so the heart stops because of overstrain. Lack of water to drink is therefore more harmful than shortage of food.

The body can protect itself to some extent against shortage of water by reducing its water output. It cannot stop losses due to breathing and sweating, but it can limit the production of urine. The medical condition known as dehydration occurs when more water is being lost from the body than is being replaced by drinking.

Functions of water in the body

- Water helps regulate the body temperature. Sweat evaporates and cools us. Without this cooling system we would become ill from heat stroke.

- Water helps the kidneys flush out harmful excess or foreign substances from our blood. The kidneys filter waste products and eliminate them from the body as urine.

- Water transports nutrients, oxygen and carbon dioxide round the body.

ACTIVITY

Design and make a product that meets the specification in Figure 2.14.

Draw your design on plain paper and annotate. Explain in detail how your design meets the requirements of the specification. It is important that you label and colour your design.

Work out the calcium content of your design:

(a) For the whole product.

(b) For a portion size.

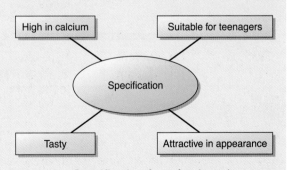

Figure 2.14 Specification for a food product

- Water is needed by nearly all body processes, e.g. digestion.

It is difficult to say how much water we need. It depends on the weather, our physical activities and even the amount of salt we eat. If we eat a lot of watery food we can drink less. Many foods are very watery, especially fruits and vegetables. On average 1–2.5 litres of water pass out of the body each day as urine. Some water is also removed with faeces. At least 1 litre of water is lost from the body each day as breath and sweat.

In this country the tap water is germ free. The water in some districts contains valuable fluoride, either naturally or added.

Figure 2.15 We need to replace the water lost during physical activity

QUESTIONS

1. Explain why it is important to make sure that we drink sufficient fluids each day.

2. Make a list of the types of food that have a high water content.

3. Give reasons why it is considered desirable to add fluoride to drinking water.

ACTIVITY

1. **Investigate the range of bottled waters available in the supermarket. Make a list of some of their claims.**

2. **Explain why you think there has been an increase in the sale of bottled water.**

3. **Discuss the environmental implication of the increased sale of bottled water.**

KEY TERM

DEHYDRATION – a medical condition resulting from insufficient water in the diet.

KEY POINTS

- Water is essential for life.
- Water provides us with no energy.
- There must be a balance between input and output of water or else dehydration will occur.

2.7 DIET

By the end of this section you should have developed a knowledge and understanding of:

- the importance of a balanced diet and of current healthy eating recommendations
- the relationship between food intake and physical activity.

A healthy, balanced diet is one that provides the correct combination of food and nutrients for optimum growth and health. To get a balanced diet, it is important to eat a mixture of foods, as foods rich in one nutrient 'balance' the lack of that nutrient in another.

Carbohydrates in the form of starchy foods such as rice, pasta, cereals and potatoes should form the basis of our diet. We should also eat at least five portions of fruit and vegetables each day.

Figure 2.16 **The Eatwell Plate**

The Eatwell Plate is based on the government's Eight Guidelines for a Healthy Diet, which are:

1 Base your meals on starchy foods.

2 Eat lots of fruit and vegetables.

3 Eat more fish, including a portion of oily fish each week.

4 Cut down on saturated fat and sugar.

5 Try to eat less salt – no more than 6 g a day for adults.

6 Get active and try to maintain a healthy weight.

The Eatwell Plate

The Eatwell Plate is a pictorial food guide showing the proportion and types of foods that are needed to make up a healthy, balanced diet. The plate has been produced by the Food Standards Agency as a guide to help people to understand and enjoy healthy eating.

7 Drink plenty of water.

8 Don't skip breakfast.

The Eatwell Plate supports previous advice to reduce fat, salt, sugar and alcohol and to increase fibre.

Figure 2.17 A healthy breakfast

The Eatwell Plate is based on the five food groups. It encourages you to choose different foods from the first four groups every day, to help ensure you obtain the wide range of nutrients your body needs to remain healthy and to function properly.

Bread, rice, potatoes, pasta and other starchy foods

Foods from this group should make up 33 per cent of the food that we eat and should be included at every meal. This is the bulk of your diet.

Fruit and vegetables

Eating at least five portions of fruit and vegetables every day is recommended for health. Fruits and vegetables do not have to be fresh or raw – they all count except for potatoes. Canned, dried, frozen, juices, soups, stews are all good and count towards your 5–a–day. You can count dried fruit, pulses and juice only once each but you can count as many canned, fresh or frozen as you like.

Milk and dairy foods

These foods should be eaten in moderate amounts every day. Try to eat 2–3 servings. A serving is a 200 ml glass of milk, 150 g yoghurt or 30 g cheese (the size of a small matchbox!). Always choose lower-fat versions whenever you can.

Meat, fish, eggs, beans and other non-dairy sources of protein

Choose lower-fat meat products, leaner cuts of meat, trim off any visible fat and skin. Use cooking methods that do not use any fat, drain away fat. Grill, poach, steam, bake or microwave. It is recommended that we eat fish at least twice a week and that one of these is oily fish, such as mackerel.

Foods and drinks high in fat and/or sugar

These foods should be eaten in small amounts. Choose lower-fat or lower-sugar alternatives wherever possible. Use spreads and oils sparingly and opt for vegetable fats and oils. Try to limit your consumption of sugary foods and drink in between meals. Try not to add any fat to foods when cooking.

Choosing a variety of foods from within each group will add to the range of nutrients you consume. Foods in the fifth group – foods and drinks high in fat and/or sugar – are not essential to a healthy diet. The Eatwell Plate applies to most people, including vegetarians, people of all ethnic origins and people who are a healthy weight for their height as well as those who are overweight.

Figure 2.18 Fruits and vegetables can be eaten in a variety of ways

ACTIVITY

1. Use the website www.foodstandards.gov.uk to find out more about the Eatwell Plate.

2. Research what is meant by lower in fat, salt and sugar. What quantity in 100 g is permitted? Make a chart to remind yourself.

3. Choose a recipe for a snack and adapt it to meet the Eatwell Plate.

KEY POINTS

- No more than 35 per cent of our food energy should come from fat.
- No more than 11 per cent of food energy should come from saturates.
- Carbohydrates should supply 50 per cent of our food energy.
- No more than 11 per cent of food energy should come from sugars.

▌ Balance

The Eatwell Plate is all about balance. There are no good or bad foods and all foods can be included in a healthy diet as long as the overall balance of foods is right. All foods supply energy and nutrients and it is achieving the correct intake of those nutrients that is important for health.

QUESTIONS

1. Explain why no more than 35 per cent of our energy should come from fat.

2. Suggest ways that a parent could encourage a primary school-aged child to include at least five portions of fruit and vegetables a day. List one day's meals.

3. List ways that someone could reduce the fat in their diet.

Figure 2.19 A range of healthy foods as part of a balanced diet

How do we know the amount of food that we should be eating?

COMA

The Committee on Medical Aspects of Food and Nutrition Policy (COMA) is a government committee within the Department of Health. The committee put together lists of the quantities of different nutrients and energy from food needed by various groups of people. This list gives DRVs or daily recommended values (also known as dietary reference values). This is a series of estimates about the amount of energy and nutrients needed by different groups of people in the UK population.

Included in this are:

- **RNI** (Reference Nutrient Intake) which shows estimated quantities needed for 97 per cent of the population. This will be far too much for a lot of people.

- **EAR** (Estimated Average Requirements) which gives an average estimate of amounts. Some people will need more and some people will need less.

- **LRNI** (Lower reference nutrient intake) is the amount of a nutrient that is enough for only a small number of people who have low needs.

When you use a nutritional software program, it will usually give you the results of how your product compares to the EAR, which is the amount of nutrients needed by the average person. You must remember that you will eat only one portion of your product, not the whole dish!

ACTIVITY

1. Research current dietary guidelines by using the internet. Useful sites include:

   www.foodstandards.gov.uk

   British Nutrition Foundation at www.nutrition.org.uk

2. Produce a fact sheet giving advice on a balanced diet to friends who do not study Food Technology.

The relationship between food intake and physical activity

This is known as **energy balance**. Energy is measured in kilocalories (kcal) or kilojoules (kJ). Carbohydrates, fats and protein from all the food and drinks we consume are broken down in the digestive system and contribute to the total daily amount of our energy:

- 1 g of fat supplies 9 Kcal
- 1 g carbohydrate supplies 3.7 Kcal
- 1 g protein supplies 4 Kcal
- 1 g of alcohol supplies 7 Kcal.

The amount of energy we need varies with age, gender and the amount of activity we carry out. Of the energy we consume, 70 per cent is used for all bodily functions (breathing, warmth, nerves, brain cells, digestion). This is called our basal metabolic rate (BMR) and the rest is used for all other activities.

If you eat and drink foods higher in energy than the body needs, the energy is stored as fat and you gain weight. If you use more energy than calories consumed, you will lose weight.

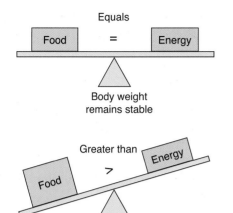

Figure 2.20 It is all a matter of balance

Remember:

- If food consumed equals the energy used, your weight stays the same.
- If food consumed is greater than energy used, then weight increases.
- If food consumed is less than energy used, there is weight loss.
- These amounts are given as Estimated Average Requirements (EAR).

	Males MJ/day	Kcal/day	Females MJ/day	Kcal/day
0–3 months	2.28	545	2.16	515
4–6 months	2.89	690	2.69	645
7–9 months	3.44	825	3.20	765
10–12 months	3.85	920	3.61	865
1–3 years	5.15	1230	4.86	1165
4–6 years	7.16	1715	6.46	1545
7–10 years	8.24	1970	7.28	1740
11–14 years	9.27	2220	7.72	1845
15–18 years	11.10	2755	8.83	2110
19–50 years	10.60	2550	8.10	1940
51–59 years	10.60	2550	8.00	1900
60–64 years	9.93	2380	7.99	1900
65–74 years	9.71	2330	7.96	1900
75+ years	8.77	2100	7.61	1810
Pregnancy	.....	.....	+0.80	+200
An additional amount is also needed by lactating mothers				

Table 2.5 Estimated Average Requirements (EAR) for energy

KEY POINTS

- Requirements for nutrients differ for different groups.
- We need to maintain a balance of energy input and energy output.
- If too much food is consumed it is stored as fat, resulting in weight gain.

ACTIVITY

Use nutrition software to analyse the amount of energy that you should be consuming. Input everything that you consume in one day. Remember to include all of your drinks and snacks. Analyse your results and make a list of the ways that you could improve your diet.

Research how much energy you use doing the following activities each hour:

- playing squash
- walking slowly
- sitting at your computer
- dancing.

Figure 2.21 The more physical activity we do, the more energy we use

KEY TERMS

ENERGY BALANCE – the relationship between energy input and energy used by the body

KCAL/KJ – measurement of energy in foods

QUESTIONS

1. What is meant by 'energy balance'?
2. Give five factors that affect how much energy someone needs.
3. How can being obese affect a person's health?

2.8 MODIFYING RECIPES

By the end of this section you should have developed a knowledge and understanding of:

- how to modify dishes to promote health through altering or substituting ingredients
- how to modify dishes to promote health through changing the method of cooking.

The Eatwell Plate can be applied to all main course dishes, such as lasagne, casseroles, pasta products. You will have to think carefully how to adapt desserts, snacks, cakes, biscuits and pastry products.

Remember that you are aiming to:

- *lower the fat*
- *lower the sugar*
- *lower the salt*
- *increase the fibre.*

When you develop or modify the products you must also consider who the product is designed for as you will need to meet their identified needs. This could mean changing the flavour, colour, texture, costs, shape or appearance or how it is assembled or cooked. You may also need to improve the nutritional content or adapt to meet cultural or dietary needs.

Figure 2.22 Pizza is a well-balanced product

A good example of a balanced product is a pizza, which contains ingredients from the four main food groups:

- a thick dough base from the bread, rice, potatoes, pasta and other starchy food group
- tomato puree and plenty of other vegetables such as mushrooms and peppers from the fruit and vegetable group
- a moderate amount of cheese, or even fat-reduced cheese, from the milk and dairy group

- a moderate amount of ham or tuna from the meat, fish, eggs, beans group and other non–dairy sources of protein.

ACTIVITY

Design and make a pizza which follows the advice of the Eatwell Plate.

Try using the Eatwell Plate shown in Figure 2.23 when you are designing/adapting recipes.

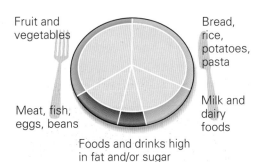

Fruit and vegetables

Bread, rice, potatoes, pasta

Meat, fish, eggs, beans

Milk and dairy foods

Foods and drinks high in fat and/or sugar

Figure 2.23 A blank Eatwell Plate

▶ Ways to modify recipes

Bread, rice, potatoes, pasta and other starchy foods

- Use different types of flour to increase variety, e.g. in bread products try using wholemeal or granary.
- Use more pasta in relation to meat/fish sauce in pasta products.
- Use more potato in relation to meat in cottage or shepherd's pie.
- Use naan bread and plenty of rice with curries.

Fruit and vegetables

- Incorporate extra vegetables into casseroles, soups, meat sauces.
- Add salads (with low-fat dressings) and vegetables to main meals.
- Add fresh or dried fruit to puddings, cakes and biscuits.
- Use fresh and dried fruit to sweeten products instead of using sucrose.

Figure 2.24 Add more vegetables to casseroles and stews

Meat, fish, eggs, beans and other non–dairy sources of protein

- Add pulses to meat dishes to increase the fibre content, reduce the overall fat content and add extra protein, e.g. red kidney beans in a chilli.
- Use lean meat and remove visible fat or skin where necessary, e.g. remove skin from chicken.
- Use alternatives to meat such as mycoprotein (Quorn®), tofu or textured vegetable protein to increase variety. Use eggs, nuts, pulses and seeds more frequently.

- Include fish in products, both oily and white varieties.

Milk and dairy foods

- Switch to semi-skimmed or skimmed milk and use lower-fat dairy products.

- Use fromage frais, quark or plain yogurt in place of cream in some dishes (you may need to test this out first as the recipe may not always work).

- Use a smaller amount of a strong-tasting cheese, such as mature Cheddar or Parmesan, in cooking instead of normal cheese.

- Use reduced-fat cheese wherever possible.

- Grate cheese for use in a wide range of products so less is used. Mix grated cheese with breadcrumbs for a lower-in-fat crunchy topping.

Foods and drinks high in fat and/or sugar

If you make products that fit into this category, think carefully about how you can improve them. You could:

- reduce the quantity of sugar in the recipe

- replace sugar with dried or fresh fruit

- use unsaturated oils and fats instead of butter or hard margarine (this won't reduce the fat content but will help lower cholesterol)

- use less high-fat and sugar ingredients, e.g. more fruit less topping on a crumble, lattice top on a pie, change a pie into a flan

- replace cream with yoghurt

- choose lower-fat versions of ingredients.

▶ Ways to improve the method of cooking

- Some traditional methods of cooking use a lot of additional fat so try to avoid roasting and deep or shallow fat frying and choose lower-fat methods.

- Grill or oven bake foods instead of frying, which will remove some of the fat from the foods.

- Steam fish instead of frying.

- Poach, bake or boil so that no fat is added.

- Dry-fry meat in a non-stick pan to remove the fat.

- Use fats and oils sparingly. Try to spray oil, this just puts a thin film on the pan.

- Ensure the temperature is correct when frying so that foods absorb less fat.

Figure 2.25 Change your method of cooking – try steaming

There are many ways to modify recipes. You will discover many more as you try different ideas.

QUESTIONS

1. State one other method of cooking for each of the following foods that would lower the fat content: fried bacon, fried sausages, fried egg, fried chicken, roast potatoes.

2. Explain ways in which the spaghetti bolognese recipe could be adapted to meet the Eatwell Plate. Consider the method of making as well as the ingredients.

Spaghetti Bolognese
220g minced beef
50g bacon
1 tablespoon oil
1 chopped onion
1 small tin tomatoes
1 tablespoon tomato puree
Salt and pepper to taste
200g spaghetti
50g grated parmesan cheese

3. Give two reasons why we should cut down on the amount of salt in our diet.

4. Suggest two different flavourings which could be added to a savoury product instead of salt.

5. Make a list of the ways of reducing fat in a recipe of your choice.

ACTIVITY

Use the basic spaghetti bolognese ingredients but modify them to produce an innovative, healthier pasta product that will appeal to teenagers.

KEY POINTS

- Keep the balance of starchy foods and fruit and vegetables high in comparison to proteins, dairy foods, fat and sugar.
- Adapt recipes by replacing or reducing high fat, sugar and salt ingredients.

KEY TERM

MODIFY – change an ingredient to improve or develop a recipe

2.9 FOOD CHOICE

LEARNING OUTCOMES

By the end of this section you should have developed a knowledge and understanding of:

- factors that affect people's choice of food: availability, cost, personal preferences, cultural preferences, religion, lifestyle, health, storage, cooking facilities, recent food trends and issues, food scares, advertising and promotions, seasonability, local food, sustainability.

Most people make a choice of food at least two or three times a day. The availability of a wide range of foods makes it easier to choose foods that are nutritionally good for us but we are all influenced by a variety of other factors.

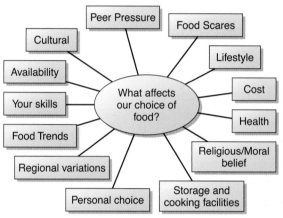

Figure 2.26 Chart to show the factors affecting food choice

Availability

Choice depends on the type of food available in the country and place that you live. In developing countries, such as in parts of Africa, there is very little choice and often insufficient food available. Countries may not be able to grow produce because of the climate, or because they cannot afford expensive agricultural equipment. In developed countries like the UK, we have a wide variety of food because of technological developments and improvements in the growth, transport, preservation and storage of food. Food technologists have also created many new foods, such as Quorn® and TVP. We can import foods that we cannot grow

ourselves. In the UK we can go to the supermarket at any time of the year and buy whatever food we want as long as we are prepared to pay for it.

Figure 2.27 Modern transportation has improved consumer choice

Cost

We all have a specific amount of money available to spend on food and so this affects our choice. People have to think of ways that they could save money on their food bill:

- using cheaper protein foods, e.g. eggs, cheese and pulses
- buying locally grown vegetables or even growing your own
- buying special offers such as 'buy one get one free'
- using a variety of supermarkets and planning meals around their special offers
- buying foods with a short shelf life that have been reduced in price
- not wasting foods – the average family in the UK throws away £600 worth of food in a year

- following the advice of the Eatwell Plate and using cheaper carbohydrates in meals
- adapting recipes by swapping expensive ingredients for cheaper ones, e.g. yoghurt instead of cream
- planning meals and shopping carefully
- using 'own-brand' economy-range products
- buying loose produce which is often cheaper than pre-packaged
- using economical methods of cooking.

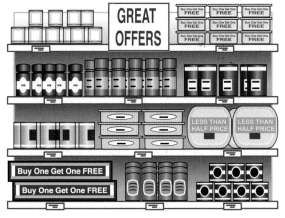

Figure 2.28 Special offers in a supermarket

Rich people tend to buy more protein foods, so their starch and fibre intake tends to decrease, while those on lower incomes tend to buy less fruit and vegetables, thus having a lower intake of vitamins and minerals.

Personal preferences

We all have our personal likes and dislikes. We are influenced by our senses.

The senses

We use all of our five senses when we eat. These give us information about the food. The five senses are:

- **Sight** – the appearance (aesthetics) of food can make it look more or less appetising. Aspects such as colour, size, shape, age, texture, garnish and decoration will all affect how you feel about the product. Some foods are expected to be a certain colour, such as tomato soup (red), white flour, etc. The colour of food is a guide to its freshness.

- **Sound** – some food products make sounds during preparation, cooking, serving or eating, for instance the crackle of popcorn, the sizzle of bacon, the crunch of crisps and raw carrot.

- **Smell** – sensed through the nose. You can detect the

ACTIVITY

Use the internet to compare the prices in three different supermarkets of:

12 eggs	250 g soft margarine
1.5 kg self-raising flour	500 g castor sugar
500 g cooking apples	500 g Cheddar cheese

You could choose your own ingredients list to do a comparison.

aroma of foods, such as ripeness and freshness of apples and cabbage. The flavour is often detected by the aroma as well as the taste. Aroma stimulates the digestive juices and makes the food appear more appetising.

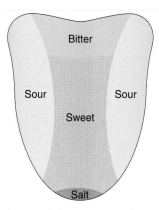

Figure 2.29 **Areas of the tongue**

- **Taste** – taste buds detect four groups of flavours: bitter, sweet, sour and salt. Flavour develops when the food is combined through chewing and mixing with saliva. Taste is very important and is detected by 9000 nerve endings in our tongue.

- **Touch** – the surface of the tongue is sensitive to different sensations, such as moist, dry, soft, sticky, gritty, crumbly, mushy, etc. As we bite and chew food we can feel how hard or soft a food is through our teeth and jaw. These qualities are known as **mouthfeel**. Texture is important – we appreciate qualities such as smoothness and crispness and if they are missing, food is considered to be unpalatable.

The characteristics of food that affect our organs or senses are known as 'organoleptic' qualities.

ACTIVITY

Carry out a survey of 20 of your school friends to find out their likes and dislikes when choosing foods. Analyse your results and present your findings as a letter to a food company advising them of teenage food preferences.

EXAMINER'S TIPS

Refer to Chapter 1 and try to include both open and closed questions.

KEY POINTS

- When you eat, you both taste and smell the food. If your nose is blocked with mucus from a cold, you can't smell properly and so food seems to have less taste.
- Smell and taste work together to develop the flavour of food.
- The sensitivity of the tongue is reduced when the food is either very hot or very cold.

Cultural preferences

A cultural group is a group of people that share the same norms, beliefs and values.

We adopt the eating patterns of our parents from infancy; we learn to like the foods that our families like. Every culture in the world has its own type of eating patterns and styles of cooking, for example use of staple crops. Styles of eating and cooking tend to be determined by the availability of cheap, locally grown food products. Rice is the staple crop in India, China and Japan, the potato in Britain and yams in parts of Africa.

Wheat is grown in many countries but is used in a variety of ways:

- pasta in Italy
- bread in Europe
- noodles in China
- unleavened bread (naan and chapattis) in India and the Middle East.

Eating patterns vary regionally within one country according to local availability of different types of food and different lifestyles of people. In some cultures and religions certain foods are not permitted because they are considered 'dirty or unclean' or sacred. Manufacturers are influenced by cultures because if there is a demand for a certain type of food they will respond.

ACTIVITY

Make a list of celebrations in different cultures and find out what special foods are served.

For example, Christmas – mince pies.

Certain foods have become an important part of the celebrations in many cultures.

Figure 2.30 **Staple foods from around the world**

Religious issues

Religious beliefs influence eating habits, as religions often have laws related to foods.

Hinduism

The cow is sacred to Hindus, so they will not eat beef or any product from slaughtered cows. They are usually vegetarians and have many days of fasting.

Sikhism

Similar to Hindus, but more meat is generally eaten.

Islam (Muslims)

The pig is considered unclean, therefore Muslims do not eat pork or any pork products. Other meats must be slaughtered in a particular way so no blood remains. This is called Halal meat.

Jews

The only meat that Jews are allowed to eat must be specially slaughtered, soaked and then treated with kosher salt. They do not eat pork. Meat and dairy produce must not be eaten at the same meal.

Moral issues

Some people may make moral decisions, for example vegetarians who decide that it is morally wrong to kill animals to eat their flesh. Current moral issues affecting food production are: intensive farming, genetically modified (GM) foods, Fairtrade, animal welfare, factory farming, irradiation, selective breeding, biotechnology and slaughtering of animals.

Factory-farmed animals can be kept in very distressing conditions, cramped with limited lighting and no room for the animals to move or exercise. There are also problems with the spread of infection because lots of animals are kept together.

Free-range animals are allowed to live and grow in natural surroundings. These products will cost the consumer more money because the farmer will not produce as much and they will need more resources than factory farmers.

Figure 2.31 **Free-range hens**

Selective breeding has resulted in egg-laying hens which will produce 300 eggs a year. A broiler chicken, reared for meat and not eggs, will reach its slaughter weight in about 40 days.

Figure 2.32 **Factory-farmed egg production**

Lifestyle

Eating habits have been affected by social changes within households during the past 30 years. Changes in lifestyle due to both parents working and the consequent increase in income (two wages) have resulted in people spending less time in the kitchen preparing food from raw ingredients. People choose to buy more foods that are ready to eat or just need reheating, and to eat out more. In some homes, due to members of the family eating at different times, some of the traditional mealtimes of breakfast, lunch and dinner are being replaced by snack meals and takeaway dinners.

Factors include:

- more mothers are employed outside the home
- more people live alone
- people travel greater distances to work
- people have social activities outside the home
- the use of convenience foods, ready meals and availability of 'takeaways' allow people to have more flexible lifestyles

- there has been an increase in snack foods available
- there is a wide variety of foods available to choose from
- most cities have a wide selection of restaurants
- there is less emphasis on the family meal and family members eat when they want to (grazing).

Figure 2.33 Shopping has become a family occasion with everyone choosing food

do so. The government produced a white paper, 'The Health of the Nation', as far back as 1992 expressing concerns that the nation's eating and drinking habits were affecting many aspects of health and disease. It committed the government to promote health and reduce coronary heart disease and obesity by improving the national diet. It set targets to reduce the number of people aged 16 to 64 who were obese by a quarter by 2005. We know that this did not work and that even now the numbers of obese and overweight people, especially children, is still increasing.

Eating for health means making small changes to the meals that we already eat. We should all choose foods carefully:

- Overweight people should choose low-calorie, low-fat foods.
- People recovering from an injury or illness should choose high-protein foods.
- Someone recovering from a heart attack would choose lower-in-fat products.

ACTIVITY

Consider the lifestyle of your family. How are the eating patterns affected by the work and social activities of the family members? Are there any ways that you could improve the eating habits of any of your family?

Health

The nutritional needs of individuals and groups of people should play an important part in choosing foods but does not always

Figure 2.34 The NHS is spending valuable funds on helping people with diet-related disorders

- Anyone suffering from high blood pressure is usually advised to have a lower-in-salt diet.

Many people are in hospital because of diet-related conditions. We do not have deficiency diseases in the UK, but there is a problem because of people eating the wrong foods.

Storage and cooking facilities

Food technologists are continually developing new food products that require little preparation and are easy to store and cook.

Most households have a microwave to reheat convenience foods. A refrigerator is considered an essential item of equipment to ensure food safety; if you do not have a refrigerator your choice is restricted to canned and dried foods. Many households have a freezer which means that they can shop weekly.

If you do not have the skills to prepare ingredients, you can buy them ready prepared, such as frozen vegetables. Students at university, for instance, and the elderly often have limited cooking facilities. However, these can be expanded through the purchase of a wide range of cooking equipment that will perform different tasks, including low-fat grilling machines, electric woks and electric barbeques.

Figure 2.35 **Lots of new equipment is available**

Recent food trends and issues

The number of new food products and the range of foods available have increased as influence on consumers' lifestyles affect their food choices. You will know about new products in the supermarket that you have noticed recently and perhaps you can think of some that have disappeared!

These are some of the food trends in the past few years:

- an increase in the development of authentic ethnic foods. As we travel more around the world and learn about food from other cultures we want to try these dishes for ourselves

ACTIVITY

Research a range of different cooking equipment. For each piece of equipment consider:

- What is its function?

- How much does it cost?

- Who would benefit from using the equipment?

- more and more sandwiches are being eaten

- traditional food products such as bread and butter pudding and steamed puddings have become more popular

- healthy eating claims, especially low-fat or no-fat claims, are increasing

- the variety of vegetable dishes is increasing

- there are more new products targeted at children, e.g. breakfast bars

- organic foods and products suitable for vegetarians are increasing

- party food is proving popular

- healthier low-fat versions of products are available

- meals that can be taken at convenient times and are often eaten 'on the move'.

Trends for the future?

Here are some predictions for the future:

- greater variety of choice and convenience, more products that can be cooked by microwave

- demand for healthier foods and organic ingredients

- greater demand for single portions

- nostalgia products, food products from the past that will look and taste more 'home made'

- eco-friendly packaging

- increased consumption of locally produced sustainable foods

- healthy ready meals targeted at children

- innovative low-calorie products for weight watchers

- with heart disease and other diseases still a major issue, foods that can fight diseases are going to be popular

- people want more indulgent foods such as luxury desserts and chocolate products

- less meat and a rise in the consumption of fruits, vegetables, whole grains

- useful bacteria are going to be used in many other food items that are part of our daily diet

- more snacking for busy people who just cannot stop for food

- increase in the consumption of raw food in the form of salads and other enticing dishes are going to be another of the food trends witnessed globally. The benefits of raw food will be explored across the globe.

Figure 2.36 Traditional steamed puddings with a new twist

ACTIVITY

1. Using examples, write your own past and future food lists. Write your own ideas for the future.

2. Carry out a survey of people to find out what their favourite nostalgia food is. Ask older people what foods they can remember from the past. Write an article on nostalgia foods suitable to go in a food magazine.

3. Cook a traditional British pudding but try to adapt it to meet the Eatwell Plate.

Figure 2.37 There was a dramatic fall in the sale of eggs when there was a salmonella scare.

Food scares

Food scares in the media have a dramatic influence on food choice and sometimes result in product sales dropping so dramatically that the company ceases to exist. Recent food scares include:

- salmonella in eggs
- botulism in hazelnut yoghurts
- listeria in chilled foods
- dioxins in coke (in 1999)
- E. coli in meat products
- food contamination during production, e.g. metals, insects, glass, fabric will cause a drop in product sale
- BSE reported in the media resulted in a drop in meat sales.

Genetically modified foods

The use of new technology in the food industry is controversial, especially products made by modifying or engineering the genetic make-up of food. This might actually improve the quality of the food, for instance blackcurrants can be modified to make them higher in vitamin C, tomatoes can be modified to improve their flavour or keeping qualities. It is now possible to 'switch off' the gene which is responsible for making a tomato go soft when it is ripe, thus making the tomato last longer.

QUESTION

Explain, using examples, why consumers are influenced by food scares.

EXAMINER'S TIPS

In the Unit A524 examination you will have 'explain' questions. Look at Chapter 15 to see how to answer this question.

Advantages of GM crops are:

- improvements to quantity and quality of food.
- can grow in adverse conditions, e.g. drought
- herbicide and insect resistance, therefore will keep longer
- high nutritional quality
- cheaper to produce.

However, there are concerns about GM foods:

- long-term safety is unknown
- environmental concerns as the pollen does not stop in one place
- ethics – we need adequate labelling. From January 2000 if a product has over 1 per cent of gm food it must be stated on the label, if it is under 1 per cent it does not need to be stated
- there is a lack of communication between provider and consumer.

Figure 2.38 Genetically modified crops

ACTIVITY

Carry out research to find out what common foods contain GM ingredients.

Advertising and promotions

We are strongly influenced by our peer group and by the media. Manufacturers spend many millions every year on advertising, especially on chocolate, crisps, snacks and sweets. Where a product will be advertised depends on who the product target group is and how much the advertising budget is. Also manufacturers may promote the product by special offers, free gifts and competitions.

Different ways of advertising and promoting food products are:

- advertisements on the television and cinema, in newspapers, magazines and internet or on posters and flyers
- displays in supermarkets and shop windows
- special money offers such as 'buy one get one free' (bogof) or money-off coupons
- celebrity endorsements by sports or pop stars
- competitions
- free samples or tastings in supermarkets
- free gifts
- eye-catching attractive packaging.

We watch chefs on the television and see advertising all around us. This influences our choice of food. We buy two for the price of one or buy this week's 'best buy', whether we need them or not.

Advertising must be legal, decent, honest and truthful and this is monitored by the Office of Fair Trading.

ACTIVITY

Collect two different advertisements for food products. Consider their suitability for the target market. What is it describing? Who is the product aimed at? What is the message? Is it a good or a bad advert? Would you buy the product?

Figure 2.39 A selection of products targeted at children

QUESTIONS

1. Why is advertising and promotion important when a manufacturer makes a new product?

2. Why are there standards and controls on advertising to children?

3. Discuss the influence that Jamie Oliver has had on school lunches.

Seasonability

This relates to the availability and use of products when they are in season. The production of crops in the UK is limited to short seasons during the year. We have become accustomed to going into supermarkets and buying anything at any time. The range of products and ingredients available for us to buy is due to the impact of globalisation. This has been made possible by improved storage, preservation and transportation of foods. Our food products travel many miles to reach our table. Think about the effect on the environment of the miles that food travels. This is called the carbon footprint of the product or food miles.

Local food

Using local products means that you are getting quality products with a low carbon footprint.

We can eat with the seasons (see Table 2.6).

A new trend is for households to have boxes of organic local produce delivered to the door.

Figure 2.40 Local organic fruits and vegetables delivered to your door

January	February	March	April
Cabbage Kale Parsnip Swede	Artichoke Spring greens Watercress	Cauliflower Purple sprouting broccoli	Greenhouse lettuce Spring greens Salad onions
May	**June**	**July**	**August**
Asparagus Tomatoes Spring cabbage	Finger carrots Gooseberries Broad beans Lettuce Spinach Strawberries	Cherries Cauliflowers Mange tout/peas Raspberries Salad potatoes	Charlotte potatoes Courgettes Discovery apples French beans Romaine lettuce
September	**October**	**November**	**December**
Beetroot Pears Apples Runner beans	Celery Pumpkin Turnip Squash	Chinese Leaves Green cabbage Brussels sprouts	Brussels sprouts on a stalk Leeks Savoy cabbage Chantenay carrots

Table 2.6 **Fruit and vegetables grown in the UK**

Sustainability

The choices we make as consumers and designers have an impact on other people, especially elsewhere in the world. If we buy chocolate, coffee or tea in the supermarket there are consequences for the people in Kenya, Sri Lanka, Nicaragua and many other places. These consequences extend to their families, schools, communities, etc. We have a moral dilemma whether we should buy British or support developing countries in some way. By eating food out of season and from far away we are using up the world's resources.

Figure 2.41 **Buying local produce from sustainable sources**

What is Fairtrade?

Fairtrade is about better prices, decent working conditions, local sustainability and fair terms of trade for farmers and workers in the developing world. By requiring companies to pay sustainable prices (which must never fall lower than the market price), Fairtrade addresses the injustices of conventional trade, which traditionally discriminates against the poorest, weakest producers. It enables them to improve their position and have more control over their lives.

Figure 2.42 The FAIRTRADE Mark

The Fairtrade Foundation has licensed over 4,000 Fairtrade certified products for sale through retail and catering outlets in the UK. The UK market is doubling in value every two years, and in 2007 reached an estimated retail value of £493 million. The UK is one of the world's leading Fairtrade markets, with more products and more awareness of Fairtrade than anywhere else. Around 20 per cent of roast and ground coffee sold in the UK retail market is Fairtrade. Stable prices mean coffee farmers can plan for the future.

Food products include:

- bananas
- cocoa
- coffee
- dried fruit
- fresh fruit and fresh vegetables
- honey
- juices
- nuts/oil seeds
- quinoa
- rice
- spices
- sugar
- tea
- wine.

KEY POINT

- The FAIRTRADE Mark is an independent consumer label which appears on products as a guarantee that disadvantaged producers are getting a better deal. It guarantees that farmers in developing countries get a fair price for their products, which covers their costs.

Figure 2.43 Traidcraft logo

Organisations such as Traidcraft use only ethically produced materials and ingredients which help both the producers and manufacturers in developing countries. Adriano Kalilii, a tea plucker from Kibena in Tanzania, can afford iron sheets to roof his house thanks to Fairtrade.

Figure 2.44 Tea in Tanzania (Traidcraft photo)

- Animals are reared without the routine use of drugs, antibiotics and wormers common in intensive livestock farming.
- Organic producers can only use natural fertilisers, not synthetic ones.

Organic foods are considered to taste nicer, avoid the risk of a combination of chemicals and respect soil structure and wildlife.

Organic Products

Figure 2.45 The Soil Association organic logo

Figure 2.46 Organic crops grown on a local allotment

Organic production is better for the environment. It means less intensive farming and the food contains far fewer pesticides. So what does organic mean?

- All food sold as organic must be approved by organic certification bodies and produced according to stringent EC laws.
- Organic farming severely restricts the use of artificial chemical fertilisers and pesticides.
- It will not contain any genetically engineered ingredients.

KEY POINT

- Organic foods avoid health risks associated with a combination of chemicals used as pesticides and herbicides.

ACTIVITY

Investigate the range of organic products in the supermarket. Compare prices with non-organic products.

QUESTION

1. Discuss the reasons why a family may choose to buy organic foods.

KEY TERMS

ORGANOLEPTIC – qualities of food associated with the senses
GENETICALLY MODIFIED – crops where the genetic structure of the cells has been changed
ORGANIC – grown or reared without the use of artificial aids, fertilisers, pesticides and antibiotics
FAIRTRADE – guarantees that disadvantaged producers get a fair deal
SUSTAINABILITY – is reducing the impact of a product on the environment
GLOBALISATION – process by which different parts of the globe become interconnected by economic, social, cultural and political means

2.10 SPECIAL DIETARY NEEDS

LEARNING OUTCOMES

By the end of this section you should have developed a knowledge and understanding of:

- food products aimed at different age groups and people with different dietary requirements:
  - diabetics
  - coeliacs (gluten)
  - allergies to nuts
  - vegetarians
  - calorie controlled
  - heart disease (CHD)
  - pregnancy.

▌ Ages and stages of life

*During the different stages of life people require different foods and quantities of nutrients to keep healthy, and different nutritional theories exist on how best to do this. (See nutrients section in 2.1.) From a manufacturer's point of view this offers the opportunity to **target groups** with products designed for their particular needs.*

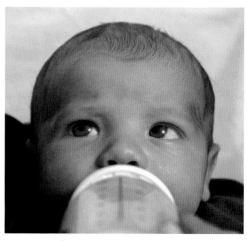

Figure 2.47 A baby gets sufficient nutrients from milk for six months

Babies are totally reliant on their parents to provide food and so manufacturers must take into account the **needs and wants** of the baby and the parents. A baby needs essential nutrients for growth and development, energy-dense, filling food that is easy to swallow. It must be hygienic and safe. Babies initially drink only milk but as they grow more energy is required so they are weaned on to solid food.

Parents will want the food to be nutritious, appetising, easy to prepare, without additives, low in sugar, hygienic, safe and sold at a reasonable price.

Toddlers are growing fast so they require a lot of energy from their food. They need a balanced diet but a high proportion of complex carbohydrates to provide this energy. The food must be easy to hold, available in suitable sized portions, with interesting shapes, colour, texture and flavour.

School-aged children are still reliant on their parents but they are influenced by the media

Figure 2.48 Weaning – from six months a baby is introduced to finger food

and peer group. They need products that meet current dietary guidelines on healthy eating and that also provide filling food, particularly for packed lunches.

Adolescents are becoming aware of environmental, moral, economic and health issues. There is a gradual move away from parental influence. They become more aware of peer group pressure and body image. Body growth is rapid so they still require a lot of energy from their food, particularly boys during their growth spurt. Girls have a greater need for the mineral iron to replace that lost during menstruation.

Puberty is also the time when peak bone mass is reached and without sufficient calcium and phosphorus in the diet at this crucial time there will be a weakening of the bones, leading to bone disease and osteoporosis in later life.

Food must be affordable, fashionable, quick and easy to prepare and suited to a busy and energetic lifestyle.

Adults' needs vary the most, depending on their lifestyle and occupation. Many adults face the problem of consuming too much energy from food, leading to weight gain. They often look to buy products to help with weight loss. Some want lower-in-fat, salt or sugar foods and are eager to follow current healthy eating guidelines. They may also want luxury products as meals become more of a social occasion.

Single people will want products sold in small packs, ready or partly made products that are easy to store.

Senior citizens are growing in number and many live on a limited income. They still require a balanced diet supplying a good range of nutrients but they often suffer from loss of appetite. They need appetising products in smaller quantities. They want easy-to-prepare, nutritional meals with easy-to-open packaging.

▶ Special dietary requirements

Some people cannot eat certain types of food without becoming ill. This may be because of a medical condition or a reaction to food. This is known as food intolerance.

Figure 2.49 Senior citizens cooking a meal together

 QUESTIONS

List four specification points for a new product to meet the needs of the following target groups.

1. A teenage student before a game of football.

2. An office worker's packed lunch.

3. A single senior citizen's main meal.

4. Party food for a toddler.

Give reasons for each of the specification points.

 ACTIVITY

- Produce design ideas to meet the specification points you have listed. In your practical lesson, prepare one of the design ideas. Evaluate the product against the specification point.

- Design some promotional material to convince teenagers about the importance of drinking milk.

Diabetics

Diabetes is a medical condition where the glucose in the blood stream is not balanced correctly. Glucose is carried in the blood to all body cells to supply them with energy. Insulin, a hormone produced by the pancreas, controls the amount of glucose in the bloodstream and stops it going too high. There are two types of diabetes: insulin dependent where there is a severe lack of insulin which is treated by insulin injections and diet, and type 2 or non-insulin dependent diabetes which usually occurs late in life and is treated with diet or diet and tablets. Meals for diabetics should include high-fibre, starchy carbohydrate foods such as potatoes, rice and pasta but should be low in sugar and sweet foods. Sorbitol (artificial sweetener) can be used instead of sucrose and glucose.

Figure 2.50 Diabetics must control their intake of sugar

Figure 2.51 Look for the gluten-free logo (Coeliac UK)

KEY POINT

- People with diabetes do not need a special diet – they should follow normal health eating guidelines.

Coeliacs (gluten allergy)

Coeliac disease is an autoimmure disease triggered by sensitivity to the protein gluten which is found in wheat, barley and rye. The gluten damages the lining of the intestine and prevents other nutrients from being absorbed. Adults with coeliac disease often have anaemia, abdominal pain weight loss and/or diarrhoea. Gluten is found in barley, rye and wheat as well as oats. It is commonly used in food manufacturing as a thickening agent and so people with coeliac disease should read ingredient lists carefully. Special gluten-free products are available.

Allergies to nuts

Our body has an immune system to protect us from harmful things but sometimes a person's body reacts too strongly to a particular substance. This is what happens when a person becomes allergic to a substance. Babies are sometimes allergic to lactose, the sugar in cow's milk. Allergies to eggs, soya and certain artificial food flavours, colours or preservatives can cause reactions.

Some allergies are very serious, for example the allergic reaction to nuts. Some people have an anaphylactic reaction to even a minute quantity of an allergen in nuts. Their whole body reacts immediately and severely, blood vessels start to leak and they have difficulty breathing. They must be treated immediately with an injection of adrenaline, otherwise they could die. In some cases even touching or breathing in particles of the allergen can cause a reaction. Consequently even the smallest amount of nuts or nut contact must be included on food labelling.

Figure 2.52 People with allergies to nuts must read all food labels carefully

QUESTIONS

1. Why is it necessary for people with special dietary needs to read food labels? Give examples using a food label.

2. Write a specification for a main course product for a coeliac.

3. Explain the function of insulin in the control of glucose levels in the blood.

ACTIVITY

Make a cake product suitable for a coeliac.

Research a range of special dietary needs and produce a factsheet for a supermarket to hand out.

KEY POINTS

- People with allergies or food intolerances must read ingredient lists carefully.
- There is a wide range of products available for people with special dietary needs.

Vegetarians

There are three main reasons why a person becomes a vegetarian: moral reasons, religious belief and medical reasons. There are two main types of vegetarians:

- lacto-ovo vegetarians
- vegans.

Lacto-ovo vegetarians will not eat meat, meat products, fish, poultry, lard, suet, fish oils or gelatine because they involve killing the animal. They will, however, eat food products from animals such as eggs, milk, cheese, butter, cream, yoghurt and fromage frais. Another problem is that cheese is made using rennin, an enzyme from a calf's stomach, but vegetarian cheese is made using a vegetable rennet. Lacto vegetarians can choose from a wide range of food products and recipes and they have no problem at all in obtaining the essential amino acids for proteins or a wide range of vitamins and minerals. Quorn®, a commercially made micoprotein, is an excellent meat substitute for lacto vegetarians. Vegans cannot eat Quorn® as it contains egg white. Cheese, eggs, nuts, beans, lentils, tofu and textured vegetable protein can all be used to make an exciting range of products.

Figure 2.53 **There is a wide range of vegetarian products available in the supermarkets, such as vegetarian lasagne**

Figure 2.54 **Look for the vegetarian logo**

Vegans are strict vegetarians who avoid eating all animal products, including meat, fish, cheese, dairy milk and cream. Vegans must ensure that they have an adequate nutritional balance in their diet. Particular problems are obtaining:

- an adequate supply of a range of proteins to ensure that they get all the essential amino acids
- vitamins A and D which are plentiful in animal fats
- mineral elements calcium, phosphorus and iron found in dairy products and meat
- vitamin B12 as there is no B12 in cereals or vegetables.

There are many types of nuts, pulses and cereals for vegans to use, particularly products made from soya which is high in biological value. They need to make sure that they use herbs, spices and a variety of vegetables to avoid their diet being monotonous. A further problem is that vegan diets are sometimes very bulky and excessive amounts of fibre can cause digestive upsets. A vegan diet can include bean and vegetable stews, salads with nuts, nut roasts, pasta and rice dishes and soya milk instead of cow's milk.

Figure 2.55 **The combination of pulses, nuts and cereals in this chick pea salad will give the vegan the essential amino acids**

 QUESTIONS

1. List the reasons why a person may become a vegetarian.

2. Explain the differences between a lacto-ovo vegetarian and a vegan.

3. Explain how the nutritional needs of a vegan can be met.

ACTIVITY

Modify a main course meat recipe to meet the needs of a vegan. Explain the reasons for your adaptation. Cook the product and evaluate it against the needs of a vegan.

Calorie controlled diets

The number of people who are overweight or obese is increasing in the UK. People are now taking less exercise than they used to but are still eating the same amount of food. This means that their weight gradually increases and the ratio of their weight in relation to their height is high. Figure 2.56 shows the chart that the medical profession use to check our weight. It records your body mass index (BMI). If someone is excessively overweight with a BMI over 30, they are classed as being obese.

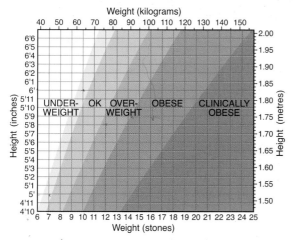

Figure 2.56 Chart to work out body mass index

This is general advice for adults only – it doesn't apply to children. If you know your height and weight, you can work out which weight range you're in using the simple steps outlined below.

- Take your weight in kilograms (kg) and divide it by your height in metres (m).
- Then divide the result by your height in metres (m) again.

For example, if you weigh 70 kg and you're 1.75 m tall, your BMI would be 22.9 (70/1.75 = 40 and 40/1.75 = 22.9).

The BMI weight ranges, as set out by the World Health Organisation (WHO) are outlined below.

- If your BMI is less than **18.4**, you're underweight for your height.
- If your BMI is between **18.5 and 24.9**, you're an ideal weight for your height.
- If your BMI is between **25 and 29.9**, you're over the ideal weight for your height.
- If your BMI is between **30 and 39.9**, you're obese.
- If your BMI is over **40**, you're very obese.

Notes: Being overweight is unhealthy because it puts a strain on the organs of the body. It can cause heart disease, high blood pressure, diabetes, osteoarthritis, varicose veins, breathlessness and chest infections. It also causes unhappiness and low self-esteem and may lead to depression.

The main cause of being overweight is eating more food than the body requires so that excess energy is stored as fat. (See the section on energy balance on page 45.)

Losing weight

The only way to lose weight is to reduce the number of calories consumed and combine this with increased physical exercise. Many people try to lose weight and the 'slimming industry' is a big part of the food market. There are clubs to help and support people by group therapy, slimming magazines, crash diets in the media, but it all relies on people controlling their intake of calories.

Meals for people who are trying to lose weight should include a variety of foods and follow the Eatwell Plate, reducing their intake of fat and sugar. Some slimming products have been developed where the fat and sugar have been reduced to lower the calorie content. We can also buy low-fat cheese, margarine-type spreads, salad dressings, low-sugar drinks, desserts, biscuits and yoghurts. A calorie-controlled diet should consist of foods naturally low in fat such as fruit and vegetables, white fish, poultry, skimmed milk and cheese, cereal, nuts and pulses.

People trying to lose weight should use low-fat methods of cooking such as grilling, steaming, boiling and stir frying.

Most foods have the amount of energy per 100 g on their nutritional label so you can count the calories.

Figure 2.57 Losing weight can be very hard work

QUESTIONS

1. List the reasons for the increase in the number of overweight primary school-aged children in the UK.

2. Explain the ways that primary school children are being encouraged to lead healthier lifestyles.

3. Describe what the term 'obesity' means.

ACTIVITY

Visit the supermarket and investigate products aimed at adults on slimming diets. Using the information from the labels, compare the calories and nutritional values with similar 'non-diet' products.

Adapt a cake recipe to reduce the sugar and include more fruit and vegetables.

▶ Heart disease (CHD)

In the UK, coronary heart disease (CHD) is a major health problem – one of the main causes of death. The risk of heart disease is increased by:

- smoking
- high blood pressure
- raised levels of cholesterol
- obesity
- a family history
- low levels of exercise.

CHD is related to the amount of fat in the diet. A diet high in saturated fats is also likely to be high in cholesterol. Cholesterol is a substance made in the liver and carried in the bloodstream. The cholesterol can build up and be deposited with other material as 'plaque' on the walls of the arteries, causing them to narrow. If the arteries then become blocked by a blood clot or more plaque, the person has a heart attack, which if severe can cause death.

Animal fat → Blood cholesterol → Heart attacks

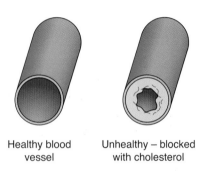

Healthy blood vessel   Unhealthy – blocked with cholesterol

Figure 2.58 Plaque build-up in arteries

The level of cholesterol in the blood depends on the amount of fatty acids in the diet. Replacing saturated fatty acids with unsaturated fatty acids can lower blood cholesterol. You can do this by using polyunsaturated fats and corn oil as alternatives to animal fat-based products. Some low-fat spreads contain animal fat. Soluble fibre is thought to remove cholesterol from arteries.

Cutting visible fat off meat, using semi-skimmed milk and spreading butter very thinly on bread can reduce cholesterol level, but only by 5 per cent. The general advice is to:

- eat more fruits and vegetables
- take regular physical exercise
- do not smoke
- eat a varied diet
- cut back on the fat in your diet and cooking
- eat more starchy carbohydrate
- use monounsaturated fats (olive oil)
- have fish instead of meat.

Does this sound familiar? It's the Eatwell Plate again!

Figure 2.59 Pregnant women should eat a varied, balanced diet

▶ Pregnancy

Pregnant and breastfeeding mothers must adapt their diet to provide adequate nutrients for themselves and the baby. A new mother does not need special food products but must ensure that she has a varied, balanced diet. She must pay particular attention to the following:

- an adequate supply of protein for the growth of the baby
- calcium and vitamin D for both her and the baby's bones and teeth development. If the mother does not have sufficient calcium in her diet for the baby's needs it will be taken from the mother's bones and teeth

- she should take folic acid before and in the early stages of pregnancy to reduce the risk of spina bifida in the baby

- iron, as the developing baby needs it for its blood supply. It also needs a store of iron in the liver as there is no iron in milk. If the mother does not get sufficient iron she will become anaemic

- a good supply of fruit and vegetables to provide vitamin C and fibre. Pregnant women are prone to getting constipation

- not eating too many fats and sugary foods as it is essential that she does not put on more than 10–12 kg in weight.

Recent research has shown that mothers who follow a poor diet or who under eat both before and during pregnancy may give birth to low birth weight babies. Low birth weight is linked to health problems for the baby.

QUESTIONS

1. What nutrients are particularly important during pregnancy?

2. Give reasons for each of the nutrients that you have listed.

3. What foods should be avoided during pregnancy?

ACTIVITY

Produce a leaflet for pregnant mothers – a guide to healthy eating in pregnancy.

Design and make a main course dish that is high in iron and suitable for a pregnant mother.

KEY POINTS

- Pregnant women need to take care of what they eat.

- They should ensure that they have good sources of energy and nutrients.

- They should maintain levels of calcium and iron.

- Going on a slimming diet during pregnancy is not advisable.

CHAPTER 3

NUTRIENTS FOUND IN AND STRUCTURE OF A COMMON RANGE OF FOODS

By the end of this chapter you should have developed a knowledge and understanding of:

- the nutrients found in and the structure of the following foods:
  - cereals
  - fruit
  - vegetables
  - meat
  - fish
  - cheese
  - milk
  - eggs
  - fats and oils
  - alternative protein foods.

3.1 CEREALS

Cereals are an important food around the world. They are often the staple food within a country because they are cheap to produce in comparison to protein foods. The main types of cereal foods are:

- wheat
- rice
- maize
- oats
- barley
- rye.

Structure and nutritional content of cereals

All cereal products are similar in structure. Wheat is one of the main cereals throughout the world.

◗ Flour

Wheat is made into flour. There is a large variety of flours available and they are used for making many different products. Flours can be described by:

- their extraction rate, i.e. how much of the whole grain is used:

  - Wholemeal flour – extraction rate of 100 per cent means that nothing has been removed from it. It is light brown in colour.

  - Brown flour – extraction rate of 85–90 per cent (10–15 per cent of the grain is removed as bran). It is also light brown in colour.

  - White flour – extraction rate of 70–75 per cent (the bran, germ, fat and some of the minerals have been removed). In the UK white flour has to be fortified by law with iron, calcium, thiamine and niacin. This is replacing the iron and B vitamins which have been lost in processing. It is white in appearance.

Structure of the Wheatgrain	Part of the Wheat-grain	Nutrients found
	Bran	• fibre
	Endosperm	• B vitamins • Starch • Protein (low biological value)
	Scutellum	• B vitamins • Protein (LBV)
	Germ	• B vitamins • Protein (LBV) • Vitamin E • Fat • Iron

Figure 3.1 Structure and nutrients found in wheat

All flours are fortified with calcium. There is a large range of different flours which can be bought in supermarkets, including:

- strong flour – this has a higher gluten content which is needed in bread making and in flaky and choux pastry. The gluten is able to stretch after it is mixed with water and developed, e.g. by kneading or rolling and folding, and helps to produce an elastic mixture

- soft flour – is used for cake and pastry making and has a lower gluten content

- self-raising flour – has a chemical raising agent added to it

- gluten-free flour – this has had the protein removed from it and it is made for people who have coeliac disease. Products which are gluten-free have a gluten-free symbol on them.

ACTIVITY

1. Investigate what other types of flour are available in shops. Produce a chart or poster to show:
   - how they can be used in food products
   - their nutritional values.

2. Flour is used to make a wide range of products – produce a mind map to show the uses of flour in food products.

3. Many children do not like wholemeal bread. Take a traditional baked product and adapt it to:
   - use wholemeal flour
   - be attractive to children.

   Evaluate how successful your product is. Suggest ways that it could be improved further.

Figure 3.2 Gluten-free symbol

QUESTIONS

1. What is meant by the term extraction rate?

2. Explain why you are encouraged to eat more wholemeal cereals.

KEY TERM

GLUTEN – protein in wheat products

▶ Rice

Rice is similar in structure to wheat. It is a good source of:

- carbohydrate – starch and fibre (if brown rice)
- B vitamins (thiamin and niacin)
- protein (LBV).

QUESTION

1. Explain why rice is considered a healthy food.

Rice is a very versatile product and can be used as part of a main dish or in soups, starters and desserts. There is a wide variety of types of rice sold in supermarkets.

There are different varieties of rice:

- short grain rice – used in puddings and risottos as the grains tend to clump together when they are cooked
- long grain rice – the grains remain separate when they are cooked. Examples are Carolina rice and basmati.

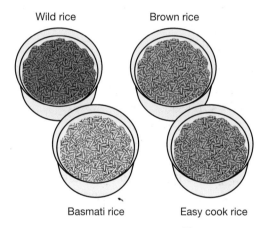

Wild rice   Brown rice

Basmati rice   Easy cook rice

Figure 3.3 Different types of rice

ACTIVITY

1. Investigate how rice is sold in convenient forms for the consumer. Produce a chart to show your findings.

2. Rice can be used in many different types of dishes. Prepare a dish to illustrate how versatile rice is. Produce a recipe leaflet for your dish which a manufacturer could attach to the packet of rice.

▶ Maize

The nutrient content of maize is similar to other cereals. It is also a good source of vitamin A.

Corn on the cob is a popular way to eat maize. Maize is available in a variety of forms: fresh, frozen and canned. It is also used to make breakfast cereals such as cornflakes.

In its ground form it is a white powder called cornflour, which contains starch. The other nutrients are removed during processing of the maize. It is often used to thicken liquids and sauces.

▶ Oats

Oats contain a good source of carbohydrates (starch and fibre), B vitamins (thiamin, riboflavin and B6), calcium, iron and small amounts

Oats are .... rather .... ned when the .... sold by grade ....ats are mainly u........... muesli, ...h as flapjacks...........d to make a non-dairy substitute.

make Oat + wheat rolls (handwritten note)

▶ Barley

The main nutrients found in barley are carbohydrate (fibre and starch). Today barley is mainly used in the brewing industry and for cattle food. It is used in foods as pearl barley which can be added to stews and casseroles or as flaked barley which is added to breakfast cereals.

KEY POINTS

- There is a wide variety of cereal products available for consumers to choose from.
- They are used in a wide variety of different food products.
- They are an important source of nutrients in our diet.

ACTIVITY

1. Other cereal products are available which can be used in food products. Investigate some of the other cereal products and produce an information leaflet about them informing consumers about their value in the diet and how they can be used.

2. Choose one of the products from your cereals leaflet and design and make a product which shows creative use of the cereal.

3. Prepare a recipe leaflet which illustrates your dish and could be given to consumers in the supermarket.

QUESTIONS

1. What are the functions of the main nutrients found in cereals?

2. Why are cereal products an important part of our diet?

3.2 FRUIT

There is a large range of fruits which come in a variety of flavours, colours, size and texture. They are mostly eaten raw, but on some occasions are cooked.

Structure of fruits

Fruits are made up of cells:

- cell wall – mainly cellulose
- cytoplasm – jelly-like and contains the colour pigments and fat droplets

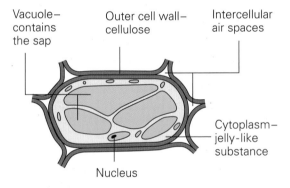

Vacuole– contains the sap

Outer cell wall– cellulose

Intercellular air spaces

Cytoplasm– jelly-like substance

Nucleus

Figure 3.4 Structure of fruit

Fruits can be categorised by their type. There are four main types:

- citrus – lemons, limes, oranges
- soft or berry fruits – raspberries, strawberries, blueberries, blackcurrants
- hard fruit – apples, pears
- some fruits which do not fall into any category, such as kiwi, pomegranate, melon, banana.

Nutritional

The nutritional content of fruits varies depending on the type of fruit. In general fruits are high in vitamins, carbohydrates (sucrose, fructose and fibre) and minerals. They are low in protein and fat.

Nutrient	Sources
Vitamin C	Rich sources – blackcurrants, rosehips. Good sources – citrus fruits, strawberries, gooseberries, raspberries. Remember vitamin C is destroyed by heat.
Vitamin A	Apricots
Carbohydrate	Found in the form of sucrose and fructose in ripe fruit. Fibre is found in the skin and fibrous parts of the fruit.

Table 3.1 Nutrients found in different types of fruits

ACTIVITY

We are being encouraged to eat more fruit. Prepare a dish which would be interesting and appealing to young children who claim they do not like to eat fruit.

3.3 VEGETABLES

There is a wide variety of vegetables available for us to use all through the year. They include those which are grown in this country and those which are imported from around the world. You are also able to buy these in a variety of ways, such as fresh, frozen and canned.

Structure of vegetables

Vegetables are similar to fruit in structure. However, they do vary depending on the type. For example, the cellulose which makes up the cell walls is thin and delicate in leaf products like spinach and lettuce, while in older vegetables it becomes thicker. The cells also contain a lot of water; if the water is lost the leaves become limp.

Vegetables also come in a variety of colours. The colour depends on:

- chlorophyll – provides the green colour – cabbage, sprouts, lettuce
- carotenoids – yellow and orange, e.g. carrots
- anthocyanins – red and blue, e.g. beetroot, red cabbage.

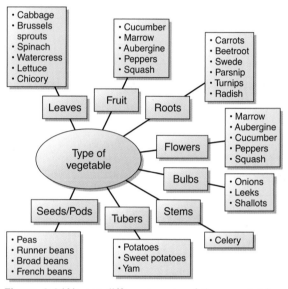

Figure 3.6 We eat different parts of the vegetable plants and this is how they are classified

Nutritional value of vegetables

Vegetables are eaten mostly as part of main meals though we are being encouraged to eat them as snacks instead of high-calorie foods.

The nutrient content of vegetables varies depending on their type and how they are cooked. Many vitamins are water soluble and destroyed by heat.

Figure 3.5 Many vegetables are brightly coloured

Protein	Only found in pulses and beans. It is of a low biological value except in soya beans which are HBV.
Carbohydrate	Root vegetables and tubers are the best sources of carbohydrate in the form of starch. Vegetables are a good source of fibre.
Vitamin C	Rich sources – sprouts, cabbage, green peppers, spinach, watercress. Reasonable sources – peas, beansprouts, potatoes – because we consume them in quite large quantities.
B Vitamins	Pulses provide a good source of thiamine. Most vegetables contain some of the B group.
Vitamin A	Carrots and dark green vegetables.
Calcium and iron	Are found in some vegetables such as watercress, cabbage and spinach but it is not always available to the body.

Table 3.2 Nutrients found in vegetables

KEY POINTS

- Fruits and vegetables provide us with important vitamins, carbohydrates and fibre.
- We need to prepare and cook them carefully so that their nutrients are not lost.

QUESTIONS

1. Why are vegetables an important part of our diet?
2. How should vegetables be prepared and cooked to preserve the vitamin content?

ACTIVITY

1. Some vegetables can be eaten raw. Design and make an interesting salad using a range of vegetables and other ingredients.

2. Calculate the cost and nutritional value of the salad using a nutrition program.

3.4 MEAT

There is a large range of meat and meat products available to purchase in the shops. The quality of the product will depend on how the animal has been kept, what it was fed on, its age, and how it is processed and cooked.

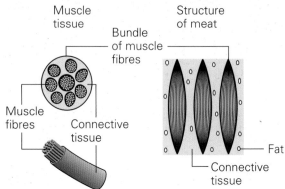

Figure 3.8 Structure of meat

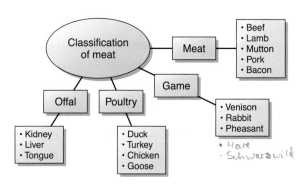

Figure 3.7 Classification of meat

Structure of meat

Meat is the muscle tissue of animals. The muscles are fibres which are bundled together and surrounded by connective tissue.

The parts of the animals which do the most work, that is the neck and the shin, have large long fibres. These tend to be tougher cuts of meat. They need long, slow methods of cooking to make them tender. Alternatively, the meat is processed, for example minced. This breaks down the fibres and means shorter methods of cooking can be used. For instance, minced beef is used to make beefburgers which are then grilled. The

meat that comes from young animals or the parts of the animal that do not do as much work, such as the breast, rump or ribs, have shorter fibres. This meat is suitable for quick and dry methods of cooking.

In making sure meat is tender you must choose the correct method of cooking for the type of meat. You can also help to make meat tender by:

- reducing the length of the muscle fibres by mincing or cutting across the muscle fibres

- marinading meat, e.g. in alcohol or with vinegar or lemon juice.

Poultry muscle fibres are similar to meat except that there is less connective tissue; this means that it is more tender.

Fat is found between the bundles of tissues. The fat helps to keep the meat moist when cooked and it adds flavour.

Myoglobin is the colour pigment that gives red meat its red colour. Different meats vary in colour.

Figure 3.9 Different types of meat – beef, pork and lamb

QUESTIONS

1. Describe how muscle fibres affect the tenderness of meat.

2. Why are tough cuts of meat cooked by long slow methods of cooking?

▶ Nutritional value of meat

The main nutrients found in meat are:

- protein (high biological value)
- fat – the amount of fat varies and many farmers are now producing meat which has a lot less fat than in the past
- vitamins – fat-soluble vitamins remain stable, B vitamins may leach into the cooking liquid
- iron – red meat is a good source of iron. Offal (liver, kidney) is an excellent source of iron
- water – makes up approximately 74 per cent of meat.

Poultry is similar to meat in nutritional value except that it contains less fat, except in goose and duck. Poultry also contains less iron than meat.

We can also eat the internal organs of animals. This is called offal and includes:

- kidneys
- liver
- heart
- tongue
- tripe.

Offal contains similar nutrients to meat but it is:

- usually lower in fat than meat
- liver is a good source of vitamin
- liver is a good source of iron.

QUESTIONS

1. What are the main nutrients found in meat?

2. If you were anaemic, which types of meat would you try to include in your diet?

3. If you were trying to reduce the amount of fatty foods you consume, which types of meat would you choose?

KEY TERMS

COLLAGEN – protein found in meat

CONNECTIVE TISSUE – surrounds the muscle fibres

ACTIVITY

1. Meat can be expensive. Using the internet or by visiting shops, compare the costs between different types and cuts of meat. Why do you think the prices vary? Which types and cuts of meat are the most and least expensive?

2. Cheaper cuts of meat can be made into interesting, filling and nutritious dishes. Using a cheaper cut of meat, make a dish which would appeal to a family. Calculate the nutritional value and cost per portion.

KEY POINTS

- Meat is made up from bundles of muscle fibres. Lean meat comes from young animals and the parts of the animal that do not do as much work.

- Meat is a good source of protein in the diet and also contains other important nutrients.

3.5 FISH

There are many varieties of fish available and fish can be bought in many different forms, for instance fresh, frozen, dried and canned.

- white – cod, haddock, coley, whiting, plaice
- oily – sardines, tuna, mackerel, sardines, trout
- shell fish – prawns, crab, lobster, shrimps, oysters.

Structure of fish

Fish is similar in structure to meat. It is made up of fibres and connective tissue. However, the fibres are much shorter and the connective tissue is much finer. This means that it is a more delicate and tender food. It is the short fibres that give fish its flaky texture. Fish is also quick to cook because of the short fibres.

Nutritional value of fish

The nutritional value of fish depends on their type. Fish can be classified into three groups:

Fish is a good source of:

- protein – fish is high in biological value protein
- fat – white and shell fish contain very little fat. Oily fish are good sources of essential fatty acids, those that the body cannot make
- minerals – calcium is a good source in fish where the bones are eaten, e.g. in sprats and tinned fish when the bones are softened in processing
- vitamins A and D – oily fish are good sources.

Nutrient	White (cod)	Oily (mackerel)	Shell (prawns)
Energy (kJ)	322.00 kJ	926.00 kJ	321.00 kJ
Energy (Kcal)	76.00 Kcal	223.00 Kcal	76.00 Kcal
Protein	17.40 g	19.00 g	17.60 g
Carbohydrate	0 g	0 g	0 g
Fat (g) of which:	0.70 g	16.30 g	0.60 g
– saturates	0.10 g	3.30 g	0.10 g
water	82.10 g	64.00 g	79.20 g

Table 3.3 Nutrients found in raw fish per 100 g

KEY POINTS

Fish can be classified by:

- habitat – sea, fresh water
- fat content.

Fish is a good source of protein and iodine.

The government advises that we should try to eat two portions of fish a week and one of these should be an oily fish.

QUESTIONS

1. How are fish classified? Give examples of fish for each group.
2. Why are we being encouraged to eat at least two portions of fish a week?
3. Explain why fish takes less time to cook than meat.

ACTIVITY

Many children say they do not like fish. Design a dish which would encourage children to eat fish.

3.6 MILK

There is a wide variety of milks available. Cow's milk is the most popular milk consumed in this country. Other sources of milk come from goats and sheep. There are also milk-type products made from oats, rice and soya.

Structure of milk

Milk is mainly water. It is an emulsion and has tiny drops of fat suspended in it. As oil and water do not mix, the fat will rise to the top of the milk. This is seen as the cream line in the milk. Today much of the milk we buy is homogenised so that the fat is distributed evenly throughout the milk and therefore this fat line is not visible.

Homogenisation involves forcing the milk at high pressure through small holes. This breaks up the fat globules in order to spread them evenly throughout the milk.

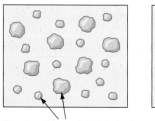
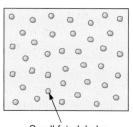

Small and large fat globules in milk which rise to the top of milk that has not been homogenised

Small fat globules evenly dispersed through the milk

Figure 3.10 Comparison of milk and homogenised milk

Nutritional value of milk

Milk contains the following nutrients:

* water
* protein
* fat
* carbohydrate
* vitamins and minerals.

Milk provides you with energy.

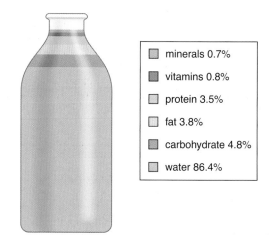

minerals 0.7%
vitamins 0.8%
protein 3.5%
fat 3.8%
carbohydrate 4.8%
water 86.4%

Figure 3.11 Average nutrient content of milk

Milk is often described as a perfect food because it is designed to feed the young of the animals it is produced from.

Nutrients	Information
Protein	• High biological value protein
Fat	• The amount of fat depends of the type of milk • By law whole milk must contain 3 per cent fat • Contains both saturated and unsaturated fats • The sales of reduced fat milks have increased as we are encouraged to consume less fat
Carbohydrate	• In the form of lactose • It does not taste sweet • Lactose-free milk can now be purchased for those people who have intolerance.
Vitamins	• Vitamin A (retinol and carotene) – the amount varies – more in summer • Skimmed milk contains less vitamins as the fat is removed and vitamin A is fat soluble • Vitamin D – it contains more in summer • Water soluble vitamins riboflavin (B2), thiamine (B1) and nicotinic acid (B3)
Minerals	• Calcium and phosphorus • Approximately 43 per cent of the calcium intake of adults is provided from milk and milk products

Table 3.4 Nutrients found in milk

Varieties of milk

There are many different types of milk available for us to buy. These vary according to how they have been produced and in their fat content.

Whole milk:

• has had nothing added or removed.

Semi-skimmed milk:

• is the most popular type of milk in the UK

• has a fat content of 1.7 per cent.

Skimmed milk:

• has fat content of 0.1–0.3 per cent

• contains slightly more calcium than whole milk

• has lower levels of fat-soluble vitamins

• is not recommended for children under the age of five.

Channel Island milk:

• is higher in calories and fat than whole milk

• has a higher content of fat-soluble vitamins

• has a visible cream line and is commonly sold in supermarkets as Channel Island or Jersey milk. There are also products sold as breakfast milk – this is Channel Island milk which has been homogenised so that the cream is evenly distributed throughout the milk. The milk has a very creamy flavour throughout.

	Milk, Channel Island	Whole, pasteurised, winter	Semi-skimmed	Skimmed
Energy (kJ)	327.00 kJ	275.00 kJ	195.00 kJ	140.00 kJ
Energy (Kcal)	78.00 Kcal	66.00 Kcal	46.00 Kcal	33.00 Kcal
Protein	3.60 g	3.20 g	3.30 g	3.30 g
Carbohydrate of which: sugars starch	4.80 g 4.80 g 0.00 g	4.80 g 4.80 g 0.00 g	5.00 g 5.00 g 0.00 g	5.00 g 5.00 g 0.00 g
Fat (g) of which: saturates unsaturates polyunsaturates	5.10 g 3.30 g 1.30 g 0.10 g	3.90 g 2.50 g 1.10 g 0.10 g	1.70 g 1.00 g 0.50 g trace	0.10 g 0.10 g trace trace
Sodium	54.00 mg	55.00 mg	55.00 mg	54.00 mg
Vitamin A Retinol Carotene	46.00 µg 71.00 µg	41.00 µg 11.00 µg	21.00 µg 9.00 µg	1.0 µg trace
Vitamin D	0.03 µg	0.03 µg	0.01 µg	trace
Thiamin	0.04 mg	0.04 mg	0.04 mg	0.04 mg
Riboflavin	0.19 mg	0.17 mg	0.18 mg	0.17 mg
Calcium	130.00 mg	115.00 mg	120.00 mg	120.00 mg
Phosphorus	100.00 mg	92.00 mg	95.00 mg	94.00 mg

Table 3.5 Nutritional value of different types of milk

QUESTIONS

1. Explain why milk is a valuable food in the diet.

2. Why does the fat content of the milks differ?

3. The sales of semi-skimmed and skimmed milk have increased. Explain why this has happened.

4. Why is vitamin A (retinol and carotene) reduced in skimmed and semi-skimmed milk?

5. Which type of milk would you recommend for children under five years of age? Give reasons for your answer.

ACTIVITY

Milk can also be obtained from other sources, e.g. sheep, goat and soya milk. Using a nutrition software package, investigate the nutritional content of three different types of milk.

How does their nutrient content compare to the types of milk shown in Table 3.5?

Why do you think there is a market for different types of milk?

Milk can be processed to produce other types of milk, such as dried milk powder, condensed and evaporated milk. It can also be made into other products such as yoghurt, cream and cheese. We will look at cheese in detail later in this chapter.

ACTIVITY

Investigate the range of milk products available. Produce a mind map to show the main characteristics of these products.

Alternatives to animal milk – rice, oat and soya milk

Figure 3.12 Alternatives to animal sources of milk

Some people have problems digesting cow's milk, being allergic or lactose intolerant. This means they may want to find another alternative which will give them similar nutrition.

Rice milk is dairy free, low in fat and calories and cholesterol free. It is a source of easily digestible carbohydrates but it is lower than normal milk in protein and essential fatty acids.

Oat milk is a dairy-free alternative to milk and soya products which can be used in the same way as cow's milk. Research has shown that oats can help reduce cholesterol; they are rich in folic acid, vitamin E, low in saturated fat, and unlike other milks, it is a good source of fibre.

Soya milk has a lower fat content compared with full-fat cow's milk. It is low in carbohydrate and provides a good source of HBV protein. It can be bought sweetened or unsweetened. Soya milk can be used as a straight substitute for cow's milk when cooking.

KEY TERMS

LACTOSE – type of carbohydrate found in milk

HOMOGENISATION – involves forcing the milk at high pressure through small holes. This breaks up the fat globules in order to spread them evenly throughout the milk and prevent separation of a cream layer

Method of heat treatment	Treatment	Effect of the treatment
Pasteurisation	• Heated to at least 71.7°C for a minimum of 15 seconds and maximum of 25 seconds • Milk is cooled quickly to below 6°C	• Kills harmful bacteria • Little effect on the nutritional value of the milk • Extends the shelf life of the milk
Sterilised milk	• Heated to a temperature of 113–130°C for approximately 10–30 minutes • Then cooled quickly	• Destroys nearly all the bacteria in it • Changes the taste and colour • Destroys some vitamins • Unopened bottles or cartons can be kept for several months without being in a fridge • Once opened it must be treated as fresh
UHT milk (ultra heat treated)	• Heated to a temperature of at least 135°C for 1 second • Put into sterile sealed containers	• Unopened packs have a long shelf life • Once opened it must be treated as fresh • Little effect on flavour or nutritional value

Table 3.6 Heat treatment of milk

ACTIVITY

1. There is a wide variety of other types of milk available to buy in shops. Investigate the range of products available and produce a chart to show information on:
   • their nutritional values
   • how they are purchased
   • their uses in food preparation
   • how they are produced.

2. Some children do not like to drink milk. Prepare an interesting milk-based product which uses milk as its main ingredient.

Heat treatment of milk

Most milk sold is heat treated to kill harmful bacteria and to increase its shelf life.

KEY POINTS

• Milk is a good source of protein, calcium, vitamin B12 and riboflavin.

• Vitamins A and D are found in whole milk and its products.

• Milk can be processed in a variety of ways to produce other products.

3.7 CHEESE

There are many different varieties of cheese you can buy, some traditionally produced in this country and others from around the world. They are made by different methods and with different types of milk, such as cow's, sheep, goats.

Structure of cheese

All cheese is made from milk. To change it from a liquid to a solid, rennin is added to the milk. In cheeses suitable for vegetarians, chymosin is added which, unlike rennin, does not come from animals. The milk then separates into curds and whey. It is the curd which is used to make the cheese. The cheese is then pressed. The harder it is pressed, the less water it contains.

Nutrients found in cheese

Cheese is made from milk solids and therefore contains similar nutrients. However, their amounts depend on the type of cheese. A hard cheese will contain more fat and protein as more of the liquid has been pressed out during the processing.

Cheese is a concentrated source of protein and also a good source of calcium, vitamin A and riboflavin. However some types – the harder varieties and cream cheeses – have a high fat content. In a response to consumers wanting to reduce the amount of fat in their diets there are many reduced-fat varieties available today.

ACTIVITY

1. Cheeses are made in many different parts of the world. Plot where different types of cheese come from on a map of the world.

2. Investigate which varieties of cheese can now be purchased with reduced-fat options.

QUESTION

1. Why is cheese an important food in our diets?

	Cheese, Cheddar (hard)	Brie (soft)	Cream cheese	Cottage – reduced fat
Energy (kJ)	1708.00 kJ	1323.00 kJ	1807.00 kJ	331.00 kJ
Energy (Kcal)	412.00 Kcal	319.00 Kcal	439.00 Kcal	78.00 Kcal
Protein	25.50 g	19.30 g	3.10 g	13.30 g
Fat (g)	34.40 g	26.90 g	47.40 g	1.40 g
(of which saturates)	21.70 g	16.80 g	29.70 g	0.90 g
Water	36.00 g	48.60 g	45.50 g	80.20 g

Table 3.7 Composition of cheese per 100 g

3.8 EGGS

Most of the eggs we use come from hens. However, we can also use duck, goose and quail eggs. They are a very versatile food and can be used in a wide variety of ways in food preparation.

Structure of eggs

Eggs are made up of three parts:

- Shell – the colour of the shell does not affect the nutritional value of the egg.

- Egg white – there are two parts to the egg white, the thick and thin.

- Egg yolk – the colour of the yolk is related to what the hens are fed on. The yolk also contains lecithin which is an emulsifier. This is useful when combining ingredients which would normally separate, for instance when it is used in mayonnaise to prevent oil and water separating.

The air space in the egg will get larger as the egg gets older. This is because the shell of the egg is porous. A stale egg will float in a bowl of water. The chalazae are two spiral bands in an egg that extend from the yolk to the inner membrane and help to keep the yolk in the centre of the egg. As the shell of the egg is porous, eggs should be stored away from strongly flavoured foods.

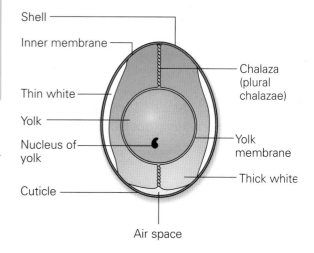

Figure 3.13 Structure of an egg

Because of their structure, eggs are a very useful food in preparing other dishes. They are particularly useful for setting, combining, aerating and thickening mixtures. See Chapter 4 on the function of ingredients.

Nutrients found in eggs

Eggs are a good source of protein and fat-soluble vitamins. They are also a high-risk food and must be stored and used correctly. They should be stored in the fridge. Eggs that are stamped with a lion mark come from hens which are salmonella free.

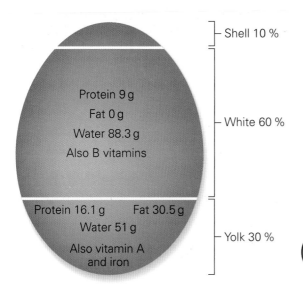

Shell 10 %

Protein 9 g
Fat 0 g
Water 88.3 g
Also B vitamins

White 60 %

Protein 16.1 g   Fat 30.5 g
Water 51 g

Also vitamin A
and iron

Yolk 30 %

Figure 3.14 Nutritional composition of eggs (nutrients per 100 g)

ACTIVITY

Eggs have many uses in food preparation. Produce a mind map to show how they can be used. Prepare a range of dishes which show the different uses of eggs.

KEY POINTS

- Eggs are a good source of protein, vitamin A, vitamin D, niacin and vitamin B12.
- It is possible to change the nutrient content of eggs by manipulating the feed of hens.
- Eggs have a wide variety of uses in food preparation.

QUESTIONS

1. Why are eggs considered to be a valuable food in your diet?
2. Explain where you would store eggs in your home.
3. How can you tell if eggs are fresh?

3.9 FATS AND OILS

There is a great variety of fats and oils that we can purchase and the market is continuing to expand. Fats and oils have lots of different uses in food preparation.

Structure of fats and oils

Fats and oils can come from both animal and vegetable sources. Oils are a liquid and fats are solid. Oils come from vegetable sources such as olives, corn, rape, nuts, soya, ground nut and from fish. Fats come from animal sources.

There are three main types of fats:

- saturated
- unsaturated
- polyunsaturated.

The more saturated fatty acids a product has, the more solid the fat will be. Animal fats contain more saturated fats than vegetable and fish oils.

Fats

- **Animal fats** – these make butter, animal suet from cattle and lard from pigs. They are traditionally high in saturated fats. Today manufacturers make lighter varieties of butter by adding ingredients such as water and vegetable oil.

- **Margarine** – this can be made from either a mixture of animal and vegetable fats and oils or all vegetable oil. By law margarine has to have vitamins A and D added to it and must not contain more than 16 per cent water. Some margarines are made using hydrogenated fats however; as technology develops many more margarines are made using emulsifiers. This means fewer hydrogenated fats and trans-fats are contained in margarines.

- **Low-fat spreads** – there are many low-fat spreads available to buy. These contain a lower fat content than butter or margarine. The percentage of water in these products is higher. Often they cannot be used for cooking, but the labels on these products need to be read carefully.

- **White fats** – these are made from oils and can be used to replace lard. They can be used in products such as pastry and for frying. The consistency of the products can vary. Some have air added, making them softer and easier to combine in ingredients, for instance when rubbing in pastry.

Oils

Oils contain 100 per cent fat. They mostly contain unsaturated fats. Some oils are hydrogenated. This means they are processed so they become hard. Hydrogenated fat is often seen in manufactured cakes, biscuits, pastry and margarines. They also contain trans fatty acids. These have no value in our diet. We therefore need to reduce the amount of saturated, hydrogenated and trans fatty acids in our diets.

ACTIVITY

Use the following headings to investigate the different fats and oils which can be purchased:

- **name of fat**
- **ingredients**
- **uses in food preparation.**

Record your results.

Nutrients found in fats

The main nutrient in fats is fat. However, the amount of different types of fat they contain varies.

Fats also contain fat-soluble vitamins. Vitamins A and D are added to margarine by law.

Nutrients	Olive oil	Corn oil	Butter	Low-fat spread	Hard margarine (animal and vegetable fats)
Energy	3378 kJ (822 Kcal)	3408 kJ (829 Kcal)	3031 kJ (737 Kcal)	1605 kJ (390 Kcal)	3039 kJ (739 Kcal)
Protein	nil	less than 0.1 g	0.50 g	5.80 g	0.20 g
Carbohydrate	nil	0.0 g	trace	0.50 g	1.00 g
Fat of which saturate	91.3 g 15.2 g	92.1 g 13.3 g	81.70 g 54.00 g	40.50 g 11.20 g	81.60 g 30.40 g
mono-unsaturates	60.7 g	27.5	19.80 g	17.60 g	36.50 g
polyunsaturates	11.4 g	47.3 g	2.60 g	9.90 g	10.80 g
Cholesterol	nil	nil	230.00 mg	6.00 mg	285.00 mg
Water	trace	trace	15.60 g	49.90 g	16.00 g

Table 3.8 Nutrients found in a variety of common fats and oils (per 100 g)

KEY POINTS

- Fats which are liquid at room temperature are called oils.
- Fats contain fat-soluble vitamins.
- Fats have different sensory characteristics.

QUESTIONS

1. What are the main sources of fats and oils?

2. Why are many people choosing to use vegetable fats and oils?

3. Some oils are hydrogenated. What does this mean?

4. What sort of fat would you recommend for the following groups of people:
   - A vegan.
   - Someone wanting to reduce the amount of fat they eat.

Give reasons for your answers.

3.10 ALTERNATIVE PROTEIN FOODS

Alternative protein foods provide protein from sources other than animals. There is a variety of meat-like products available in supermarkets. They have been developed to resemble meat products.

Structure of alternative protein foods

Figure 3.15 Range of soya products – soya beans, chunks, milk and tofu

Soya beans are made into a variety of products including milk, soy sauce and tofu.

Textured vegetable protein is made from soya beans. The soya beans are made into a flour-like substance and then mixed with water so that the starch can be removed. The mixture is then made into a variety of shapes. It can be bought as a dried or frozen product. It is very bland and needs ingredients with strong flavours to be added to it to make it into an interesting product.

Tofu is made from ground soya beans. It resembles a soft cheese in texture. As it is soft it absorbs flavours.

Myco-protein is produced from micro-organisms. When it is made into a food product it has egg white added to it to bind it together. The myco-protein is then shaped into a variety of shapes, such as mince, slices and fillets. It is also used to make ready-to-use products such as sausages.

Nutrients found in alternative protein foods

Alternative protein foods contain the following nutrients:

- Protein – soya beans are a high biological value protein.
- Vitamins and minerals – they often have been enriched with these, e.g. soya fortified with B12.
- Fibre, often found in soya mince and Quorn®.

They are also low in fat.

KEY POINTS

- Soya and myco-protein foods provide protein and are low in fat.
- They are a valuable source of protein for vegetarians.

Nutrients	Quorn®	Tofu	Soya mince frozen
Energy KJ/Kcal	433 KJ/103 Kcal	438 KJ/105 Kcal	727 KJ/175 Kcal
Protein	14.0 g	12.1 g	18.0 g
Carbohydrate of which sugars	5.8 g 1.3 g	0.6 g 0.5 g	3.0 g 2.0 g
Fat of which saturates	2.6 g 0.6 g	6.0 g 1.0 g	10.0 g 1.0 g
Fibre	5.5 g	0.5 g	3.0 g
Sodium	0.4 g	trace	0.12 g

Table 3.9 Nutrients found in a range of alternative protein foods (per 100 g)

ACTIVITY

Many people are choosing not to eat meat.

1. Investigate the range of soya and myco-protein foods available in supermarkets.

2. Design a dish using either a soya or myco-protein which a supermarket could use to promote these alternative meat products. Produce a recipe leaflet that could be given out with the product.

QUESTIONS

1. Give two reasons why someone may eat myco-protein instead of meat.

2. Explain why alternative protein foods are important to vegetarians.

3. Which of the alternative proteins would not be suitable for a vegan to eat? Give reasons for your answer.

CHAPTER 4

FUNCTION OF INGREDIENTS

By the end of this section you should have developed a knowledge and understanding of the:

- function of ingredients in a range of products: flour, sugar, fats/oils, eggs
- use of raising agents, additives and the fortification of foods
- use of standard and pre-manufactured components.

Every ingredient used in a recipe has a specific function, for instance to thicken, aerate, coagulate, add nutritional value. You need to have an understanding of the function of ingredients in order to choose the correct ingredient when designing and making food products.

The food industry uses additives and fortification to improve the quality and nutritional content of food products.

4.1 FUNCTION OF INGREDIENTS

Ingredient	Function	Example
Flour	Forms the main structure of a product due to its gluten content	Bread – strong plain flour – high gluten content Cakes – soft plain flour – low gluten content to give a soft, tender crumb
	Bulking	Crumble – topping Pastry – casing
	Raising agent if self-raising flour is used	Cakes
	To thicken (gelatinisation)	Sauces

Table 4.1 Ingredients and their functions

Ingredient	Function	Example
Fat	Adds colour and flavour if butter or margarine is used	Cakes, biscuits
	Holds air bubbles during mixing to create texture and volume	Cakes, biscuits, pastry
	Helps to extend shelf life	Pastry
	To shorten a flour mixture and make crisp or crumbly in texture	Pastry
	Shortening	Certain types of biscuits and pastry
	Frying/sautéing	Stir-fry
	To form emulsions	Salad dressing
Oils	Binds ingredients	
Egg	Adds colour and flavour	Cakes
	Holds air when whisked	Meringue, whisked sponge
	Forms an emulsion when mixed with fat	Mayonnaise
	Binds ingredients together	Beefburgers, fish cakes
	Coagulating/setting	Quiche Lorraine
	Glazing	Pastry
	Coating/enrobing	Holding dry coatings such as breadcrumbs onto a surface and forming a barrier during cooking processes, e.g. fried breaded fish
	Enriching – thickening	Sauce
	To give a smooth, glossy finish to aid piping	Choux pastry
	Adding nutritional value	
Sugar	Sweetens	Desserts, cakes
	Develops flavour	Soft brown sugar, or treacle in a gingerbread
	Increases bulk of the mixture	Cakes
	Holds air	When creamed with fat, e.g. Victoria sandwich
	To aid fermentation	Bread
	To preserve	Jam
Liquid	Acts as a raising agent when converted to steam	Cakes, batters
	Binds ingredients together	Pastry
	Glazing (milk)	Scones
	Enrich (milk)	Bread
Salt	Helps develop flavour	Pastry
	Strengthens gluten in flour and controls the action of yeast	Breads
	To preserve	Fish, fork, Beef...

Table 4.1 continued

Ingredient	Function	Example
Baking powder	To aerate	To make cake rise
Yeast	To aerate	To make bread rise
Fruit and vegetables	Adds colour and flavour Adds texture To thicken Adds nutritional value To garnish To add a topping	Savoury and sweet dishes Savoury and sweet dishes When cooked and puréed, e.g. soups, sauces Tomato Potato on shepherds pie
Herbs and spices	Improve and add flavour To garnish	Curry, chilli Parsley
Gelatine	Setting	Jelly, chilled desserts, e.g. cheesecakes, soufflé
Chocolate, icings	To coat or decorate	Biscuits, cakes, desserts

Table 4.1 continued

If we now look at three types of pastry in more detail you will see that similar ingredients are combined in different ratios by different methods to produce a variety of textures and finishes.

Ingredient	Shortcrust	Flaky	Choux
Flour	Soft plain flour Low gluten content to produce short crumb texture	Strong plain flour High gluten content to produce crispy, flaky layers	Strong plain flour High gluten content which stretches to hold the expanding steam and air
Fat	Mixture of white fat and margarine or butter. Fat coats the flour granules to reduce the water mixing with the gluten	Mixture of white fat and margarine. When placed as small pieces on the dough the fat traps air between the layers of dough	Butter or margarine for flavour
Water	Binds the rubbed-in fat and flour	Combines with gluten to form stretchy, elastic dough. Lemon juice is added to strengthen the gluten	Boiled to 100 °C so the heat causes the starch in flour to gelatinise. Mixes with flour to develop the gluten
Salt	Helps develop flavour	Helps develop flavour and strengthen gluten	
Egg			Helps to hold air in the starch mixture. Gives a smooth, glossy finish and aids piping of the mixture

Table 4.2 The function of ingredients in shortcrust, flaky and choux pastry

▶ Recipe engineering

Manufacturers may change ingredients in standard recipes for various reasons. This process is known as recipe engineering. New ingredients may be substituted or proportions of ingredients changed, for example:

- to change the nutritional profile of a product (e.g. high-fibre bread)
- to alter the amounts of additives and seasonings to develop flavour, texture and colour to make the recipe suitable for large-scale production (e.g. using vegetable oil instead of solid fat in biscuits)

- to use cheaper ingredients (e.g. soya in beefburgers)
- to make products suitable for people with special dietary needs.

When changing ingredients great care is needed. For instance:

- fat gives flavour – reducing fat needs to be done carefully to avoid loss of flavour
- fibre – increasing makes a big difference in texture and may be unacceptable – use half white and half wholemeal flour
- sugar – care is needed when reducing because of its function in cooking.

QUESTIONS

1. Copy and complete Table 4.3 by adding two examples of ingredients that can perform each of the listed functions. You may need to find examples of ingredients other than the ones detailed in Tables 4.1 and 4.2.

   Work in pairs or small groups to look through recipes to help you. The first one has been done to get you started.

Function	Ingredient	Ingredient
Aerating	Water (steam)	Baking powder
Binding		
Bulking		
Setting		
Thickening		
Sweetening		
Glazing		
Preserving		
Adding flavour		
Adding colour		
Adding texture		
Adding extra fibre		

Table 4.3 Ingredients and their functions

2. Table 4.4 lists ingredients required to make a lemon meringue pie. Copy and complete the table to show the function of each ingredient.

Ingredient	Function
Pastry base	
Flour	
Fat	
Water	
Filling and topping	
Lemon	
Eggs	
Cornflour	
Sugar	

Table 4.4 Ingredients for a lemon meringue pie

3. A manufacturer wants to develop a new range of cake products.

Cake ingredients
100 g soft margarine
100 g caster sugar
100 g self-raising flour
2 eggs
Filling
2 tablespoons jam

a) Suggest two flavourings that could be added to the cake mixture.
b) Suggest one ingredient that could be added to the cake mixture to change the texture.
c) Give one function of the sugar in the cake.
d) When the cake is cooked the colour is too pale. The manufacturer decides to improve the colour of the cake. Suggest one way to make the cake darker.

4. The list of ingredients here has been taken from a nutritional label for a suet sponge roll filled with jam: wheat flour, raspberry jam, suet, water, sugar, skimmed milk powder, raising agent, salt.

Copy and complete Table 4.5 to show how the ingredients can be modified to improve the nutritional content of the roll.

Change	Explanation
Reduce sugar	
Increase fibre	
Reduce fat	

Table 4.5 Modifying ingredients

ACTIVITY

Look at the list of ingredients on a packaged food product of your choice:

- List the ingredients.

- State the function of each ingredient used in the making of the food product.

KEY POINT

- Ingredients have a function within a recipe.

4.2 RAISING AGENTS

A raising agent is added to a cake, bread mixture, etc. to give lightness to the mixture. The lightness is based upon the principle that gases expand when heated. The gases used are air, carbon dioxide or water vapour. These gases are introduced before baking or are produced by substances added to the recipe before baking.

Air

Air expands very quickly. Figure 4.1 shows the different ways that air can be added to mixtures.

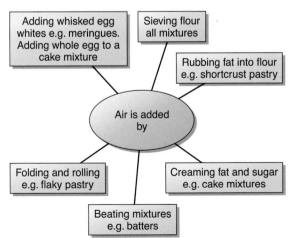

Figure 4.1 Ways of adding air to mixtures

Whisked egg whites have the property of holding air, as in soufflés, meringues, etc. Whole eggs do not hold air as easily because of the fat in the yolk.

Dishes almost entirely dependent upon air as a raising agent include:

- whisked sponges

- soufflés

- meringues.

Carbon dioxide

This may be introduced by the use of:

- bicarbonate of soda (sodium bicarbonate) used alone – as in gingerbread. A strong flavour of washing soda is produced and a dark colour, but the flavour and colour are disguised by the use of spices such as ginger and by treacle

- bicarbonate of soda plus acid, e.g. bicarbonate of soda and cream of tartar

- baking powder – this is usually a commercial preparation of bicarbonate of soda + cream of tartar or tartaric acid, with rice flour or a similar substance added to absorb any moisture and prevent lumps. The quality of commercial baking powder is controlled by law and is of standard strength.

Recipe: 50 g cream of tartar, 25 g bicarbonate of soda, 25 g rice flour – to absorb any moisture and prevent lumps.

Self-raising flour

This is a prepared mixture of a soft flour and raising agent. It will give good results for plain cakes or scones but there is too much raising agent for rich cakes. NEVER use self-raising flour for bread, pastries, biscuits and batters.

Yeast

When yeast is given the right conditions – food, warmth, moisture and time – it can break down sugar by a process known as fermentation, producing carbon dioxide and alcohol.

Water vapour (steam)

This is produced during cooking from liquids in the mixture. It has about 1600 times the original volume of water. It is used in éclairs, batters, choux pastries, flaky and puff pastry and cakes.

Addition of raising agent

1. Buy a reliable brand.
2. Store in an airtight container, in a cool dry place, to prevent loss of strength and reaction.
3. Use the correct proportion and sieve dry ingredients.
4. Add and distribute moisture evenly to give even reaction.
5. Keep mixture cool before baking if there is a time lag.

KEY POINT

- Bubbles of gas expand when heated and make food mixtures rise.

Too little raising agent	Too much raising agent
Lack of volume	Over-rising then collapsing, giving a sunken cake, or sunken fruit
Close texture	Coarse texture
Insufficient rising	Poor colour and flavour
Shrinkage	

Table 4.6 Using a raising agent

4.3 USES OF ADDITIVES

Additives are substances which are added to foods during manufacturing or processing to improve their:

- keeping properties
- flavour
- colour
- texture
- appearance
- stability.

Additives are used in a large range of food products today. The main groups of food additives are:

- antioxidants
- colours
- flavour enhancers
- sweeteners
- emulsifiers and stabilisers
- preservatives.

Over 300 additives are allowed in the UK. Flavourings are not included in this figure. More than 3000 flavourings are used in many different combinations. All additives have to be checked for safety before they can be used in any foods. Additives which are allowed to be used are given a number. Some are also given an 'E' if they have been accepted as safe for use within the European Union. All additives also have a chemical name. Table 4.7 shows you how the numbers are allocated.

Colours	E100 – E180
Preservatives	E200 – E299
Antioxidants	E300 – E322
Emulsifiers and stabilisers	E400 – E495

Table 4.7 Classification of E numbers

Figure 4.2 Colourings used in sweets

Why are additives used?

Additives are used for the following reasons:

- They can help make food safe for longer.
- They can make the food more attractive or taste better.
- They can help to keep the price of the food competitive.
- They give the food an improved nutritional profile (higher in vitamins or lower in fat).

Additives may be:

- natural – obtained from natural sources, for instance red colouring made from beetroot juice (E162) is used in making ice cream, sweets and liquorice
- nature identical (synthetic) – made in a laboratory to be chemically the same as certain natural materials, such as vanillin which is found naturally in vanilla pods
- artificial – synthetic compounds which do not occur in nature, such as saccharin (E954), a low-calorie sweetener.

Many consumers prefer food products to contain additives obtained from natural sources. Many manufacturers now try to use fewer synthetic additives. For example, a cake manufacturer may use additives from natural sources and will then advertise the range of cakes as 'Home Style Baking'.

Artificial additives are used a lot by the food manufacturing industry. Their use is controlled by government departments. Some people have unpleasant reactions to certain additives but this is less common than in the past. The long-term effects of additives are not known.

The additives must be listed on the label by their:

- type
- chemical name or number.

They must appear on the label in descending order of quantity (greatest amount first).

ACTIVITY

Look at a variety of different food labels and see if you can recognise the different types of additives used.

Advantages of using additives for the manufacturer

- Used in a wide range of food products to meet consumer needs, e.g. quick, easy, convenient meals, such as pot noodles, instant whipped desserts, instant mash.
- To improve a specific characteristic of a food, e.g. vanilla-flavoured ice cream, orange-flavoured soft centres in chocolates, coffee liqueur-flavoured hot chocolate drinks.
- To produce the expected qualities in foods, such as colour and flavour, e.g. soft-centred chocolates with pink colouring and strawberry flavouring or green colouring with mint flavouring.
- To produce a product range by using different additives in the basic food, e.g. potato crisps flavoured with salt and vinegar, cheese and onion, smoky bacon, chicken, prawn cocktail, etc.
- To help maintain product consistency in large-scale production, e.g. the use of

emulsifiers to prevent salad cream separating.

- To restore original characteristics of a food after processing, e.g. adding colour to processed vegetables such as canned peas which lose their green colour in production.
- To prevent food spoilage, to preserve foods and give them a longer shelf life, e.g. bread, cakes and biscuits.
- To disguise inferior ingredients. This can help to reduce the costs of food products.

Disadvantages of using additives for the manufacturer

- Some people may have an allergy to additives and may therefore choose not to purchase the product. It is often difficult to find out which additive is causing the allergic reaction. Examples of allergies caused by food additives include asthma attacks, skin rashes and hyperactivity in children.

KEY TERMS

ADDITIVES – substances added to food in small amounts to improve colour, flavour, texture or to make the food stay safe for longer.

E NUMBER – a number given to an additive to indicate it has been approved for use in the EU.

ACTIVITY

Working in groups, look at the following task and prepare a short presentation to other pupils in your class.

Task

Two manufacturers are trying to persuade a major supermarket to sell their new pasta bake. Manufacturer A does not use any additives in his product, manufacturer B uses additives.

Decide whether you are going to be Manufacturer A or B.

Prepare a presentation to persuade the supermarket to take your product.

QUESTIONS

1. Why are additives added to food products?

2. Why do some people have concerns over the use of some additives?

▶ Types of food additives and their functions

Colours

Colours are added to make foods look more attractive. They are used in manufacturing to:

- replace colour lost during heat treatment, e.g. in canned peas
- boost colours already in foods, e.g. strawberry yoghurt
- maintain consistency between different batch productions as they are added in

precise quantities, e.g. yellow colouring in tinned custard

- make foods that are normally colourless look attractive, e.g. carbonated drinks.

Colours are not allowed to be added to baby foods.

Figure 4.3 Colourings added to tinned peas and yogurt to make them more appealing to the consumer

QUESTION

1. Some consumers believe that the use of colour additives is not necessary for foods to taste good. What are the arguments for and against using artificial colours from the consumer's and the manufacturer's perspective?

Preservatives

Preservatives help to keep food safe for longer. They are added to foods to:

- extend shelf life, which means that the consumers do not need to go shopping as often
- prevent the growth of micro-organisms which can cause food spoilage and lead to poisoning.

Preservatives are found in:

- many processed foods with a long shelf life
- cured meats, such as bacon, ham, corned beef
- dried fruit, such as sultanas, raisins, etc.

Sugar, salt and vinegar are still used to preserve some foods, but most people tend to think of preservatives as chemicals. Some additives used for preservation have been used for a long time, for instance:

- sugar to make jam and marmalade
- vinegar to make pickles, e.g. cabbage, eggs and onions
- salt in meat, fish
- alcohol such as peaches in brandy.

Sweeteners

There are two types of sweeteners, **intense sweeteners** and **bulk sweeteners**.

Intense sweeteners are aspartame and saccharin. They are:

- approximately 300 times sweeter than sugar and therefore used in only very small amounts
- very low in energy
- used in low-calorie drinks and reduced-sugar products, and are also available as sweetening tablets
- useful for consumers who want to reduce the amount of sugar in their diet.

However they:

- lack the bulk that is needed in recipes which normally use sugar cane or beet
- do not have the same characteristics as sugar for cooking
- may leave a bitter aftertaste.

Bulk sweeteners are hydrogenated glucose syrup, sorbital (E420) and sucralose. They are:

- similar to sugar in levels of sweetness
- used in similar amounts to sugar
- used in sugar-free confectionery and preserves for diabetics.

There have been developments in half-sugar products recently. Ordinary sugar has a small amount of aspartame added to it, which makes it twice as sweet and means half the calories. This means that half the amount of sugar is needed.

ACTIVITY

Investigate how successfully half sugar can be used in traditional sweet baked products such as Victoria sandwich cake, scones or biscuits.

Emulsifiers, stabilisers, gelling agents and thickeners

These help to improve the consistency of food during processing and storage. Emulsifiers and stabilisers help mix together ingredients like oil and water that would normally separate, for instance when a salad dressing is left to stand the oil rises to the top. Lecithin is a natural emulsifier found in eggs, for example, and is used to make mayonnaise, low-fat spreads, salad dressings, etc.

Figure 4.4 Oil and water do not mix

Thickeners increase the viscosity of foods. These are important for giving foods a smooth, creamy texture. They are often used in thick and creamy desserts and in low-fat products which often have a high percentage of water, such as low-fat spreads.

There are occasions in food preparation when a product needs the assistance of a **gelling agent** in order to produce the correct consistency. Some uses of gelling agents are:

- to create a smooth set texture, e.g. in a cheesecake

- for setting meat and fish in savoury jelly

- as a stabiliser to stop separation, e.g. yoghurt

- as a stabiliser to ensure smooth texture

- to give set liquid a pliable texture, e.g. marshmallows (sweets).

Gelling agents are often extracted from foods such as beans, seaweed and plants.

Flavourings and flavour enhancers

- Flavourings and flavour enhancers must meet the requirements of the Food Safety Act 1990 and all other flavouring regulations.

- They are used widely in savoury foods to make the existing flavour in the food stronger. Monosodium glutamate (MSG) is an example of a flavour enhancer. It is often used in Chinese foods. Some consumers may be allergic to MSG, causing them sickness and dizziness.

- They add flavour to food, for instance vanilla in ice cream.

- They replace flavours lost during the processing of the food.

Antioxidants

Most foods containing fats and oils, such as pies, cakes, biscuits, dried soups, preserved meat and fish products and cheese spreads, are likely to contain antioxidants. Some antioxidants are natural, such as vitamins C and E.

These are used to:

- help prevent fat-soluble vitamins (A and D), oils and fats from combining with oxygen and making the product become rancid. Rancid fats have an unpleasant smell and taste

- prevent some foods from going brown,

e.g. apples and pears when they are exposed to air.

Anti–caking agents

These are used to stop crystals and powders from sticking together. They are found in cocoa, dried milk powder, etc.

Anti-foaming agents

These are used in jam making. They stop a large amount of foam forming when the fruit and sugar are being boiled.

Commercial glazing agents (E901, E903, E904)

These are used to give a shiny appearance to food and to protect the food from drying out.

These additives are obtained from beeswax, leaves or insects and are used in making confectionery, chocolates and sweets.

▶ Fortification of foods

In the UK there is a range of fortified foods. Some are fortified by law, such as white and brown flour with calcium. Today there are many foods which are voluntarily fortified as food manufacturers seek to promote foods which are linked to healthy lifestyles, for instance fruit juices and the majority of breakfast cereals have added vitamins and other nutrients.

Why are food products fortified?

- To increase the nutrient content, especially when added to staple foods such as bread. When wheat is processed iron, thiamine and niacin are removed with the bran. These nutrients have to be replaced in white and brown flour by law in the UK.

- Where there is nutrient deficiency in a country fortification can help to reduce the deficiency.

- Manufacturers may see it as an advantage in helping them to sell more of their product as it can be marketed as containing the nutrient or having added nutrients.

- The addition of some nutrients may help with other aspects of the product. Vitamin C is an antioxidant, it will therefore reduce the rate of spoilage in some products.

- To replace the nutrients lost during the processing of the food. This is very important if the food was a good source of the nutrient before it was processed.

- To produce a product that is similar to another. By law margarine has to have vitamins A and D added to similar levels as in butter. Manufacturers of some soya-based drinks add calcium, as the drinks are sold as a substitute for milk.

Examples of voluntary fortification

- Fruit juices made from concentrate are often fortified with vitamin C so that it has the same nutritional profile as freshly squeezed fruit juice.

Figure 4.5 Examples of foods which have been fortified

- TVP when used for savoury products is fortified with iron and the vitamin B complex so that its nutritional profile is similar to meat.

- Low-fat spreads often have vitamins A and D added to them so they are similar to margarine and butter.

- Many breakfast cereal products are fortified. These are clearly labelled on the packet.

KEY POINTS

- Some foods are fortified by law.
- Safety and technical considerations are taken into account when deciding which foods to fortify and to what level.
- Fortified foods make an important contribution to diets in the UK.

ACTIVITY

Look at a variety of fortified food ingredient labels and complete Table 4.8 to show how they have been fortified and the function of the nutrient added.

Product	Ingredient added	Function of the nutrient in the diet

Table 4.8 Fortified food ingredients and their function

QUESTIONS

1. Explain why flour is fortified.
2. Manufacturers sometimes choose to fortify foods. Give three reasons why they may choose to do this.
3. Discuss how fortified foods can make a contribution to the nutritional intake of consumers in the UK.

4.4 FOOD COMPONENTS

The word 'components' is used to describe an individual part that makes up a product. For example, flour is a standard component of pastry and pastry is a standard component of apple pie.

Manufacturers often find it quicker, cheaper or simpler to 'buy in' ready prepared ingredients or parts to make their food product. These are called pre-manufactured components. For example, when producing a pizza a manufacturer may buy in ready-made pizza bases, grated cheese, chopped ham and vegetables

Standard components	Pre-manufactured components
concentrates e.g. tomato puree	ready-made pastry
stock e.g. cubes	tinned tomatoes
seasonings e.g. salt	ready to serve custard
herbs e.g. parsley	pre-washed and prepared vegetables
spices e.g. coriander seeds	dried cheese sauce
raising agents e.g. baking powder	crumble mix
thickeners e.g. cornflour	frozen cream decorations
flavourings e.g. vanilla essence	part cooked base
juices e.g. lemon juice	ready to roll icing

Table 4.9 Examples of some standard components and pre-manufactured components

Advantages/Benefits	Disadvantages/Limitations
Save preparation time	You rely upon a manufacturer to supply the product so their problems become yours
Saves staff skill, costs and equipment	The taste and quality may not be as good as using your own ingredients
You get the same result every time	Other food companies may use the same components
The quality is guaranteed	The components may be expensive
You are getting the components from experts who know how to make them	May contain certain ingredients consumer wishes to avoid, e.g. artificial colourants
Some have a relatively long shelf life	May contain added fat, sugar or salt
Can be used as part of more complex products	Could have poor proportions, e.g. little meat compared to sauce
It saves relying on several suppliers to provide the separate ingredients	
It can make food preparation safer because the high-risk processes – such as vegetable preparation that needs soil removal – are carried out in another place	
If egg products are cooked elsewhere, this removes the risk of contamination from raw egg	

Table 4.10 Advantages/benefits and disadvantages/limitations of using pre-manufactured components

QUESTIONS

1. A savoury flan is made by using the following basic ingredients:

Pastry	Filling
150 g plain flour	200 ml milk
75 g fat	2 eggs
6 tsp water	75 g cheddar cheese
	1 g pepper

a) Identify one pre-manufactured component which could be used in the savoury flan.

b) Give two benefits to a manufacturer of using pre-manufactured components.

c) Give one limitation to a manufacturer of using pre-manufactured components.

2. State two ways pre-manufactured components can maintain the consistency of a food product.

3. Copy and complete Figure 4.6 by:
   - naming a pre-manufactured component
   - stating three different food products in which it could be used.

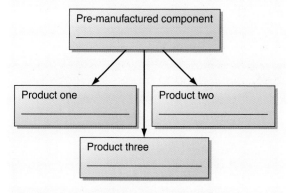

Figure 4.6 Pre-manufactured components

 ACTIVITY

A pizza is made by using the following basic ingredients:

Base	Topping
100 g strong plain flour	100 g cheddar cheese
100 g wholemeal flour	1 onion
2 tablespoons oil	8 chopped tomatoes
125 ml warm water	1 teaspoon fresh herbs
yeast?	

Draw an annotated sketch to show how pre-manufactured components could be used when making the pizza.

 KEY POINTS

- Components help to produce products of a consistent standard.
- Components are used by the food industry to save preparation time and costs.

KEY TERMS

STANDARD COMPONENTS – describe ingredients that make up a product, for example flour

PRE-MANUFACTURED COMPONENTS – ready-prepared ingredients, such as ready-made pastry

PROCESSES AND SKILLS

5.1 HEAT TRANSFERENCE

By the end of this section you should have developed
a knowledge and understanding of:

- heat transference through the different methods of cooking:
  boiling, baking, grilling, microwaving, steaming, frying and roasting
- the effect of heat on different foods
- baked products: rubbing in, creaming, melting, whisking, all-in-one,
  kneading, folding, rolling, shaping, cutting
- sauce making – roux, blended, all-in-one
- fruit and vegetable preparation
- preparation of meat, fish, alternative protein foods
- finishing techniques: garnishing, glazing, decorating of food products.

*When preparing foods to eat,
there are many different
processes and skills involved. It is
essential that preparation is
carried out correctly so that food
is safe to eat and also presented
in a way which is appealing and
appetising.*

Heat

*Heat is a type of energy. When it
is applied to foods, the foods will
change. The most noticeable
changes in foods are:*

- *colour and*
- *texture.*

*However, the nutritional content
of the food may also change and
this needs to be considered when
deciding on the method of
cooking.*

◗ Cooking method

The choice of method of cooking will depend on the following:

- the type of food which is being cooked
- the facilities that are available
- how much time is available
- the needs of the individual, e.g. special dietary requirements
- choice of the consumer, cooking a healthy diet
- skill of the cook.

There are three basic methods of heat transference:

- conduction
- convection
- radiation.

The different methods of cooking available to us use at least one of these methods of heat transference.

Table 5.1 shows the different methods of heat transference for the most common methods of cooking foods.

Cooking methods are classified as either dry or moist depending on whether water is involved.

- Moist-heat cooking methods include boiling, simmering, steaming.
- Dry-heat cooking methods include baking, roasting, deep-fat frying, sautéing and stir-frying.

Moist methods of cooking

These use fairly low temperatures to cook foods. The liquid used to cook the food can

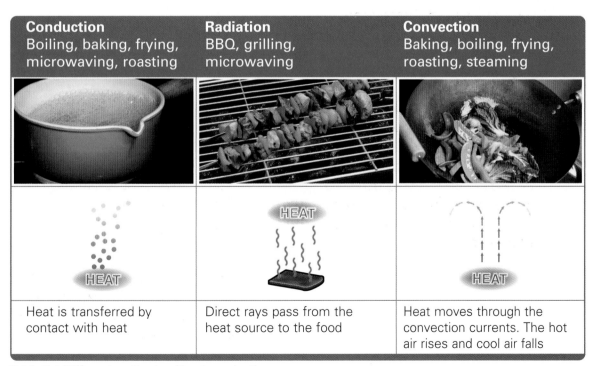

Conduction Boiling, baking, frying, microwaving, roasting	Radiation BBQ, grilling, microwaving	Convection Baking, boiling, frying, roasting, steaming
Heat is transferred by contact with heat	Direct rays pass from the heat source to the food	Heat moves through the convection currents. The hot air rises and cool air falls

Table 5.1 Different methods of heat conduction

vary, for instance water, fruit juice, milk and stock.

Boiling

Boiling is probably the most popular of the moist-heat cooking methods. Boiling uses large amounts of rapidly bubbling liquid to cook foods (100 °C). Examples of foods cooked by this method are rice, pasta and potatoes.

Simmering

Simmering is one of the most widely used moist-heat cooking methods. Properly simmered foods should be very moist and tender. The foods are cooked in hot liquid (85–99 °C) but require gentler treatment than boiling, for example to prevent food such as fish or meat from toughening or vegetables from disintegrating.

Poaching

The temperature of the liquid is just below simmering. Foods which are often poached include eggs, fish and fruit. These foods do not need a long cooking time.

Steaming

The food does not come into contact with the boiling water but is cooked by the steam which is rising from the boiling water.

Steaming can be carried out in a variety of ways, as shown in Table 5.2.

In a tiered steamer it is also possible to cook several foods at once, such as potatoes in the base and various vegetables in the different layers of the steamer. This can help to reduce energy costs.

The types of foods suitable for steaming include:

- puddings – suet, sponge
- fish
- vegetables.

Dry methods of cooking

Higher temperatures are used in dry methods of cooking compared with moist methods.

Baking

When food is baked it mainly uses dry heat. The temperature can easily be controlled. The temperature used varies depending on the type of food product being cooked – a very low temperature is used to cook meringues so that they will dry out and have a crisp texture, while Yorkshire puddings are cooked on a high temperature so that the steam is produced in the mixture to cause the batter to rise. On some occasions moisture may be

| Plate method | Saucepan method | Tiered steamer | Electric steamer |

Table 5.2 Different methods of steaming

added to help develop certain textures in a food, for instance placing egg custards in a bath of water to prevent them from curdling. Baking is regarded as a healthy way of cooking as fat is not usually involved.

Roasting

Food is cooked by dry heat. A small amount of fat is also used to prevent the food drying out and to develop the flavour. Foods which are commonly roasted include vegetables and meat.

Grilling

This is a quick method of cooking. The source of heat can come from above and/or below the food. Suitable foods for grilling are tender cuts of meat, such as chops, chicken breast, sausages, beefburgers, mushrooms, tomatoes, bread. When the foods are cooked the surface is quickly sealed due to the dry heat. The food must be turned often to ensure even cooking. It is recommended that foods which are to be grilled are no more than 3.5 cm thick.

Frying

This is still a popular method of cooking although we are being encouraged to reduce the amount of fried food we consume. There are four different types of frying:

- dry
- shallow
- deep
- stir-frying.

When frying it is important that the correct type of fat is used. A low-fat spread is unsuitable for frying due to its high water content. The water causes the fat to split and separate when it is heated. The fat used must be suitable to heat to a temperature of 200 °c without it burning or changing in taste. The most common type of fat for frying is vegetable oil, although in the past lard was often used.

Dry frying

Some foods can be fried without any fat being added to the pan. These foods have to have a fairly high fat content, such as sausages and bacon. Non-stick frying pans are the best as they help to prevent the food from sticking. It is possible to purchase fat sprays which can be used to put a very thin layer of oil onto a frying pan. See Figure 5.1 for an example of a spray.

Figure 5.1 Example of spray which can be used when frying

Shallow frying

This is when foods are cooked in a shallow layer of hot fat or oil. The fat comes about half way up the food. As this is a very quick method of cooking it is not suitable for tough cuts of meat and poultry. The following are suitable foods for shallow frying:

- eggs – omelettes, fried, pancakes, crepes
- fish – fresh/frozen – various cuts – fillets, small whole fish

- meat and poultry – prime cuts, e.g. fillet steak, chicken breast
- fishcakes
- sausages
- bacon.

Figure 5.3 Example of stir-frying

 QUESTION

1. Why is stir-frying considered a healthy method of cooking?

Figure 5.2 Example of shallow frying

Stir-frying

This method of frying originated in the Far East. Small pieces of finely chopped food are cooked in a wok. The temperature of the oil is high and the food is constantly moved around the pan. This is becoming a popular method of cooking foods as:

- it is a quick method of cooking
- it is an energy-saving method of cooking food
- it is a relatively healthy method of cooking food as very little fat or oil is added to the wok
- very few nutrients are destroyed by this method.

Deep frying

Figure 5.4 shows a commercial deep-fat fryer which is commonly seen in fish and chip shops and commercial kitchens. When food is deep fried it is totally covered in fat during the frying process. The types of foods suitable for deep-fat frying include:

Figure 5.4 Example of commercial deep-fat frying

- chips
- doughnuts
- small poultry joints
- fish
- scotch eggs.

It is recommended that we reduce the amount of deep-fried foods we consume.

ACTIVITY

Make a list of the types of foods which are commonly fried. Suggest an alternative way each food could be cooked to reduce the amount of fat in the product.

Microwaving

Microwaves are in common use in many homes – statistics from the Expenditure and Food Survey carried out by the Office for National Statistics showed that in 2006 91 per cent of households had a microwave. They are also widely used in catering kitchens, shops, offices and work canteens.

They are popular because foods can be defrosted, cooked and reheated quickly. They are also continually being developed to include extra features such as:

- child locks
- weight sensors
- different cooking modes, e.g. defrosting foods, cooking vegetables, meat, fish, pasta
- defrost modes
- turbo reheat
- auto sensor cooking.

Microwave ovens work by the microwaves penetrating into the food and causing the molecules in the food to vibrate. As the molecules vibrate against each other this causes friction which produces heat. Standing time is part of the cooking process. When food comes out of the oven, the water molecules continue to vibrate which generates the heat, allowing the cooking process to be completed. During this time the centre of the food will gain rather than lose temperature. Standing times given on food labels should always be followed.

Microwave ovens should have a label on the front as shown in Figure 5.5.

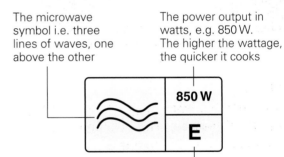

Figure 5.5 A microwave oven label

There are many different types of microwaves available today, as Table 5.3 on page 120 illustrates.

When deciding which method of cooking to use there are always advantages and disadvantages to each method. Table 5.4 on pages 120 and 121 shows some of the advantages and disadvantages of each method.

Type of microwave	Example	Uses
Standard		To defrost, reheat and cook foods
Standard with grill		All the features of a standard microwave oven, but with an internal grill. This can be used as a stand-alone grill or for browning or crisping food, e.g. crisping pizza, in conjunction with the microwave
Combination		A combined microwave, grill and convection (hot-air) oven gives more flexibility; the functions can be used independently or together. Some combination ovens offer a steaming function

Table 5.3 Different types of microwave

Method of cooking	Advantages	Disadvantages
Boiling	• A quick method of cooking as the transfer of heat is quite quick • Food is not likely to burn • A simple method of cooking	• Food may disintegrate if it is not carefully timed • Water-soluble vitamins (B and C) may be lost • Some flavour from the foods will leach into the water
Steaming	• As the food does not come into contact with the liquid, the loss of water-soluble nutrients is reduced • Food cooked by this method is usually light in texture and therefore easy to digest • Different foods can be cooked in the different tiers of a steamer, therefore reducing energy costs	• Depending on the product being cooked, it can take a long time to cook, e.g. a steamed pudding • Care with timings must be taken so that delicate foods such as fish are not overcooked

Table 5.4 Advantages and disadvantages of different methods of cooking

Method of cooking	Advantages	Disadvantages
Grilling	• A quick method of cooking food and therefore reduces the energy costs • No added fat, therefore it is a healthier method than frying – as the food cooks, fat drains off the grilling rack • It is possible to trim excess fat off some meats, e.g. bacon, before grilling	• Not suitable for tough cuts of meat • Careful timing of cooking is needed so that foods are not overcooked
Frying	• A quick method of cooking food • Food is usually attractive in colour – golden brown • Soluble nutrients are not lost	• Heat-sensitive nutrients are destroyed • We are being encouraged to reduce the consumption of fats – therefore this method of cooking does not assist this • Fats need straining and changing regularly • Fried food is more difficult to digest • Great care has to be taken with frying food from a safety perspective
Microwave	• Food is cooked very quickly – saves energy • Useful for people who have busy lifestyles • Less destruction of heat-sensitive nutrients as the cooking time is short • Less loss of water-soluble vitamins when cooking vegetables • The bright colour of vegetables is retained as cooking time is short • Very useful for defrosting frozen foods	• Careful timing is required as foods can easily be overcooked • As the food is cooked so quickly the flavours may not develop in the food • The colour of the food may be pale if it is cooked in a standard microwave

Table 5.4 continued

QUESTION

1. We are being encouraged to eat fewer fried foods. Suggest suitable alternative methods to frying for cooking the following foods:
   - sausages
   - eggs
   - beefburgers
   - potatoes.

KEY TERMS

CONDUCTION – heat transferred from one molecule to another

CONVECTION – where warm molecules rise and the cooler molecules fall closer to the source of heat

RADIATION – heat is passed by electromagnetic waves from one place to another

ACTIVITY

1. Many consumers are trying to reduce the amount of fat they consume. Produce a fact sheet to help inform consumers of which methods of cooking will help them in achieving this goal.

2. We are all being encouraged to reduce the amount of energy we use. Discuss how this can be done when preparing different meals. Give reasons and examples.

3. Produce a chart to show the advantages and disadvantages of the different methods of cooking vegetables.

5.2 EFFECTS OF HEAT ON DIFFERENT FOODS

LEARNING OUTCOMES

By the end of this section you should have developed a knowledge and understanding of:
- how cooking can affect the structure of foods.

Many foods can be eaten raw, but many others need to be cooked for the following reasons:

- *to make them safe to eat*
- *to stop the food from decaying*
- *to destroy any harmful toxins in the food, e.g. red kidney beans contain a poison which is destroyed by soaking the beans for 24 hours and then boiling them for 90 minutes*
- *so the food can be digested*
- *so the food is attractive and appealing*
- *to develop the flavour in the foods*
- *to provide variety in the diet – different foods can be cooked in different ways, providing a range of flavours and textures.*

When foods are prepared and cooked you are often able to see one or more of the following changes:

- *changes in colour – toast becoming brown*
- *food increases in size – rice swells*
- *food decreases in size/shrinks – meat*
- *food becomes thicker – sauces*
- *food curdles – eggs*
- *foods becomes firmer – fish.*

Other ways foods change which are not visible are:

- *loss of nutritional value*
- *food becomes tender*
- *foods absorb other substances, such as water (a visible effect of this is that the structure and appearance of the food changes).*

The effect of heat on protein foods

When moist or dry heat is applied to proteins the proteins in the foods coagulate (set). They are overheated and become tough and more difficult to digest.

Food	What happens to the food when it is heated?
Meat	• The muscle fibres will begin to coagulate between 40°C and 60°C. • After 60°C the fibres in the meat shrink and the juice in the meat is squeezed out. • Tougher cuts of meat or meat from older animals, e.g. mutton, needs long, slow, moist methods of cooking, e.g. casseroling, so that the meat becomes tender. • Lean cuts of meat (those with less connective tissue) are suitable for dry cooking and a short amount of cooking time. • The fat in the meat melts. • The colour of the meat changes if meat is cooked by a dry method – beef for example goes from red to brown. • There is little change to the protein content. • B vitamins (water soluble) may be leached into the cooking liquid in moist methods of cooking.
Fish	• The muscles in the fish shrink as fish have very short fibres and only a small amount of connective tissue. Short cooking times are required. • If it is cooked for too long it will become tough. • Some of the B vitamins are lost as they are destroyed by heat.
Eggs	• The egg white begins to coagulate at 60°C. The egg white changes from an opaque colour to a white colour. • The egg yolk begins to coagulate at 70°C. • If eggs are heated too quickly the liquid from the egg separates out and the protein becomes tough. This is called syneresis. It is sometimes seen when cooking scrambled eggs. • There is little effect on the nutritional value.
Milk	• When milk is heated a skin develops on its surface.
Cheese	• The fat in the cheese melts and the proteins coagulate. • If the cheese is heated at a high temperature or for a long time the cheese will become stringy and more difficult to digest. • You may be able to see the fat that has been squeezed out of the cheese. If this gets too hot it smells bitter and starts to decompose. • If cheese is added to a cheese sauce it should be added at the end of the sauce-making process and should be grated – this will make the melting process quicker and less heat will be required.

Table 5.5 What happens to different protein foods when heat is applied?

The effect of heat on starchy foods

Wheat flour is one of the most common starchy foods used in cooking. The way it reacts to heat depends on the type of heat applied and the ingredients it is mixed with.

Dry heat on flour

When dry heat is applied to products such as baking bread, the crust of the product becomes brown – this is called **dextrinisation**.

Moist heat on flour

When flour is mixed with a liquid as in a sauce, the mixture will thicken. This is known as **gelatinisation**. This occurs because:

• the starch grains are not able to dissolve in the liquid

• as the liquid is heated the starch grains swell and as more heat is applied the starch grains break open, causing the mixture to thicken.

The mixture must be stirred as it is being heated to prevent lumps forming.

Cornflour is often used as an alternative to flour in sauces. Cornflour is the finely powdered white starch obtained from maize kernels. It is virtually tasteless. Unlike other flours, it blends to a smooth cream with liquid, although it does still need to be stirred when it is being heated so lumps do not form.

Other starch foods which thicken mixtures are:

- potatoes – potato flour is used to thicken sauces; it thickens soups and casseroles as the starch is released from the potatoes into the cooking liquid
- other root vegetables – swede will thicken soups and stews; sweet potatoes will thicken soups; tapioca is made from the cassava plant and is used in puddings, stews and soups
- rice flour – used to thicken sauces, useful to those who are on a gluten-free or wheat-free diet; thickens milk puddings such as rice pudding; used to thicken savoury dishes such as risotto
- arrowroot – made from the maranta plant, used to make clear glazes which are often used on fruit tarts.

Food manufacturers use a lot of starches in products. They have been adapted to meet specific requirements, for instance:

- pregelatinised – thickens instantly when hot water is added, e.g. in pot noodles, instant soups
- can be mixed with cold liquid and will thicken, e.g. in instant whip, angel delight
- prevents sauces separating (syneresis) in ready meals
- used to thicken low-fat desserts and salad dressings – to stop them separating.

These starches are called modified starches.

ACTIVITY

In groups prepare a variety of dishes which show how carbohydrate foods can be used to thicken mixtures.

▶ The effect of heat on sugars

Sugar helps with the browning of sweet foods.

Sugar which has been browned under a hot grill to create the hard caramel on top of a crème brulée	Sugar which has changed to a syrup and caramelised in a crème caramel	Maillard reaction which occurs in biscuits when they contain carbohydrate and protein

Table 5.6 Table to show how sugar has changed colour in three different products

Moist heat on sugars

When moist heat is applied to sugar the following happens:

- The sugar melts and becomes syrup. It is sometimes used in this syrup state, such as in fruit salads, though most people today put fruit salads into fruit juices to reduce the sugar and calorie content of the product.
- At 154 °C the sugar starts to change colour – this process is called caramelisation.
- The longer the sugar is heated, the deeper the colour of the caramel and the harder it will set when it is cooled.

Dry heat on sugars

When dry heat is applied to sugars, sugar will also caramelise. When sugars are mixed with other products such as eggs and flour (which both contain protein) in baked products, browning occurs in these products. This is called a Maillard reaction.

▶ The effect of heat on fruits and vegetables

Fruits and vegetables provide important sources of vitamins in our diets. It is therefore important that they are cooked so these vitamins are not destroyed. Vitamin C and B are water soluble and are easily destroyed by heat.

When cooking foods with high vitamin C content the following can be done to help to retain the vitamin C:

- Add vegetables to boiling water – this destroys the enzymes and will help preserve the vitamins.
- Steam the vegetables – vegetables are not in contact with the water therefore vitamins will not leach into it.
- Serve them immediately – if they are kept hot there will be further loss of vitamin C as it is also destroyed by heat as well as being water soluble.
- Cook for as little time as possible.
- Use as little water as possible – and use the liquid so that the vitamins are still consumed.

It is not possible to eat all vegetables raw. Some vegetables, such as potatoes, are cooked to make them more digestible. When potatoes cook, the starch grains absorb water, which causes the grains to swell and the cellulose in the potato to soften.

When fruits and vegetables are cooked they may also change in colour. In green vegetables if they are overcooked the colour of the vegetables will fade, making them less appealing to the consumer.

KEY POINT

- Fruits and vegetables need to be cooked carefully to retain their nutritive value.

Figure 5.6 The difference between correctly and overcooked broccoli

ACTIVITY

Using a nutritional computer program, compare the vitamin C content in:

a) a range of raw vegetables

b) a range of vegetables cooked in different ways

c) a range of different processed vegetables, e.g. fresh, canned and frozen.

Produce an information sheet explaining your findings.

KEY TERMS

COAGULATE – to set

GELATINISATION – this is what happens to starches and water when cooked together

CARAMELISATION – this happens when sugar is heated

MAILLARD REACTION – this happens when foods containing proteins and carbohydrates are cooked by dry methods

QUESTIONS

1. What does the word coagulation mean?

2. Explain what happens to the ingredients in a sauce when they are cooked.

3. What are modified starches?

4. What advice would you give to a consumer on how to cook vegetables to retain their nutritional value?

5.3 BAKED PRODUCTS

There are a large number of baked products which you can successfully prepare in the home and in school. When making any baked product such as cakes, biscuits, pastry and bread it is important that the ingredients are added in the correct proportion and that the mixtures are handled correctly.

KEY POINT

- When producing baked products it is important that ingredients are weighed accurately so that the ingredients will work correctly together.

◗ Cake making

There are six main methods of cake making (see Table 5.7 on page 129). Each method produces products which have a different texture. The nutritional profile of the products also varies. The amount of fat in the product will determine how long the cake will stay fresh – without drying out. Cakes cannot be successfully made with reduced-fat spreads as the water content of these is too high. It is important to check on the labels of the different types of fats to see whether they are suitable for cooking.

QUESTIONS

1. Using a nutritional program, compare the nutritional profile of each of the different methods of cake making.

   Suggest how the recipes could be adapted to improve their nutritional profile

2. A cake manufacturer wants to develop a new range of cake products which:

   - are attractive to school children
   - include fruit
   - are suitable for a packed lunch box.

   Working in small groups, each group using a different method of cake making, design and make a range of products which will fit the specification.

   Evaluate your products against the specification and suggest any further improvements which could be made to the products.

◗ Pastry

There is a wide variety of pastry products available in shops and they can be purchased from many different sections of a supermarket, such as:

- chiller cabinet
- delicatessen
- bakery section
- freezer.

Method of making	Example of product	Ratio of fat to flour	Raising agent	Basic recipe	
Creaming	Victoria sandwich, small buns	1:1	Self-raising flour – contains baking powder	100 g SR flour 100 g fat (margarine or butter) 100 g sugar 2 eggs	
All in one	Victoria sandwich, small buns	1:1	Self-raising flour – contains baking powder	100 g SR flour 100 g fat (margarine or butter) 100 g sugar 2 tsp baking powder 2 eggs	
Whisked sponge	Swiss roll Fruit flan Gateaux Sponge cake	No added fat	Air Steam	50 g flour 50 g sugar 2 eggs	
Rubbed in	Scones Rock buns	1:2 in cakes 1:4 in scones, contains baking powder	Self-raising flour	Cakes 200 g SR flour 100 g fat (margarine or butter) 100 g sugar 2 eggs 50 ml milk	Scones 200 g SR flour 50 g margarine or butter 125 ml milk
Melted	Flapjack Gingerbread	Varies depending on the product being made	Bicarbonate of soda in gingerbread. Flapjack does not contain a raising agent	Varies depending on the product	
Batter	Muffins		Baking powder Steam	225 g plain flour 120 ml vegetable oil 2 tsp baking powder ¼ tsp salt 1 egg 250 ml milk	

Table 5.7 Information on the methods of cake making

Pastry products can be served on many different occasions during the day. Pastry products are often high in calories. The main ingredients in all types of pastry are:

- flour
- fat
- water
- salt.

Eggs, sugar and other ingredients such as cheese and herbs can be added to some pastries for extra flavour. The ingredients are used in different ratios and are mixed in

Type of pastry	Basic recipe	Ratio of fat to flour	How fat is incorporated	Texture required
Shortcrust	200 g plain flour 100 g fat (mixture of margarine and white fat) water	1:2	Fat rubbed into flour	Light texture, crisp, short
Flaky	200 g plain flour 150 g fat (mixture of margarine and white fat) 2 tsp lemon juice water	3:4	¼ fats rubbed into flour, then water added. Pastry is rolled and folded adding a ¼ of the fat each time	Layers of crisp pastry
Choux	75 g plain flour 25 g butter 2 eggs 125 ml water	1:3	Fat is melted in the water	Hollow inside, well risen with a crisp texture
Suet	200 g SR flour 100 g suet water	1:2	Pre-grated suet is stirred in	Light, soft. This pastry can be steamed as well as being baked in an oven

Table 5.8 Information about the main types of pastry

different ways to produce a variety of textures and flavours.

You can also get:

- filo pastry – this originally came from Greece. When it is cooked it becomes very crisp. The fat content in filo pastry is much lower than in other pastries. This can be purchased fresh or as a frozen product
- puff pastry – similar to flaky pastry. Many people buy this as either a chilled or frozen product as it is quick to use and saves a lot of preparation time
- products made with hot water crust pastry – this is used for pork pies and is not made very often in the home.

It is possible to buy shortcrust, puff and filo pastry as a pre-manufactured component. Many people choose to do this because:

- it saves time
- they do not have the skills to make the pastry
- it saves buying lots of separate ingredients they might not use at a later date.

When preparing pastry (except for choux pastry) it is important to keep everything as cool as possible. Rolling out the pastry has to be done carefully so that it is not spoilt. Choux pastry is not rolled out – it is usually piped or spooned into the desired shapes.

Rolling out

The pastry needs to be as cool as possible when rolling out. It should be of a firm consistency. You should roll out on a lightly floured work surface with a floured rolling pin. The pastry should be rolled with short, even strokes. Once you have rolled across the pastry, turn it through a quarter turn and continue rolling. You should not turn the pastry over.

Figure 5.7 Web diagram of tips for making good shortcrust, flaky, suet and puff pastry

ACTIVITY

Investigate the nutritional values of the different types of pastry.

Record your findings and discuss how you could possibly adapt the basic recipe, reduce or change the types of pastry used in traditional dishes.

QUESTION

1. Many people choose to purchase pastry from the shops – ready to roll. What are the advantages and disadvantages of this?

▶ Bread making

There is a large variety of breads made with a wide range of flours. Many types of bread are traditional to different parts of this country and to different parts of the world. They can also be made from a wide variety of different flours.

Figure 5.8 Different types of bread

ACTIVITY

Research the different types of bread available in a supermarket. Produce a chart or poster to show where they originate from and the types of flour used in them.

The main ingredients in bread are:

- strong plain flour
- yeast – fresh or dried
- salt.

Other ingredients can be added to the bread to give variety to the taste and texture of the product.

To successfully make bread the following are important:

- using strong plain flour – this contains gluten (the protein in flour) which will provide the structure to the cooked bread
- salt – helps to improve the mixture and adds flavour
- yeast – this is the raising agent – when the warm (25°C–35°C) liquid is added to the dry ingredients and yeast it must not be too hot as this will kill the yeast and the bread will not rise
- kneading the bread – this helps to develop the gluten which stretches to hold the carbon dioxide bubbles produced by the yeast.

Figure 5.9 Kneading bread

ACTIVITY

A bakery wants to develop a hand-held snack bread product. The specification for the product is:

- can be eaten 'on the go'
- suitable for a wide range of consumers
- costs under £1 per portion
- attractive
- contains either fruit or vegetables
- includes a variety of textures.

Using a basic bread recipe, design a product which meets this specification.

List the ingredients and their costs.

Explain how your design meets the specification.

Plan and make the product.

Evaluate the product against the specification and suggest any improvements.

Shaping and cutting

There are various tools and equipment which can help you to cut and shape foods. Equipment includes: food processors which have a variety of blades for different tasks,

Figure 5.10 Range of equipment which can cut and shape foods

graters, zesters, vegetable peelers, cutters and a range of knives. It is important that the correct piece of equipment is used for the task so that it is carried out successfully.

When using sharp equipment care must be taken to ensure that the piece of equipment is used safely.

ACTIVITY

Evaluate the efficiency of using a food processor to carry out various practical tasks.

What are the advantages and disadvantages of using a food processor?

KEY TERMS

RATIO – quantities of ingredients expressed in numbers, e.g. ratio of fat to flour in a creamed cake mixture is 1:1

RUBBING IN – this is when the fat is rubbed into the flour until it resembles breadcrumbs. It is used in pastry, cake and biscuit making

CREAMING – the fat and sugar are beaten together using either a wooden spoon or a mixer. This helps to add air to the mixture. Cakes and biscuits can be made by this method

WHISKING – sugar and eggs are whisked together. This adds air to the mixture – used when making a whisked sponge

5.4 SAUCE MAKING FOR SWEET AND SAVOURY PRODUCTS

There are many different types of sauces and they are used in a wide variety of dishes. In this section we are going to focus on starch-based sauces.

The different starches which are often used to thicken sauces are:

- flour
- cornflour
- arrowroot.

Depending on the proportions of the ingredients used the thickness of the sauce varies.

Sauces can be made by three different methods:

- roux
- blended
- all-in-one.

Roux
This is the traditional method of making a sauce. The fat is melted and the flour stirred in and cooked on a medium heat. The liquid is added gradually. The sauce is returned to the heat and brought back to the boil.

Blended
This is often used for cornflour- and arrowroot-based sauces. A little of the liquid is blended with the cornflour. The remaining

Type of sauce	Proportions of ingredients	Description of sauce	Example of dish
Pouring	250 ml milk 15 g fat 15 g flour	Pours freely	Custard
Coating	250 ml milk 25 g fat 25 g flour	Coats the back of a spoon	Cauliflower cheese
Binding	250 ml flour 50 g fat 50 g flour	Very thick sauce which can bind ingredients	Fish cakes

Table 5.9 Proportions of ingredients used in sauces

liquid is heated. The liquid is poured onto the cornflour, stirring carefully. The sauce is returned to the pan and brought back to the boil.

All-in-one

All the ingredients are placed in the pan and brought to the boil. Stirring or whisking is required all the time to prevent the sauce from having lumps.

ACTIVITY

In groups, prepare a cheese sauce by the three different methods detailed in this section. Additonally prepare a sauce using a packet mix. Compare the results of making the sauce for:

- ease of making
- time it took to make
- quality of the finished sauce
- cost
- nutritional value.

Use the sauce to make a savoury dish of your choice.

QUESTIONS

1. List the three main methods of making sauces.

2. Suggest **three** different ingredients which could be used to flavour a savoury white sauce.

3. Give **two** reasons why it is important to stir a sauce when it is being cooked.

4. These are the ingredients used in a plain white sauce:
   - 25 g flour
   - 25 g fat
   - 250 ml milk

Describe what happens to the ingredients when they are heated.

5.5 FRUIT AND VEGETABLE PREPARATION

Fruits and vegetables need to be carefully prepared to maintain their nutritional profile.

Fruits and vegetables must be stored correctly before they are prepared to help retain their nutritional value. This can be done by:

- storing in a cool, dry place
- handling carefully – bruising will reduce the vitamin C content
- removing any damaged fruit or vegetables
- checking the storage instructions on the products
- keeping salad ingredients in the salad drawer.

Figure 5.11 There is a wide variety of fruits and vegetables to choose from

Preparing fruits and vegetables

When preparing fruits and vegetables:

- Wash to remove dirt.
- Remove any blemishes or outer leaves.

- Peel if necessary – many fruits and vegetables can be eaten with their skin on and this will increase the nutrient content as many of the nutrients are stored just below the surface.
- Prepare vegetables just before cooking to prevent loss of vitamins by the action of enzymes and oxidization.
- Do not soak them in water as this will result in the loss of water-soluble vitamins.
- Some fruits and vegetables will go brown once they are peeled and cut, e.g. apples, potatoes, pears. This is called enzymic browning. This can be reduced by:
  - blanching vegetables in boiling water
  - dipping fruit into lemon juice
  - cooking the foods as soon as they have been prepared.
- Handle delicate fruits and vegetables carefully so they do not get bruised.

Most fruits can be eaten raw, sometimes they are cooked, for instance stewing apples or poaching pears. Fruits should be washed before they are eaten.

KEY POINT

- Fruits and vegetables need to be carefully prepared so that vitamins are not lost.

Techniques

It is important that fruits and vegetables are prepared correctly. This will often involve using a sharp knife. Figure 5.11 shows the correct ways to hold vegetables when chopping and slicing them.

Figure 5.12 Bridge and claw grip used when preparing fruits and vegetables

ACTIVITY

1. Soups can be a nutritious snack product. Design a soup which would be attractive for teenagers using seasonal vegetables.

2. Calculate the nutritional value and the cost per portion.

3. Compare your product with different types of soup already on the market.

QUESTIONS

1. Why is it important to wash fruits before they are eaten?

2. When storing, preparing and cooking vegetables, how can the nutritional content be maintained?

KEY TERM

OXIDIZATION – occurs when fruit and vegetables are cut and the cells are exposed to the air

5.6 PREPARATION OF MEAT

A wide variety of meat, poultry and offal can be used in cooking. There are also many products made for consumers to cook at home, such as sausages and beefburgers.

Today most people buy their meat ready prepared and do not joint or bone pieces of meat. The meat will come cut into portions or joints and may also be chopped or minced. It is important when choosing meat that it is cooked in an appropriate way so that it is tender to eat. Usually lean tender cuts of meat are suitable for dry methods of cooking

Figure 5.13 Butcher's window display

and tougher cuts of meat require long, slow methods of cooking, such as stewing and braising.

Meat is classed as a high-risk food because it contains protein and is moist. It is important that it is processed, stored, handled and cooked correctly so that it is safe to eat.

The following is good practice:

- Wash your hands before and after touching any type of raw meat.

- Keep raw meat separate from other foods – cover and store the meat at the bottom of the fridge so that it cannot touch any other foods.

- Raw meat may contain harmful bacteria that can spread to anything it touches, therefore it is important to clean surfaces and equipment thoroughly after preparing meat.

- Raw meat should be stored at temperatures below 5 °C.

- Any bacteria present in the meat will be destroyed by heat. It is therefore important to check that the meat is thoroughly cooked. This can be done with a food probe or meat thermometer.

Figure 5.14 Checking the temperature of meat

QUESTIONS

1. Why is it important to store raw meat away from other foods?

2. How would you recommend meat to be stored?

KEY POINT

- Meat and poultry can be made into a wide variety of dishes. They must be carefully stored, prepared and cooked to ensure they are safe to eat.

5.7 PREPARATION OF FISH

Most people buy fish ready prepared, from supermarkets. There are fewer fishmongers with independent shops today. Fish can be bought fresh, frozen, dried or canned. Fresh fish is usually sold as whole fish, or cut into steaks or fillets.

When choosing fresh fish:

- it should have a sea-fresh smell
- the flesh of the fish should be moist and firm
- the scales on the fish should be shiny.

Figure 5.15 The fish counter

Fish, like meat, is a high-risk food and therefore the same good practices that are used when preparing meat need to be applied when preparing fish. It is also wise to thoroughly wrap fish so that the smell does not pass to other foods.

KEY POINT

- Fish is a high-risk food. It needs to be stored and cooked correctly. It should be eaten as soon as possible after purchase.

5.8 PREPARATION OF ALTERNATIVE PROTEIN FOODS

There is a wide range of alternative protein foods available. These include products made from soya beans, such as textured vegetable protein (TVP) tofu, and myco-protein such as Quorn®. These products can be bought in a variety of forms. The products will either simply need cooking or will require other ingredients to be added to them to make a dish or product.

The cooking instructions must be followed carefully for all these products. Soya beans can be bought frozen, tinned or dried. Quorn® is sold as a variety of ready-to-eat products but can also be bought as mince, chunks or fillets. These are sold from either the chiller cabinet or the freezer.

Tofu is purchased as a solid curd. It is usually sold from the chiller cabinet. It can be frozen, but must be cooked when it has been defrosted. It can be grilled or stir fried.

When purchasing alternative protein foods as cook chill products you must remember to treat these as high-risk foods.

Figure 5.16 Soya products

5.9 FINISHING TECHNIQUES

By the end of this section you should have developed a knowledge and understanding of the:

- importance of making foods look attractive
- different methods used to make food products look more attractive.

First impressions play an important part in how successful a food product is going to be. Initially we rely on the senses of sight and smell when we judge a product and then taste as we eat it. The aim when you produce food is to make it:

- *attractive in appearance*
- *thoroughly/correctly cooked – to make it safe*
- *appetising – mix of flavours.*

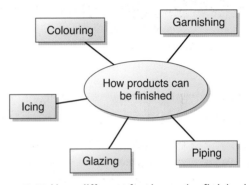

Figure 5.17 How different foods can be finished

How different food products can be finished

Some products have a finish applied to them to make them more attractive before they are cooked with other products. Figure 5.16 shows you some different ways foods can be finished.

ACTIVITY

The pictures in Figure 5.18 on page 140 show a range of food products that have different finishing techniques applied to them.

Produce a chart to show:

- the different finishing techniques used on each product
- how successful they have been in improving the appearance of the product.

Suggest any further improvements.

Gingerbread man	Cheesecake	Apple pie	Wedding cake
Bread	Iced cakes	Fish pie	

Figure 5.18 Different finishing techniques applied to products

Icing

Many cakes are iced to improve their appearance. They will be iced in different ways to:

- attract the target market
- suit the type of cake mixture used.

The main different types of icing used on cakes are:

- glacé
- butter
- fondant
- royal
- melted chocolate.

Glazing

This is a finish usually applied to the food before it is cooked. It will help to improve the colourful appearance of the food, therefore making it more attractive to consumers. Glazes can be used on both sweet and savoury foods.

Figure 5.19 A range of garnishes which can be used on foods

Type of glaze	How it is used/works	Example of foods
Egg wash	Usually a mixture of egg and milk applied to the products before baking. The product will have a shiny finish due to the coagulation of the egg	Pastry Scones
Egg white	Used on sweet pastry products with sugar sprinkled on top – this gives the product a light golden appearance and a crunchy texture	Sweet pastry products
Milk	Helps with the browning of the product but does not give a shiny appearance	Bread Pastry Scones
Sugar and water	The sugar and water are boiled until syrup is formed. When the product is cooked the syrup is brushed over it. This gives the product a shiny and sticky glaze	Sweet bread products, e.g. Chelsea buns
Arrowroot glaze	Arrowroot is mixed with water and or fruit juice and boiled to make a clear glaze. It is used to cover fruits on tarts	Fruit flans and tarts
Aspic	This is used on savoury products. It is made from gelatine and stock and sets as a clear jelly. Vegetarian versions of this can be bought	Used on savoury meat and fish dishes which are served cold
Jam – usually apricot or redcurrant	The jam is warmed and sieved if necessary and used to cover fruit	On French apple tart

Table 5.10 How different ingredients can be used to glaze food products

Garnishing

Both sweet and savoury products can be garnished. When garnishing foods you should consider the following points:

- neatness of the product – it should improve the appearance of the product, not dominate it
- garnish – it should improve the colour, flavour and texture of the dish.

Piping

Piping can be used on both sweet and savoury products. Examples of ingredients which can be piped are:

- cream (double)
- butter icing
- royal icing
- creamed biscuit mixtures – Viennese fingers
- choux pastry – for making éclairs and choux buns
- potatoes
- mayonnaise.

There are different types of nozzles available. The type and shape of the nozzle to be used will depend on:

- the ingredient being piped
- the purpose of the piping
- the type of finish required.

Coating

Some food products can be coated with other ingredients to create an attractive finish on the product or to create a layer to separate foods (see Table 5.11).

How?	Why?	What?	Examples
Applying a coating of another food	Adds texture and protects delicate food	Batter/sugar batter	Fritters, doughnut, fish
Applying layers of ingredients	Nutrition and texture	Egg and breadcrumbs	Scotch egg

Table 5.11 Coating food products to improve their appearance

Colouring

Sometimes colours are added to food products to improve the appearance, for instance colours added to icing on cakes. There is a lot of debate about the adding of artificial colours to foods as these are linked to hyperactivity in some people, particularly young children.

ACTIVITY

Plan to prepare and make a range of dishes which will illustrate a variety of finishing techniques.

After you have made the dishes, evaluate how successful they are as ways of improving the appearance of food products.

QUESTIONS

1. Different finishes are often applied to food products to improve their appearance.

   a) State a different suitable finish which could be applied to each of the following products:
      (i)   apple pie   [1]
      (ii) quiche Lorraine   [1]
      (iii) shepherd's pie   [1]

Figure 5.20 Novelty cake

   b) Figure 5.20 shows a birthday cake which has been designed to appeal to children.
      (i) List three different finishing techniques which have been applied to the cake. [3]
      (ii) The cake in Figure 5.18 was made by hand (job production). Explain three different ways the design could be simplified so that it could be made by batch production. [6]

EXAMINER'S TIPS

When a question asks you to explain something, remember to make a statement – develop the point further and if possible give an explanation to clarify your answer.

KEY TERMS

GARNISH – to improve the appearance of a dish, usually savoury
DECORATE – to improve the appearance of a dish, usually sweet
GLAZE – a finish applied to the surface of a product to improve the colour and appearance

CHAPTER 6

USING TOOLS AND EQUIPMENT

By the end of this section you should have developed a knowledge and understanding of:

- selecting and safely using tools and equipment appropriately
- alternative tools and equipment which can be used for the same task.

You need to choose suitable equipment to prepare ingredients efficiently and safely.

Using the correct equipment is essential for producing the required result in food preparation. Electrical equipment such as mixers and processors can take some of the hard work out of mixing, slicing and chopping whilst saving time. However, they cannot entirely replace hand-held equipment for efficiency, particularly for working quickly with small amounts of ingredients. During your practical sessions you need to demonstrate the correct use of appropriate equipment and look for opportunities to use a range of equipment, including labour and time-saving items. Always read recipes carefully so you are using the correct piece of equipment for the job.

6.1 EQUIPMENT

Measuring

For measuring, scales, cups, jugs or spoons may be used.

Cutting and chopping

Knives of various types and styles are used to cut and chop. They vary in size and blade type depending on what they are to be used for.

Graters are used for preparing cheese or vegetables and they can be round or box shape, or for more safety the rotary type.

Ceramic or nylon chopping boards are more hygienic than wood. In the catering industry different coloured boards are used for different tasks.

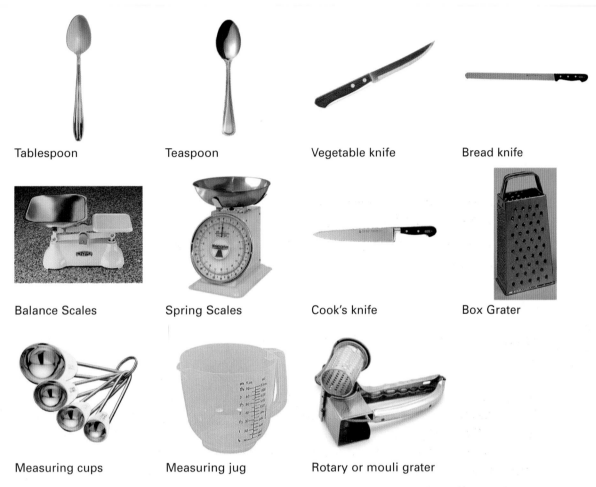

Tablespoon	Teaspoon	Vegetable knife	Bread knife
Balance Scales	Spring Scales	Cook's knife	Box Grater
Measuring cups	Measuring jug	Rotary or mouli grater	

Figure 6.1 Measuring equipment

Figure 6.2 Cutting and chopping

Red = raw meat

Blue = raw fish

Yellow = cooked meat

White = vegetables

Green = salad/fruit

Whisking

Whisks can be used for adding air to mixture. They can be operated by hand or electricity. Hand whisks can be balloon shaped, wire or rotary.

Spreading and lifting

For this a variety of equipment is available. Examples include spatulas (which are used for scraping out bowls), fish slices and palette knives (for lifting food).

▶ Other equipment

More specialist equipment can be used for fruit and vegetable preparation to save waste and make tasks easier.

Sieves can be used for aerating flour, strainers for separating solids from liquids.

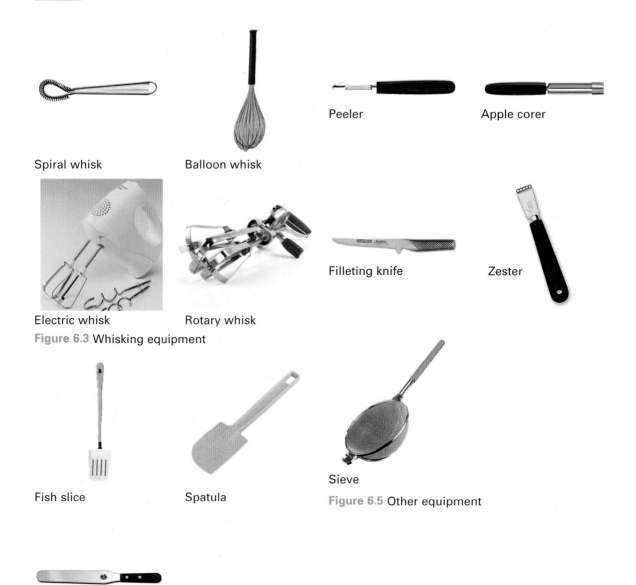

Spiral whisk

Balloon whisk

Peeler

Apple corer

Electric whisk

Rotary whisk

Filleting knife

Zester

Figure 6.3 Whisking equipment

Fish slice

Spatula

Sieve

Figure 6.5 Other equipment

Palette knife

Figure 6.4 Spreading and lifting

6.2 FOOD PREPARATION

When food is prepared it often undergoes one or more of three manipulative processes:

- mixing (e.g. beating an egg white)
- cutting (e.g. grating cheese)

- forming and shaping (e.g. rolling pastry).

All tools and equipment used in the preparation of food will fulfil one or more of these functions. The correct tool must be selected to:

- complete the task, safely, hygienically and efficiently
- achieve a consistency of finish
- achieve a quality outcome.

Mixing

There are many ways of combining foods, such as stirring, whisking, kneading, rubbing in. Sometimes personal preference determines the piece of equipment used. At other times choosing the right tool is important. For instance using a metal spoon when folding flour into a whisked sponge – it has a thinner edge, cuts through the mixture cleanly and destroys fewer air bubbles. The mixture will retain air, so when baked it has a light texture. A wooden spoon is needed when creaming mixtures (margarine and sugar).

Cutting

Different cutting tools and equipment give varying results, for instance a knife would not be a good choice for a consistent finish for cheese – results would be irregular, slices varying in thickness, shape and length. A cheese slicer will produce more consistent results and in commercial terms would be more cost effective.

Forming and shaping

Items for shaping include piping bag and nozzles, rolling pin, mould (jelly, Dariole), cake tin, sausage maker, mincer, pasta maker, burger press. Some give a more decorative finish which can look more professional (such as piping potatoes on the top of a shepherd's pie rather than forking).

Labour-saving devices

Machines can perform repetitive tasks efficiently, accurately, safely and with a consistency of outcome. They can save time and effort. In industry, labour-saving equipment is very important when large quantities of food need to be produced within a specified time. Catering outlets use machines to achieve uniformity of appearance, taste and texture. People who use these have to be properly trained. Machines often have sharper blades, operate faster and heat to a higher temperature.

▶ Alternative ways of carrying out processes

You may choose to prepare ingredients by hand or use equipment such as food processors and electric whisks (see Table 6.1). You could test different ways of carrying out a particular process to see which gives you the best result.

Large-scale equipment

The equipment used in the food industry will be different to that used in a domestic setting. Table 6.2 on page 149 shows a comparison of equipment used in a domestic setting and equipment used in industry.

Process	Hand method	Using machinery
Cutting, peeling, chopping	Using a range of knives for meat and vegetable preparation Pastry cutters, e.g. cutters for jam tarts Peeler to remove skins from potatoes, fruit, etc.	Food processor – chopping blade, used to chop food very finely Slicing blade for cucumber, carrot Electric knife can also be used, e.g. slicing meat Automatic peeler to remove skins
Whisking	Rotary, balloon or coil whisk to beat cream or egg whites as in meringue	Electric whisk can do the same jobs but will save you time and effort
Mixing	Mixing doughs, e.g. rubbing fat into flour using the fingertips and mixing in water with a round bladed knife to create the dough, e.g. shortcrust pastry Kneading bread dough	Food processor will carry out the rubbing-in and mixing process during pastry making Large food mixer will knead bread by means of a dough hook
Purée	Puréeing fruit/vegetables by using a sieve	Blender/smoothie maker will purée fruit/vegetables much quicker and the result will often be smoother
Shaping	Shaping beefburgers	Using a beefburger press
Grating	Box, flat or mouli grater	Food processor has a grater attachment

Table 6.1 Hand method versus machinery

Small scale	Large scale
Weighing ingredients using scales	Computer-controlled weighing or measuring into the hopper
Slicing vegetables using a knife and chopping board	Automatic slicer fed from the hopper
Peeling potatoes with a peeler	Mechanical peeler with specially lined drum
Rolling out with a rolling pin	Dough is sheeted using rollers
Cutting dough with tart cutters	Dough is cut using rollers with blades
Puréeing in a liquidiser	Enormous liquidiser used
Cooking in a saucepan	Large bratt pans are used
Cooking in an oven	Computer controlled travelling or tunnel ovens or rotary ovens are used
Cooling on a wire tray	Blast chilled in cooling tunnels
Cutting dough into portions using a knife	Automatic cutting
Portion controlled with a spoon measure	Squeezed out with an extruder
Using a food probe for temperature control	Sensors are computer controlled
Mixing in a bowl or processor	Giant mixing systems are used
Piping bag for cream	An injector or extruder is used
Piping bag for biscuits	A depositing machine would be used

Table 6.2 Equipment used in a domestic setting versus equipment used in industry

 QUESTION

1. Name the following pieces of equipment and give an example of jobs that they could be used for.

ACTIVITY

1. Find a recipe for each of the following food products:

   - Shepherd's pie
   - vegetable soup
   - cheesecake (with a biscuit base).

Draw a table like the one in Table 6.3. Using the recipes you have found, plus your knowledge of making practical products, write down the processes involved in the making of each food product. List the equipment required to carry out each process.

You can suggest hand and any alternative equipment if this is appropriate.

2. Look at the making instructions for a food dish. Create a table like Table 6.4 to show:

   - the list of equipment you will be using
   - the reason for using each piece of equipment.

Name of product	Processes	Equipment
Shepherd's pie		
Vegetable soup		
Cheesecake (biscuit base)		

Table 6.3 Processes and equipment

List of equipment	Reason for using

Table 6.4 Instructions for a food dish

KEY POINT

- Choose equipment appropriate to the task.

PRESERVATION AND EXTENDING SHELF LIFE

By the end of this section you should have developed a knowledge and understanding of:

- safe shelf life of a food product
- methods used to increase the shelf life of food products.

If food is not preserved it will deteriorate. Deterioration of food is caused by micro-organisms and by enzymes. Food preservation is a way of increasing the shelf life of a product.

7.1 DETERIORATION OF FOOD – FOOD SPOILAGE

Fresh foods cannot be stored for very long before changes occur which affect the texture, flavour or colour of the food. Some changes are noticeable, for instance a banana as it ripens changes from green to yellow and eventually it will turn black. Other changes are not as noticeable, but some of the changes that occur can often make the foods unfit to eat. This is known as food spoilage.

Micro-organisms and enzymes can cause changes in food.

Changes caused by micro-organisms

Micro-organisms are usually visible only under a microscope. They can be found in water, soil, air and rubbish as well as on animals, humans and equipment. Some foods may

YEASTS   BACTERIA

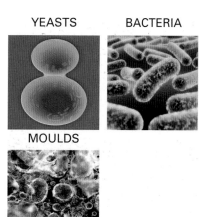

MOULDS

Figure 7.1 The three types of micro-organisms

already contain micro-organisms, for example salmonella in chicken. Other micro-organisms can be transferred to food by poor hygienic practices, by humans, flies and rodents.

Micro-organisms can perform useful functions in the production of food products such as cheese, yoghurt, bread, beer and Quorn®. Micro-organisms can also be harmful and cause food spoilage. When foods are described as contaminated it means that they are infected with micro-organisms and therefore are not safe to eat. Some micro-organisms, known as pathogenic bacteria, can cause food poisoning which can result in serious illness or even death. Micro-organisms multiply rapidly in conditions which when combined offer warmth, moisture, food and time.

Yeasts

Function:

- Through the process of **fermentation** they are used to make breads and alcohol (sugars break down into alcohol and carbon dioxide gas).

Spoilage:

- Responsible for food spoilage in high-sugar foods such as fruit, jam and fruit yogurts.

Figure 7.2 Fruit spoilage

Conditions needed for growth:

- Active in warm, moist conditions with food for growth and reproduction.
- Does not need oxygen to grow (**anaerobic**).

Moulds

Function:

- Used in food manufacture to produce specific flavours and textures, e.g. the manufacture of blue-veined cheeses such as Danish Blue, Stilton. These moulds are considered harmless.

Spoilage:

- Visible to the eye. Grow as thread-like filaments, usually on the surface of food, e.g. on cheese, bread. They can be black, white or blue.
- Reproduce by producing spores which travel in the air. Spores settle, germinate and multiply into new growths.

- Harmful only when they produce myotoxins, which are poisonous substances.

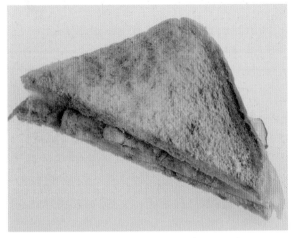

Figure 7.3 Mould on a cheese and cucumber sandwich

Conditions needed for growth:

- Grows quickly in moist conditions at temperatures of 20°C–30°C. Grows slowly in dry, cold conditions.
- Grows on food that may be dry, moist, acid, alkaline, or has salt or sugar concentrations.

Bacteria

Function:

- Used in food manufacture, e.g. making cheese and yoghurt. The lactic acid bacteria cultures used in these products are not harmful.

Spoilage:

- Often undetected because the food looks, tastes and smells as it should but the presence of bacteria makes it potentially very dangerous to eat.
- Those which cause food poisoning are known as pathogenic bacteria, e.g.

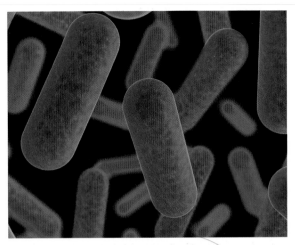

Figure 7.4 E. coli bacteria seen under a microscope

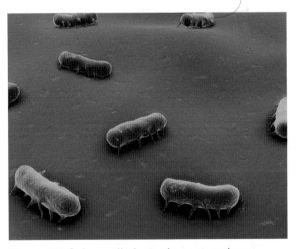

Figure 7.5 Salmonella bacteria seen under a microscope

Escherichias coli (E. coli) which can be very harmful.

Conditions needed for growth:

- Active in warmth, moisture, food and oxygen (optimum conditions).
- Reproduce rapidly by dividing in two and again in two in minutes.
- Able to grow rapidly in neutral pH conditions. Most pathogenic bacteria are unable to grow in acid or alkaline

conditions, e.g. beetroot preserved in vinegar.

- Most active in a temperature range of 5°C–65°C, known as the danger zone. The optimum temperature is 37°C, i.e. the human body temperature. Below 0°C bacteria will become dormant. Most cannot survive at temperatures of 70°C or above.

- Some are able to form spores that can lie dormant. If the right conditions are provided the spores will germinate.

Changes caused by enzymes

Enzymes are found in all foods and can also cause changes in food. They are proteins and speed up chemical reactions.

Function:

Enzymes are used in a wide range of manufacturing processes:

- bread and brewing – enzymes present in yeast are active in the fermentation process

- cheese – enzymes speed up the ripening stage.

Spoilage:

Enzymes can cause 'browning' in certain foods. Enzymatic browning can be reduced by:

- high temperatures, e.g. blanching cut vegetables in boiling water

- acidic conditions, e.g. dipping cut fruit in lemon juice.

Everyone working in the food chain must make sure that food is safe to eat as food can be infected at any stage of production. This includes farmers, manufacturers and consumers.

In Table 7.1 you can see a selection of high- and low-risk foods. High-risk foods are easily contaminated by bacteria. They are often used without further cooking, for example cooked meats. They need to be kept in the refrigerator. Low-risk foods have a longer shelf life and are not so easily contaminated by bacteria.

High-risk foods	Low-risk foods
(often high protein and moisture content)	
<ul><li>raw fish</li><li>dairy products</li><li>cooked meat and poultry</li><li>shellfish and seafood</li><li>gravies, sauces, stocks, soups and stews</li><li>egg products, e.g. raw egg in chilled desserts and mayonnaise</li><li>cooked rice</li><li>protein-based baby foods</li></ul>	<ul><li>high acid content foods, e.g. pickles and chutney, fruit juice</li><li>high sugar content foods, e.g. marmalades, jams, fruit packed syrup</li><li>sugar based confectionery, e.g. sweets, icing</li><li>unprocessed raw vegetables, e.g. potatoes, carrot</li><li>edible oils and fats</li></ul>

Table 7.1 High-risk and low-risk foods

QUESTIONS

1. Explain what you understand about the term 'food spoilage'.

2. Draw a chart like the one in Table 7.2 and complete.

Micro-organism	Function	Spoilage
Yeast		
Moulds		
Bacteria		

Table 7.2 **Food spoilage**

3. What conditions are required for micro-organisms to multiply rapidly?

4. How can enzymatic browning be reduced in cut fruits and vegetables?

5. Look at the following list of foods and note down which are classed as high risk:

- cooked rice
- chicken
- cakes
- tomato sauce
- milk
- biscuits
- cabbage
- shellfish.

7.2 STORAGE OF FOOD

Food must be stored correctly at all times to prevent spoilage.

Fridge

Refrigerators provide safe storage of food with less risk of food poisoning. There are many types of refrigerator units available – some just refrigerate (larder fridges) while others contain both refrigerator and freezer (fridge freezers). The size of the freezer section in a fridge freezer can vary. Stand-alone freezers are also available. These have no refrigerator section so can only be used to store frozen foods.

Sensible use of your fridge:

- Avoid opening the door regularly – warm air enters every time you open the door.

- Avoid putting in hot food – this raises the temperature, fills the inside with steam which condenses on the shelves and lining, and so raises the temperature of other foods in there.
- Cover food.
- **REMEMBER** – an increase in the temperature inside the fridge could lead to bacterial growth.

▶ Freezer

During freezing foods become frozen as the water content in the food becomes solid. The freezer 'star' rating indicates the temperature range of the freezer section in the refrigerator and the length of time you can store foods.

A freezer box within a fridge cannot be used to freeze fresh foods – it can only be used to store already frozen foods.

A freezer that is classed as a　　　　can be used to freeze fresh foods. This is found on all domestic freezers.

Thawing and refreezing

When food is thawed the structure is damaged and there is sometimes loss of colour, flavour, texture and nutritional value. Food poisoning bacteria will not multiply in a freezer, but it must be remembered that the bacteria present are not destroyed in the freezer and will multiply when they are sufficiently warm. Frozen foods are therefore transported in temperature-controlled vehicles to keep the foods in a frozen state. On entering the supermarkets, restaurants, etc. they are quickly packed into large freezers.

You should never re-freeze food after it has thawed – bacteria grow quickly in thawed food.

Foods which do not freeze well

Foods which contain a large proportion of water and have a delicate cell structure do not freeze well because ice crystals damage the cell structure, causing it to collapse.

Freezing vegetables

Most, with the exception of salad vegetables, freeze well and can be kept up to a year. It is important to blanch vegetables before freezing to halt enzyme activity which causes changes in colour, flavour, texture and nutritional value.

Freezer burn

Greyish-white marks appear on the food when it has been packaged badly. The food dehydrates and although safe to eat, will change colour, texture and flavour.

Headspace

Liquid or semi-liquid food expands when frozen. Allow 13 mm headspace in containers (shallow) and 25 mm in tall, narrow containers.

Star rating	Temp oC	Storage times
*	−6	up to 1 week
**	−12	up to 1 month
***	−18	up to 3 months
✳(✳✳✳)		

Table 7.3 Freezer star rating

Baked egg custards	separates
Bananas	turn black
Cream (single)	separates
Jelly	collapses
Salad	becomes limp

Table 7.4 Foods which do not freeze well

 ## 7.3 PRESERVATION

You have already seen that bacteria, yeasts and mould cause changes in food which can be harmful. Micro-organisms need food, warmth, moisture and time to multiply. If even one of these conditions is removed, the food is preserved and will keep for a longer time. If micro-organisms and enzymes are destroyed, this also allows food to last longer.

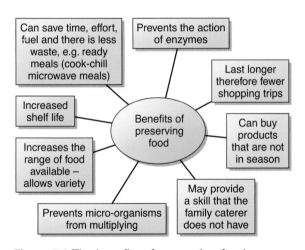

Figure 7.6 The benefits of preserving food

Limitations of processed foods

- Can sometimes be more expensive.
- Often contain a lot of fat, sugar and salt.
- Do not contain much fibre (except for canned baked beans, sweetcorn).

- Some nutrients have been lost when the food was processed.
- Additives may need to be added to restore colour, flavour and texture.
- Texture of food may change, e.g. canned strawberries are much softer than fresh strawberries.

Food is preserved in many ways so that it keeps longer.

High-temperature methods

Pasteurisation

- Pathogenic micro-organisms are destroyed (72 °C for 15 seconds).
- Storage of food is extended for a limited time, days not months.
- Used for heat-treating milk, some soups, liquid egg, and ice-cream etc.

Sterilisation

- Heated for a long period of time at higher temperatures (104 °C for 40 minutes).
- Destroys nearly all micro-organisms and enzymes.
- Extends storage period.
- Used for milk and fruit juices.

Figure 7.7 Milk

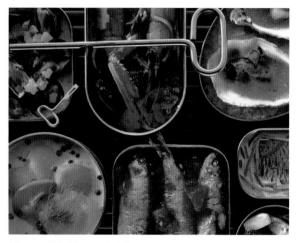

Figure 7.8 Canned fish

- Milk is changed to a creamy colour with a slight caramelisation of the milk sugar content, giving a 'cooked' flavour.

Ultra heat treatment (UHT)

- Uses very high temperatures (130 °C for 1–5 seconds). Destroys all bacteria.

- Extends storage period of milk, up to six months unopened.

- Little colour change.

- Only slight change in taste.

- Little loss of nutrient content.

- Sold in airtight cartons, e.g. soups, prepared sauces, e.g. chilli.

Canning

Canning is a form of sterilisation. Food can be:

- packed in cans and then sterilised *or*

- sterilised and then packed into ASEPTIC (sterilised) cans.

The cans are then sealed with a double seam to prevent leakage and to prevent re-contamination. Temperature and time vary depending on the food type, but it is crucial to ensure the sterilisation process is complete and that the food retains its structure and texture. After sterilisation the cans are sprayed with water to prevent the contents overcooking.

- Used for a huge range of foods, e.g. soup, vegetables, fruit, meat and fish etc. to give a long shelf life.

- Texture of some foods may change, e.g. strawberries become soft.

- Some loss of nutrients, especially vitamins B and C.

- Acid foods, e.g. grapefruit, are canned in plastic-lined cans to prevent corrosion.

Low-temperature methods

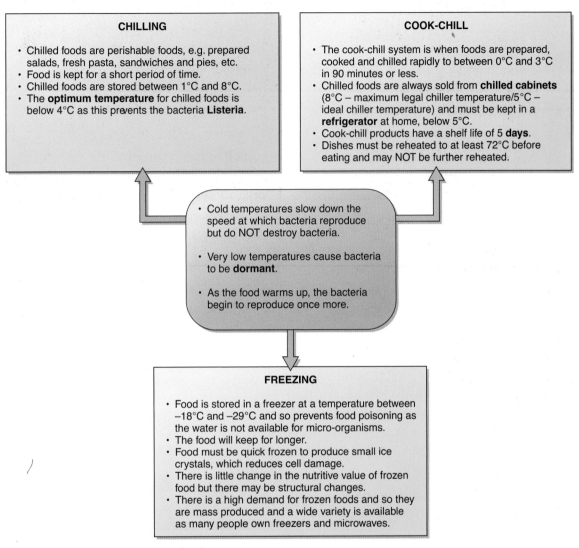

CHILLING

- Chilled foods are perishable foods, e.g. prepared salads, fresh pasta, sandwiches and pies, etc.
- Food is kept for a short period of time.
- Chilled foods are stored between 1°C and 8°C.
- The **optimum temperature** for chilled foods is below 4°C as this prevents the bacteria **Listeria**.

COOK-CHILL

- The cook-chill system is when foods are prepared, cooked and chilled rapidly to between 0°C and 3°C in 90 minutes or less.
- Chilled foods are always sold from **chilled cabinets** (8°C – maximum legal chiller temperature/5°C – ideal chiller temperature) and must be kept in a **refrigerator** at home, below 5°C.
- Cook-chill products have a shelf life of 5 **days**.
- Dishes must be reheated to at least 72°C before eating and may NOT be further reheated.

- Cold temperatures slow down the speed at which bacteria reproduce but do NOT destroy bacteria.
- Very low temperatures cause bacteria to be **dormant**.
- As the food warms up, the bacteria begin to reproduce once more.

FREEZING

- Food is stored in a freezer at a temperature between −18°C and −29°C and so prevents food poisoning as the water is not available for micro-organisms.
- The food will keep for longer.
- Food must be quick frozen to produce small ice crystals, which reduces cell damage.
- There is little change in the nutritive value of frozen food but there may be structural changes.
- There is a high demand for frozen foods and so they are mass produced and a wide variety is available as many people own freezers and microwaves.

Figure 7.9 Low-temperature methods

Chilling and freezing in industry

Cook-chill

Chilling is a short-term way of preserving fresh food.

It is critical that the correct temperature controls are followed at all stages of manufacture, storage and distribution. This is in order to:

- have records of temperature control which can be shown to the Environmental Health Officer
- prevent waste
- avoid bacterial growth
- avoid complaints
- meet the requirements of the Food Safety Act

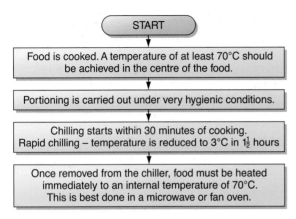

Figure 7.10 The chilling process

- keep the food at its best (texture/colour/taste/appearance).

If it goes below 0°C the product will freeze. It is not possible to detect by looking at the packaging whether a product has been stored at the correct temperature.

Products are transported by refrigerated vans and on delivery to the supermarket are transferred immediately to refrigerated storage rooms.

Cook-chill products are always sold from the chiller cabinets in shops. Once bought, cook-chill products should be transported home quickly, preferably in a cool bag, and stored at below 5°C in the refrigerator.

Cook-chill products are often thought to be of a better quality than frozen products. They have a shorter shelf life (usually a few days) but do not need to be defrosted first.

Advantages of cook-chill:

- very little change in nutritional value, flavour, colour, texture or shape
- fresh foods can be kept at maximum quality for a longer time

- the consumer can be offered a much larger range of fresh and convenience foods
- nutrients are not destroyed.
- no need to defrost as in frozen products, therefore quicker to cook/reheat
- fewer additives needed during manufacture
- available in single portions
- no skill required – easy to prepare/cook/make/little equipment or washing up
- consistent quality
- little waste
- saves energy in the home.

Example of cook-chill foods:

- a single raw food (e.g. meat, fish)
- a mixture of raw foods (e.g. coleslaw, stir-fry, vegetables, mixed lettuce leaves)
- made from cooked ingredients (e.g. recipe meals such as lasagne, soup)
- a mixture of both raw and cooked foods (e.g. potato salad).

Blast freezing

This method is suitable for most foods. Complete meals can also be frozen, provided their maximum thickness is no greater than 4 cm. Air is circulated around a freezing compartment by a fan, reducing food temperature quickly. Food must be kept in storage units at a temperature of between –20°C and –30°C after freezing.

Freezing is rapid, so texture of soft tissue is unchanged. This is not a widely used method because it is expensive. Vacuum chilling is now being used instead of blast freezing because it is a quicker method of cooling.

Cook-freeze

Meals are blast frozen and stored at −20°C until required. Dishes must be prepared with strict attention to hygiene. Many large catering operators find it convenient to use cook-freeze systems today. Meals are prepared and frozen rapidly. The food can be distributed to branch outlets in the frozen state and heated by microwave or micro-ovens when required for service (micro-ovens cook by both microwaves and convected heat).

Manufacturers have increased their range of frozen foods for the reasons outlined in Figure 7.11.

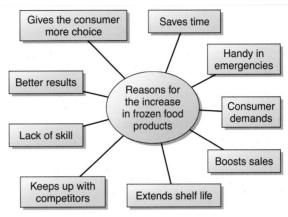

Figure 7.11 Reasons for the increase in frozen food products

▶ Dehydration (Drying)

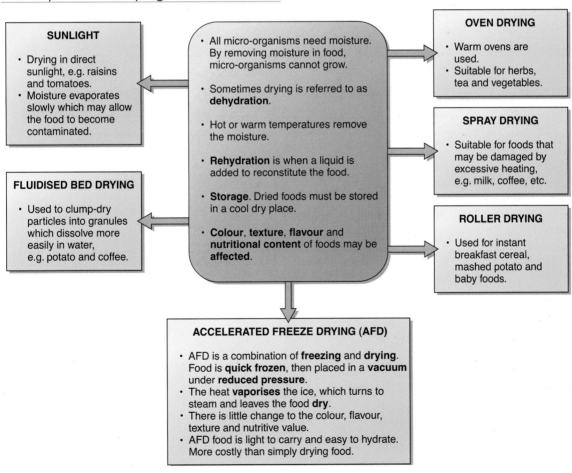

Figure 7.12 Dehydration (drying)

▌ Chemicals

Chemical preservation destroys bacteria or prevents them reproducing.

Vinegar

- Acetic acid with a low pH of 3.5. (bacteria cannot survive below 4.5).
- Used for foods such as pickled onions, cabbage and eggs, etc.

Salt

- Used to coat foods such as ham, bacon, and fish or is used in a brine solution (salt and water) such as tuna, vegetables, etc.
- Reduces moisture content by osmosis.

Sugar

- In high concentrations (60 per cent of final product) prevents bacteria from growing because it makes the water unavailable.
- Used in jams, marmalades and jellies.
- Strong sugar solutions can also be used for coating candied and crystallised fruit.

Figure 7.13 Preservation using sugar

QUESTIONS

1. How can you prevent the inside temperature of a fridge from becoming warm and why is it important to prevent this from happening?

2. Why is important to blanch vegetables before freezing?

3. Draw a chart to show four benefits and four limitations of preserving food.

4. Milk is a high-risk food. Give two processing methods which increase the shelf life of milk.

5. State how a sandwich should be packed and stored if it was to be sold in a supermarket.

6. Complete statements a) to e) with the correct ending to form a complete sentence.

   a) Freezing or chilling   moisture is not available for micro-organisms

   b) Drying food removes   in packaging for other gases

   c) Freezing turns liquids into solids   slows down the rate of bacterial reproduction
      therefore

d) Systems are available which exchange air

e) Food should be cooled below 5°C or

heated to above 62°C to reduce bacterial growth

the water, preventing bacterial growth

7. Explain why in the food industry freezing is a popular method of preservation.

8. Soup can be manufactured as a dried product. Draw a chart to show two benefits and two limitations to the consumer of using a dried soup.

9. State two methods of preserving for each of the following foods: strawberries, peas, fish, onions, milk.

▶ Modern methods

Additives

These are added to destroy bacteria or prevent them reproducing.

Modified Atmosphere Packaging (MAP)

- Altering the gas in the packet prevents bacteria being able to use the oxygen for growth which means the product has an increased shelf life.

- Also known as **controlled atmosphere packaging (CAP)**. MAP or CAP preserves food in sealed packs that contain a mixture of three gases:
  - oxygen
  - nitrogen
  - carbon dioxide

The process involves:

- packaging fresh foods in peak condition. The colour of the food remains the same until the pack is opened. Once opened, food has a normal shelf life

- replacing the air by 'gas flashing' a combination of gases around the food

- sealing the plastic bag or plastic lid to a food tray by means of a **hermetic** sealing process

- You can see the product.

- Used for chilled meats, vegetables such as lettuce and fruits.

Vacuum packed

- Removing air and sealing the package also prevents bacteria growing. Once opened, food has a normal shelf life.

- The food is kept in **anaerobic** conditions, i.e. there is no oxygen around it.

- Foods maintain colour and texture.

- Used for bacon and smoked fish.

- Coffee once Accelerated Freeze Dried (AFD) is vacuum packed so that it doesn't lose taste quality through contact with the air.

Figure 7.14 Using MAP to package apples

KEY POINTS

- Bacteria need warmth, moisture, food and time to multiply.
- The shelf life of a product is the length of time it will last without deteriorating.
- Food spoilage will occur if food is not stored correctly or if it has reached the end of its shelf life.
- Food can be processed in a variety of ways.
- Preservation is used to prolong the shelf life of products.

KEY TERMS

SHELF LIFE – how long a food product can be kept safely and remain of high quality

FOOD-SPOILAGE BACTERIA – bacteria which cause a food to go bad but do not usually cause food poisoning

PATHOGENIC BACTERIA – harmful bacteria which can cause food poisoning

CONTAMINATION – when foods are infected with micro-organisms and therefore are not safe to eat

MICRO-ORGANISMS – classified as bacteria, moulds and yeasts

ENZYMES – proteins which speed up chemical reactions

HIGH-RISK FOODS – foods that spoil in a short amount of time; those most likely to encourage bacterial growth, such as foods high in protein and moisture

LOW-RISK FOODS – foods which have a long shelf life, such as dried foods

PRESERVATION – long-term food storage

STERILISATION – heating at 104°C for 40 minutes to extend the shelf life of a product

COOK-CHILL – food that has been cooked, fast chilled in 1½ hours and stored at low temperatures

COOK-FREEZE – food that has been cooked, fast frozen and stored below freezing point

DEHYDRATION (drying) – removal of water from food

ACCELERATED FREEZE DRIED (AFD) – a technique where food is frozen then dried

IRRADIATION – a process involving passing strictly controlled x-rays from a radioactive or electron beam through food

MODIFIED ATMOSPHERE PACKAGING (MAP) – packaging containing a mixture of gases which help to preserve food

7.4 PACKAGING FOOD

Nearly all the food we buy today is packaged in some way. Food packaging and the design of the packaging are important because of the range of products on sale in supermarkets. Over the years the materials and methods of packaging have changed as new technology has been introduced.

Figure 7.15 A modern supermarket

Reasons why food is packaged

Packaging has a number of important functions. Food is packaged for the following reasons:

- Contains the product so it is easy to transport, store and display. The packaging, when sealed, prevents spillage and loss.
- Identifies the product by providing information. Labelling information is required by law to describe and inform consumers about products and the presentation of the packaging helps to attract customers to buy the product.
- Protects the product from damage so reduces food waste. This includes:

- physical damage, e.g. crushing
- contamination from chemicals, micro-organisms, insects
- atmospheric conditions, e.g. warm conditions may cause fruit to over ripen.
- Increases the shelf life of the product.

Food packaging legislation states that food packaging must not:

- be hazardous to human health
- cause the food to deteriorate
- cause unacceptable changes in the substance or quality of the product.

Tamper-evident packaging

Many manufacturers use tamper-proof packaging techniques on their products. These techniques make it easy to see if the packaging has been opened, so reducing the risk of the food becoming contaminated if it is opened by mistake and then re-closed. Examples include:

- plastic collars on sauce bottles
- film overwraps on cardboard boxes
- tear-away strips around the top of plastic bottles
- tin foil seals in pourable boxes, e.g. fruit juices.

If these are broken you should not buy the product.

Materials

A variety of materials can be used to package food products. Some food products are packaged in a mixture of materials.

Figure 7.16 An example of tamper-evident packaging

Packaging for takeaway food products

Many of us buy takeaway food products and it is particularly important that the packaging of such products can be disposed of easily. This packaging often includes the use of paper sheets, plastic trays, pots and lids or cardboard boxes that aim to:

• protect the food during transportation

• prevent leakage or spillage

• keep the food hot.

Over the last few years there has been a huge increase in the range of takeaway food products, for example burgers, fish and chips, pizza, and kebabs. Manufacturers, retailers and consumers all need to be aware of the environmental issues involved in producing, using and disposing of such a large amount of packaging

Packaging material	Benefits/ advantages	Limitations/ disadvantages	Examples of food
Glass	Can be moulded in a variety of shapes Transparent so the product can be seen Withstands high temperatures Strong Recyclable Cheap to produce	Brittle and will often break easily Heavy	Jam, sauces, pickles
Metals including foil and cans	Strong Withstands high temperatures Lightweight Available in different thickness Recyclable Can be moulded into a variety of shapes Easy to store	Cannot see the food Cannot be used in the microwave	Canned foods e.g. fruit, soup, meat, fish, ready meals

Packaging material	Benefits/ advantages	Limitations/ disadvantages	Examples of food
Plastic	Cheap to produce Can be moulded into a variety of shapes Available in different thickness Can be used in the microwave Easy to print on Lightweight Some are biodegradable (these plastics can be expensive) Most do not react with foods Transparent so the product can be seen Can withstand high temperatures	Can be difficult to dispose of Made initially from oil A lot is still not recyclable	Yoghurts, cheese, bread, fruit, vegetables, ready meals, biscuits
Paper/card	Cheap to produce Available in different thickness Easy to open Recyclable Easy to print on Can be laminated Lightweight Variety of shapes Used in sheets for flexible wrapping Biodegradable Can be made from recycled material	Can tear easily Not waterproof unless it is laminated Product could be easily crushed and damaged	Cereals, eggs, flour, sugar, baked products e.g. cakes, biscuits, pizza
Ovenable paperboard	Used in the oven and microwave Easy to print on Lightweight	Loses its shape and strength when soggy Can easily be crushed so damaging the product	Frozen and chilled meals

Table 7.5 Types of materials used in food packaging

Figure 7.17 Takeaway foods

 QUESTIONS

1. Suggest a material that a manufacturer could use to package the following foods for sale in a supermarket. Give two benefits and one limitation of using each material.

   - Pickled onions
   - Chilled sandwich
   - Cornflakes
   - Baked beans in tomato sauce.

   Present your answers in a chart like the one in Table 7.6.

Food	Material	Benefits	Limitation
Pickled onions		1 2	1
Chilled sandwich		1 2	1
Cornflakes		1 2	1
Baked beans in tomato sauce		1 2	1

Table 7.6 Benefits and limitations chart

2. Tin foil is sometimes used to package food products. Explain the benefits of using tin foil in the packaging of food products.

3. How would a cook-chill lasagne that is to be reheated in a microwave be packaged?

4. Explain why food manufacturers are using tamper-proof techniques when packaging their food products.

ACTIVITY

Using a packaged food product of your choice, explain how the packaging:

- contains the food product
- identifies the food product
- protects the food product
- increases the shelf life of the food product.

Create a mood board to show the different types of packaging materials and tamper-proof techniques used to package food products. To create the mood board you could use pictures, photographs, sketches, text from magazines, leaflets, packaging, images from the internet, etc.

KEY TERMS

RECYCLABLE PACKAGING – made from materials that can be used again, such as glass, paper

BIODEGRADABLE – with time the material, such as paper, will break down

TAMPER-PROOF SEALS – those which guarantee that the product has not been opened

CHAPTER 8

HEALTH AND SAFETY

**By the end of this section you should have developed
a knowledge and understanding of:**

- how to use a range of tools and equipment safely and efficiently
- the importance of safe and hygienic practices in the cooking, transportation and storage of food
- risk assessment (HACCP)
- food hygiene legislation including food labelling
- the role of the Environmental Health Officer.

Safe and hygienic practices are essential for the preparation, cooking, transportation and storage of food ingredients and products. The food industry has legislation that protects the consumer which must be followed when making any food product to sell.

8.1 USING TOOLS AND EQUIPMENT SAFELY AND EFFECTIVELY

Equipment used in any kitchen should be designed so that it is hygienic and safe. All equipment should be safe, properly maintained and used correctly for the purpose for which it is intended. Some materials will need regular disinfection – cleaning with a chemical (cleaning agent) to kill or reduce micro organisms to an acceptable level, to maintain the highest hygienic standards. Particular care should be given to any surface that comes into contact with food.

Equipment should:

- protect food from contamination
- be made from a material that does not contaminate
- be hard wearing
- be designed so that trapped dirt and bacteria are avoided
- be easy to move and disassemble for thorough cleaning and disinfecting.

Equipment selected for industrial use must

conform to European Union safety directives. Equipment must carry the CE mark which indicates that the required safety standards have been met.

| | Manufactured under an ISO 9001 quality system.

Conforms to all relevant British and European Standards |

Figure 8.1 **CE mark**

Knives

These must be used correctly to avoid accidents and cross contamination.

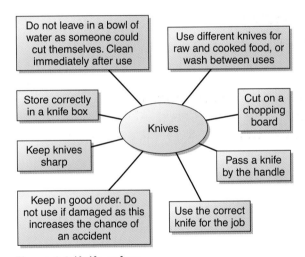

Figure 8.2 **Knife safety**

Electrical equipment

This should be bought from a reputable shop/manufacturer. Safety rules include the following:

- Set up and use equipment correctly. Always use the correct attachments.
- Do not use near water. Only use with dry hands.

- Check equipment regularly, e.g. check for loose, bare, frayed wires.
- Ensure it is in good working order before using. Check the equipment is not broken/damaged and that all correct parts are present.
- Plug in correctly. All equipment should be fitted with the correct plug and fuse.
- Only one person should operate the equipment.
- Keep hands away from moving parts, e.g. do not place hands in a bowl with a whisk or dough hook.
- Wash blades from food processors, etc. with care.
- Place equipment in a safe place on the work top, i.e. not near the edge.
- Turn off after use.

Safety rules when using a cooker

- Turn saucepan handles inwards. No handles should be placed over rings.
- Use oven gloves.

Figure 8.3 **Removing hot dishes safely from the oven**

- Do not leave oven door open/leave grill unattended.
- Turn off after use.
- Do not touch electric rings after use as they take time to cool down.
- Make sure gas is lit.
- Reposition oven shelves before heating the oven.
- Use back rings rather than front rings if these are available.

- Use correct size ring for pan size.
- Do not clean while still hot.
- Use the correct temperature – not too high.
- Stir liquids with a wooden spoon rather than metal. Wooden spoon handles will not get hot.
- Maintain/service regularly.
- Tie back hair and have no loose clothing which may catch fire.

8.2 THE IMPORTANCE OF SAFE AND HYGIENIC PRACTICES IN THE PREPARING, COOKING, TRANSPORTATION AND STORAGE OF FOOD

Food is in danger of becoming infected by yeasts/moulds/bacteria at each stage of its production from the farm to the table. If poor hygiene practices are applied, food can easily become contaminated and this could lead to food poisoning.

Food poisoning

Food poisoning is an illness caused by eating contaminated food or water. Thousands of cases of food poisoning occur each year.

Food poisoning occurs if food is contaminated by:

- harmful bacteria or other micro-organisms
- toxic chemical contamination.

Bacteria multiply or reproduce by binary fusion. They require the following conditions to grow:

- Warmth – bacteria thrive at temperatures

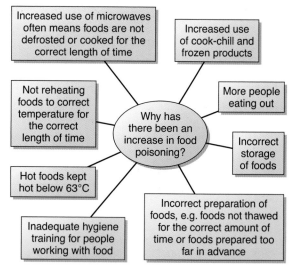

Figure 8.4 Reasons for increased cases of food poisoning

between 37 °C and 63 °C – known as the danger zone. Temperatures above 72 °C will destroy most bacteria, so food should

Buying food	Buy from a reputable shop that keeps food in safe conditions Choose food that looks fresh Check the food is within the date mark
Transporting food	Appropriately packaged and transported that it is not damaged in transit Keep chilled, perishable foods cool, below 8°C. Quickly transport from one area to another. Insulated lorries are used by food manufacturers Frozen foods are transported by special freezer lorries Use cool bags to transport frozen and chilled food from the supermarket
Storage of food	In correct conditions: • frozen food in the freezer • chilled and perishable foods in the fridge • non-perishable foods, e.g. dry packaged foods, canned foods, in a cool, dry, well-ventilated cupboard
Preparing food	Leave perishable foods in the fridge until ready for use Defrost frozen foods before preparation unless the label says otherwise Clean work surfaces before and after preparation Wash fruits and vegetables before using Take special care when preparing meat and poultry to avoid cross contamination Use colour coded chopping boards to avoid cross contamination
Cooking food	Cook thoroughly before consumption During cooking the temperature should reach 72°C for two minutes. If keeping food hot, the temperature must be at or above 63°C. A temperature (food) probe can be used to test the internal temperature of the food

Table 8.1 Safe hygiene practices

be cooked until it is piping hot – hotter than 72 °C for two minutes.

- Moisture (liquid) – one reason why dried foods have such a long shelf life.
- Food – bacteria prefer foods that are high in protein and moist, i.e. high-risk foods such as cooked meat and poultry, raw fish, cooked rice.
- Time – in the right conditions bacteria can multiply quickly in a very short time.

The bacteria that cause food poisoning are called pathogenic bacteria.

Figure 8.5 Good/bad chef

Most food poisoning is caused by bacterial contamination which occurs because of some of the following reasons:

- poor personal hygiene standards of food handlers
- poor hygiene during the production and serving of food
- cross contamination between raw foods and cooked foods, e.g. raw meat to cooked ham
- storage of high risk foods at room temperature
- poor preparation and cooking routines such as:
  - not thawing foods properly
  - preparing food too far in advance
  - under cooking high-risk foods, e.g. chicken
  - not allowing foods to cool before putting them in chill cabinets or freezers – 90 minutes to chill below 8°C
  - not re-heating foods to the correct temperature for a long enough time
  - keeping 'hot' foods below 63°C
  - leaving food on display at room temperature for longer than the maximum safe period of four hours.

Some people, for example, pregnant women, elderly people, babies and those with a low resistance to infection, are more susceptible to food poisoning and extra care must be taken when preparing and cooking food for these groups of people.

Symptoms of food poisoning include diarrhoea, vomiting, nausea, headache and fever. They may occur as quickly as one hour after eating or can take as long as 72 hours. The usual incubation period is 12–48 hours.

Many types of bacteria cause food poisoning and the incubation periods, symptoms and methods of control vary accordingly. Most bacteria are killed by thorough heating, but some, such as Clostridium botulinum, produce spores which survive high cooking temperatures.

Cross contamination

During food processing micro-organisms can transfer from raw to cooked foods, causing infection. This is known as cross contamination. To prevent cross contamination you must avoid:

- allowing raw and cooked foods to touch

Food poisoning bacteria	Possible sources
Salmonella	Poultry, eggs, meat
Staphylococcus	Food handlers
Clostridium	Raw foods such as vegetables and meat
Bacillus	Cereals, especially rice
Campylobacter	Infected animals, birds and unpasteurised milk
Listeria	Raw, processed and cooked foods, e.g. soft cheese
E.coli	Cattle, raw meat and raw milk

Table 8.2 Bacteria which cause food poisoning

each other, e.g. raw chicken and boiled ham

- allowing the blood and juices of raw foods to drip onto cooked foods, e.g. putting raw meat above cooked foods in the refrigerator
- allowing bacteria to be transferred during handling or preparation, e.g. from hands, work surfaces, equipment.

Rules for food hygiene

1. Wash hands thoroughly before handling food and between handling different types of food.

Figure 8.6 **Hand washing**

2. Keep raw and cooked foods separate and use different equipment to prepare them.

3. Pay particular attention to personal hygiene and wear clean protective clothing, cover cuts and never cough or sneeze over food.

4. Keep all working surfaces and utensils clean.

5. Cover and cool all cooked food rapidly and refrigerate as quickly as possible. Store below 5 °C.

6. Do not put hot foods in the refrigerator. It will raise the temperature of all the foods in there.

7. Keep pets away from food preparation areas.

8. Take care over waste disposal. Keep bins covered and empty and wash them regularly.

Figure 8.7 **Would these bins be acceptable in your kitchen?**

9. Keep flies out of the kitchen

10. Reheat all food thoroughly above the danger point of 63 °C, taking great care to avoid 'cold spots' in food heated in microwaves by turning and moving the food.

ACTIVITY

Look at the rules for food hygiene. Select at least four. Using the information, design a poster that could be displayed to inform people of the rules that should be followed when working with food.

QUESTIONS

1. Knives must be used correctly and stored to avoid accidents and cross contamination. Using a table like Table 8.3, place the following statements under the correct heading.

To avoid accidents	To avoid cross contamination

Table 8.3 Avoiding trouble

   - Keep knives sharp.
   - Cut on a chopping board.
   - Use different knives for raw and cooked food.
   - Store correctly in a knife box.
   - Pass a knife by the handle.

2. State four safety rules you should follow when using electrical equipment.

3. State two hygiene and safety checks that a food manufacturer could carry out when choosing and buying ingredients.

4. State three hygiene and safety checks that a food manufacturer could carry out when preparing food.

5. Name the piece of equipment that could be used to test the internal temperature of food.

6. Define the term high-risk foods.

7. State two symptoms of food poisoning.

8. Match the food poisoning bacteria with its correct possible source:

Salmonella	rice
Bacillus	eggs
Listeria	raw vegetables
Clostridium	food handlers
E.coli	infected animals
Campylobacter	raw meat
Staphylococcus	soft cheese

9. What do you understand by the term cross contamination?

10. Draw and label three items of protective clothing a food handler could wear.

11. Recent reports highlight an increase in the number of cases of food poisoning caused by salmonella, campylobacter, listeria and Escherichia coli (E. coli). Explain the factors which have led to the increased number of cases of food poisoning.

8.3 WHAT IS RISK ASSESSMENT?

Risk assessment means making an assessment of any risk to a food product during its production and the required action to ensure the safety of the food.

The risk assessment system used within the food industry is known as the Hazard Analysis and Critical Control Point (HACCP). HACCP identifies specific hazards and risks associated with food production and describes how these hazards and risks can be controlled.

Many food companies now use the HACCP system to help with safe food production. All stages of the food process are assessed, from the raw materials, through the making process to the distribution and sale of the food product.

What is a hazard?

In food production, a hazard is anything that can cause harm to a consumer.

A hazard may be:

- **biological** such as salmonella in chicken
- **chemical** such as cleaning chemicals in food
- **physical** such as glass or metal in food.

What is a risk?

In food production, the risk is the likelihood that a hazard might occur.

What is critical control point?

A control point is the step in the making process where the hazard must be controlled.

This step has to be carried out correctly to make sure that the hazard is removed or reduced to a safe level. A hazard can be chemical, physical or micro-biological. Some hazards such as micro-biological hazards are high risk. The control points for these hazards are called critical control points (CCPs) as it is critical (essential) that the hazard is removed or reduced because it could result in food poisoning.

Benefits of HACCP to the food industry

- Predicts hazards.
- Prevents problems rather than responding to problems as they occur.

Process	Hazards	Hazard Type	Control measures	CCP	Tests for control
Cook raw kidney beans 40 minutes and drain.	Dangerous chemicals in raw beans.	Chemical	Must boil rapidly for 10 minutes.	Yes	Cook the beans at the correct temperature and time.
Collect beef other and ingredients.	Beef could contain bacteria.	Biological	Make sure beef is stored separately at 5°C or below.	Yes	Check the refrigerator is at or below 5°C
Fry beef and chopped onions.	Undercooked beef can be dangerous. Could contain salmonella.	Biological	Make sure meat is cooked until it turns brown.	Yes	Visual check for browning of meat.
Add tomato paste, chilli seasoning and beans. Cook for 20 minutes.	Tomato paste may be old and mouldy. Food may be undercooked.	Biological	Check food is within shelf life. Cook for sufficient time to reach 70°C or above.	Yes	Visual check of the date marks. Cook at the correct temperature and time.
If to be reheated, cover and cool quickly.	Food may get contaminated from other foods.	Biological	Make sure food cools to below 8°C within 90 minutes.	Yes	Cool food to the correct temperature in the correct time.
Reheat to piping hot.	Bacteria may be present.	Biological	Test to see if 72°C at edge and centre.	Yes	Reheat to correct temperature.

Table 8.4 **Hazard analysis of making and reheating chilli con carne**

- Saves money by planning ahead.
- Critical control points mean that people are focusing on the important problems.
- Response can be rapid.
- Supports 'due diligence', i.e. by showing and proving that all reasonable precautions have been taken to prevent the offence arising.
- All staff are involved with product safety.
- Helps make safe food products.
- Meets legal requirements for safety.

Table 8.4 shows how hazards have been identified for making and reheating chilli con carne.

Hazard analysis helps us to think about what could go wrong and how to reduce risks. The process of identifying hazards and working out how to reduce or eliminate them is called a risk assessment.

QUESTIONS

1. What do the letters HACCP stand for?
2. What do you understand by the following terms?
   - Risk assessment
   - A hazard
   - A risk
   - A critical control point
3. Give two ways HACCP is used in the food industry.

ACTIVITY

In pairs, draw a simple HACCP system for making a hard-boiled egg sandwich. Use the following processes to help you design the HACCP:

- Store sandwich ingredients.
- Boil the egg until hard, then cool in cold water.
- Mash the egg with bottled mayonnaise for the filling.
- Make the sandwiches.
- Store the sandwiches for eating.

▶ Food health and safety legislation

Several laws cover the regulations for the preparation, storage and sale of food. You will find it useful if you can identify and understand the main pieces of legislation.

The food industry has to be responsible for making sure its customers are protected from harm by using high standards of food safety.

Food Safety Act 1990

This Act ensures that all food produced in the food industry is safe to eat. All stages of food production are covered. The Local Authority Environmental Health officers have the authority to enter premises and inspect food production methods.

Food Safety (General Food Hygiene) Regulations 1995

The regulations aim to ensure that there are common food hygiene rules across the EU. They affect anyone who runs a food business and ensure high standards of hygiene in the preparation and selling of food products.

Figure 8.8 Wear clean protective clothing

Figure 8.9 Ice cream vans must be registered

The main offences

Selling or keeping for sale food which:

- is unfit for human consumption
- has been made harmful to health
- is contaminated
- is not of the nature, substance or quality expected
- is falsely or misleadingly presented.

The law is enforced by the local Environmental Health Officer and the Trading Standards Office.

Registration

Any premises where food is being prepared for sale, including vans selling ice cream or hot dogs, must be registered.

Training

Everybody working in the food preparation industry has to go through some form of food hygiene training related to their particular job or workplace. The regulations focus on how to identify and control food safety risks at each stage of the process of preparing and selling food. The regulations let food

businesses assess the risk to food safety and apply controls relevant to their situation.

Proprietors of food businesses must:

- make sure food is supplied or sold in a hygienic way
- identify food safety hazards
- know which steps in the activities are critical for food safety
- ensure safety controls are in place, maintained and reviewed.

Key points covered by the Food Safety (General Food Hygiene) Regulations 1995:

- Food premises should be clean and in good repair.
- All preparation surfaces must be smooth, easy to clean and disinfect.
- Design and layout of the premises should allow adequate cleaning and disinfection.
- Food areas must have adequate lighting and ventilation.
- Floors and walls must be non-absorbent and stay clean. Ceilings must be designed

Figure 8.10 A University canteen

to minimise condensation and prevent the growth of moulds.

- Opening windows, should be designed to prevent insects getting in, or be covered with a screen.
- A pest control policy must be in place.
- Quality control checks to be carried out on ingredients.
- Food must be stored in hygienic conditions and protected from contamination.
- There should be adequate toilets and wash hand basins.
- A supply of drinking water must be available when preparing and cooking foods.
- Core temperatures of food to be recorded during cooking.
- Equipment to be colour coded.
- Equipment and packaging must be clean and made of a material that is easily disinfected.
- Food waste must be regularly removed from areas.
- Bins must be kept in good condition, fitted

with lids and kept away from food stores and equipment. Bins should be easy to clean and disinfect.

- All food handlers must maintain a good standard of personal hygiene.
- Food handlers must wear appropriate clean protective clothing.
- Food handlers suffering from illness must not work in food areas. If feeling ill whilst at work they must report to their supervisor who will then send them home.
- Food handlers to change protective clothing and rewash/sanitise their hands when moving from low risk to high risk areas.
- All food handlers must be properly trained in food hygiene.
- Vehicles used to transport food must be clean, in good condition and must be designed to allow for cleaning and disinfection.
- Temperature controlled vehicles must be designed so that the temperature can easily be monitored and controlled. Food should be stored at a temperature which

Figure 8.11 Refrigerated lorries

will prevent the growth of micro-organisms. This means below 8°C in a refrigerated van or freezer van below −18°C.

- A distribution system should be established to record the orders and delivery dates.

The Food Safety (Temperature Control) Regulations 1995

Some foods must be kept at controlled temperatures during preparation, transporting and storage, in order to help to control the spread of harmful micro-organisms such as listeria and salmonella, as these can cause very serious food poisoning. These micro-organisms grow rapidly at room temperature and foods must, therefore, be kept either very hot or very cold.

From 1 April 1991 a list of foods was given which must be kept either below 8°C or above 63°C if already cooked and waiting to be eaten. These foods include:

- **cooked products containing meat, fish, eggs, cheese, cereals, pulses
- **some cooked pies and sausage rolls

- *smoked fish
- *prepared salads
- **sandwiches
- *dairy based desserts
- *cream cakes
- **these should be stored below 5°C

The regulations clarify the three systems of temperature control as follows:

a) Chill-holding requirements
No person shall keep any food which is likely to support growth of pathogenic micro-organisms or the formation of toxins at a temperature above 8°C.

The Regulations include specific examples of food preparation, storage, processing and distribution.

b) Hot-holding requirements
No person shall in the course of activities of a food business keep any food which:

- has been cooked and reheated
- is for service or on display
- needs to be kept hot in order to control the growth of micro-organisms or the

Figure 8.12 Refrigerator

Figure 8.13 Keeping food at the correct temperature – above 63°C

formation of toxins at or in food premises at a temperature below 63°C.

c) Reheating of food

Food which in the course of a commercial operation has been heated and which thereafter reheated before being served for immediate consumption or exposed for sale shall, on being reheated, be raised to a temperature of not less than 82°C.

Date marking

Virtually all foods, including frozen and canned foods, now have to carry date marks, in the form of either 'use by' or 'best before' dates – see section on food labelling on page 185 for further explanation.

In April 2004 EU food hygiene legislation included primary food production for the first time to develop a 'farm to fork' approach to food safety. Primary producers are expected to base their food safety procedures on a HACCP system.

- Facilities where animals are reared and fed must be kept clean and disinfected.

- Equipment used to transport animals and harvested products must be kept clean and disinfected.

- Pest control should protect animals and harvested products.

- Waste should be removed quickly.

- Staff to be trained in the identification of hazards.

- Records should be kept on animal feed, use of pesticides, etc.

If these Acts are followed, food businesses will have satisfied customers, a good reputation and consequently increased business. There will be less wastage of food, because food will have an increased shelf life, resulting in higher profits.

If the Acts are not followed this could result in food poisoning outbreaks which might be fatal, resulting in complaints from the customers which are difficult to defend. This could lead to civil action from the food poisoning sufferers which may in turn lead to fines and legal action costs. Food could also be wasted due to pest infestations, leading to loss of production.

 QUESTIONS

1. The Food Safety (Temperature Control) Regulations 1995 outlined three systems of temperature control. Give the temperature that this piece of legislation states for:
   - chill-holding
   - hot-holding
   - reheating.

2. What are the benefits to a food manufacturer of following food hygiene and safety legislation?

ACTIVITY

Using the information in Table 8.5, create a mind map/bubble diagram to help you understand the implications of health and safety legislation for both the manufacturer and the consumer.

Relevant point	Explanation	Example/Evidence
Ensures high standards of personal hygiene	Prevents contamination Prevents food poisoning	Protective clothing worn by workers No jewellery/nail varnish, etc.
Ensures high standards of safety	Control of high risk foods, foreign bodies Health and safety of workers	Named high-risk food Any physical accident
Prevents cross contamination	From raw to cooked foods	Raw meat to cooked meat Colour-coded equipment Safety of machinery
Staff training	Staff must all undergo training before being employed in the food chain	Foundation certificate in food hygiene
HACCP procedures	Assess and monitor risks	Any named control
Ensures appropriate control of high risk foods.	Temperature control in freezing/transportation/ refrigeration/cooking/ reheating	Any named temperature example Refrigerator 8°C or below Freezer below −18°C Cooking above 72°C
Safety of equipment, machinery, storage equipment, transport	Equipment must be checked and cleaned regularly using sanitizer or disinfectant	Meat slicer, etc. Any suitable equipment
Microbial analysis must be carried out	Samples are taken regularly and checked in a laboratory	Any suitable named food product Food poisoning
Premises are inspected	Environmental health officers can visit at any time	Premises can be closed down if they are not of the correct standard
Manufacturers must provide evidence of safe practices	Products are tracked through the factory	Cook-chilled products Batch numbers

Table 8.5

Relevant point	Explanation	Example/Evidence
Food labelling	Specific information must be included on labels	Contact details of manufacturer Storage instruction Reheating instructions Use by/sell by dates
Consumers have the legal rights to complain	Legal action can be taken if there is a fault in a product	Any suitable example E.g. fly in a loaf of bread
Good standards Poor standards	High reputation Closed down Fined	Increased sales Lose/poor sales Bankruptcy Product recall

Table 8.5 continued

KEY POINTS

- Safety and hygiene rules should be followed when using tools and equipment.
- Cases of food poisoning are increasing.
- Food poisoning can result if food is not prepared, cooked and stored properly.
- Potential hazards are identified using a system known as HACCP.
- Hazards can be biological, chemical and physical.
- Many laws protect consumers and help to provide safe food.
- Rules and regulations support the preparation, cooking and storage of food so that it is safe to eat.

KEY TERMS

CRITICAL CONTROL POINT – point in the production process that is essential to control

CROSS CONTAMINATION – the transference of bacteria from raw and cooked food

DANGER ZONE – the temperature range in which bacteria thrive, 5–63°C

DISINFECTION – cleaning with a chemical (cleaning agent) to kill or reduce micro-organisms to an acceptable level to maintain the highest hygienic standards

RISK ASSESSMENT – identifying possible hazards and finding out how they can be reduced or eliminated

HAZARD – anything that is likely to cause harm to the consumer

HAZARD ANALYSIS CRITICAL CONTROL POINT (HACCP) – a food safety system based on the prevention of hazards

Food labelling

The Food Regulations 1996 describe the information that must be on a food label. By law a food label must contain the information in Table 8.6.

Information	Reason
Product Name	To inform the consumer what the product is, e.g. cornflakes, apricot jam. Differences between similar products must be clearly identified, e.g. fruit-flavoured yoghurt and raspberry yoghurt. Any pictures used must not be misleading. For example, strawberry-flavoured ice cream must not show pictures of strawberries on the packaging.
List of Ingredients	To inform consumers exactly what ingredients are contained in the product. All ingredients must be listed in descending order of weight, with the largest amount of ingredient first. Food additives and water must be included.
Storage Instructions	Informs the consumer how to store the product in order to prevent food spoilage. Temperature guidelines are important, e.g. keep refrigerated, suitable for home freezing.
Date Marking	Informs the consumer of the length of time the product can be kept, i.e. the shelf life. 'Use by Date' for high-risk foods, e.g. raw and cooked meat, chilled foods (perishable foods). The date and month will be shown; after this date the food may not look or taste different but it will be unsafe to eat and it should be thrown away. 'Best Before Date' for low-risk foods, e.g. biscuits, crisps, or foods which are processed and packaged to have a long shelf life, e.g. UHT milk. The date, month and year will be shown. After this date the food will start to deteriorate in terms of flavour, colour, texture or taste. 'Display Until' used by the food retailer as it informs the retailer when to remove the product from the shelves or chill/freezer cabinets. This date is usually a few days before the 'use by date' so the consumer has a number of days to use the product. This is not a legal requirement.
Manufacturer's Name and Address	Product can be returned if faulty or letter of complaint can be made in writing.

Table 8.6 Legal requirements on food labels

Information	Reason
Weight or Volume	Most pre-packed food is required to show the net weight or volume, i.e. within a few grams of the weight. If not sold pre-packed, most foods have to be sold by either quantity or number. Some foods are sold in standard amounts. This allows consumers to compare products in terms of value for money. A large e placed alongside the amount shows that it is an average quantity. **e** 190g
Product Description	It may not be clear from the product name what the product is. A description is required to inform the consumer.
Instructions for Use	Preparation, cooking and heating instructions inform the consumer as to how the product should be used.
Place of Origin	Informs the consumer the place the food has come from, e.g. 'product of Spain'.
Allergies	Informs the customer about any ingredients that may cause reactions to people with allergies.

Table 8.6 continued

Information	Reason
Bar Code	A way of identifying the product. Helps the retailer with stock control. An electronic scanner at the checkout reads the bar code; the price of the product is recorded and displayed and details are recorded for stocktaking.
Nutritional Information	Consumers know what nutrients are in the product so informed choices can be made. This allows consumers to select foods which have a specific nutrient content, e.g. low in sugar. Consumers can compare the nutrient content of one product against another. Many manufacturers put nutritional information on food product labels, although they are not required to do so unless a special claim is made about the product, e.g. 'low in fat'.
Serving Instructions	Gives consumers ideas of what could be served with a product.
Cost	The consumer can compare the price of different products.

Table 8.7 Other information found on food packaging

Sensory analysis and shelf life

Food technologists and microbiologists work together so food products are of a high quality and safe to eat. The shelf life, i.e. 'use by' and 'best before' (safety and quality), is determined by both these people through a range of testing.

Microbiologists examine the growth of bacteria in foods and identify a safe shelf life.

Food technologists examine by taste testing, with advice from the microbiologists, how long the product maintains its sensory qualities.

Nutrition labels

The Food Labelling Regulations specify labelling requirements for nutritional information. Nutritional information is voluntary unless a nutrition claim is made.

Nutrition labelling may be given two formats:

Group 1 – the 'Big 4'

Nutrition information	
	Typical values per 100 g
Energy	KJ Kcal
Protein	g
Carbohydrate	g
Fat	g

Table 8.8 **Group 1 – the 'Big 4'**

Group 2 – 'Big 4 + Little 4' or 4 + 4

Nutrition information	
	Typical values per 100 g
Energy	KJ Kcal
Protein	g
Carbohydrate	g
of which sugars	g
Fat	g
of which saturates	g
Fibre	g
Sodium	g

Table 8.9 **Group 2 – 'Big 4 + Little 4' or 4 + 4**

The government recommends that Group 2 information is given on all foods on a voluntary basis as this gives consumers more information so they can make informed choices.

Some manufacturers are using a traffic light colour system on the front of the packaging. This helps you to see at a glance if the food has low, medium or high amounts of fat, sugar and salt.

- Green = Low
- Amber = Medium
- Red = High

Many foods have a mixture of greens, ambers and reds. If you want to make a healthier choice try to go for products with more greens and ambers, and fewer reds. The colours make it easier to compare products at a glance.

Nutrition claims on food labels

The Food Labelling Regulations 1999 impose conditions for making nutrition claims. If manufacturers make a nutritional claim, such as low fat, high fibre, they must provide nutritional information. If a claim is made about a nutrient which is not present on the Group 1 or Group 2 format, for example high in vitamin C, then this nutrient must be included as part of the Group 2 declaration and the product must contain a significant amount of vitamin C.

Certain health and nutrition claims on food labels will need to be viewed with caution as many are not yet defined in law. This means they can mean different things on different food products. One exception is the term 'reduced calorie' which is defined by law. This means that the product should be at least 25 per cent lower in calories than the standard product.

The Food Standard Agency is working on new rules to make it easier for people to trust some of the claims we see on labels. At the moment you need to check the claims yourself by looking at the nutrition information.

- Cooking instructions

- Suitable for microwaving

- Suitable for recycling

- Vegetarian

- Suitable for freezing

- Keep Britain Tidy

Figure 8.14 shows some examples of the range of symbols used on food packaging

Symbols or words, 'flashes', may be printed on the label to give information about:

- dietary group, e.g. 'suitable for vegetarians'
- storage, e.g. 'suitable for home freezing'
- ingredients, e.g. 'this product contains traces of nuts'
- cooking, e.g. 'suitable for microwave'
- special features, e.g. 'medium hot curry'

Labelling can help prevent food poisoning:

- Looking at the list of ingredients will allow consumers to identify any high-risk foods.
- Correct storage conditions are given which the consumer should follow in order to keep food safe, i.e. where the food should be stored (e.g. fridge) and for how long.
- Best before/use by dates inform the consumer how long the food will be safe to eat.

Figure 8.15 Part of a food label showing storage information and use by/display until dates

Cooking instructions tell the consumer how the food should be cooked and at what temperatures it is safe to eat.

Figure 8.16 Part of a food label showing cooking instructions

The manufacturer's choice of food packaging is important with regards to preventing food poisoning:

- packaging protects the product from damage/contamination
- choice of material should suit the cooking method/storage
- impermeable materials should be used for some foods and some foods need to be packaged so they are airtight
- some foods need to be packaged using MAP (Modified Atmosphere Packaging)
- some materials can extend the shelf life of the product e.g. foods that are heat processed, e.g. pasteurised milk is packaged in glass. Metal is used during the canning process.
- plastics when sealed can prevent contamination.

QUESTIONS

1. A chilli con carne product is purchased from the freezer section in a supermarket. Information on the packaging informs the consumer:
   - that the product should be eaten on the day of purchase if it is not kept frozen
   - do not re-freeze after thawing.

   Why should the consumer follow these instructions?

2. Give two benefits to the consumer of having nutritional information on food packaging.

ACTIVITY

1. Find a food label, stick this onto plain paper.
   Draw arrows to show where the information required by law can be found on your label.
   Using your food label, answer the following questions.

   a) Who is the product aimed at? Explain why you have come to this conclusion.
   b) Which ingredient has the highest proportion of weight?
   c) How should the product be stored?
   d) What type of date-marking is used on your label? Why is this type of date mark used?
   e) What preparation and cooking instructions are given on your label?
   f) Are there any special claims (i.e. information) given on your label? What are these?
   g) Does the nutritional information on your label comply with government regulations? Why?
   h) How does the manufacturer describe the product?
   i) Do you think your label is attractive? Why?
   j) How could the manufacturer improve the label?
   k) What materials are used for your packaging/label? Why have these materials been used?

2. Find and draw the symbol that tells the consumer a product is gluten free.

3. Gluten-free products are manufactured for certain consumers who have special dietary needs. What is the name of the special diet that requires people to eat gluten-free products?

8.4 ENVIRONMENTAL HEALTH OFFICERS (EHOs)

EHOs are the main officers enforcing food safety law. They have powers to visit, enter and inspect food premises at any reasonable time, without notice, to ensure businesses are operating safely and hygienically.

They may also visit as a result of a complaint. EHOs look at the way food businesses are run and ensure that the law is being complied with. They also identify potential hazards. On every visit the EHO will carry out a risk assessment. Most companies are visited every nine months to a year.

EHOs:

- ensure food is safe and fit to eat
- aim to reduce possible sources of contamination
- monitor working conditions and hygiene systems
- enforce the law
- offer advice and support
- issue notices to improve conditions or stop certain practices
- can close part or all of a business if necessary
- can seize and detain food
- can prosecute employers and employees.

If premises are found to be unhygienic, they may be closed down and will be allowed to re-open only when the Local Authority agrees they have reached an acceptable standard.

EHOs' inspections usually concentrate on five main areas:

- temperature control – from storage of raw materials through to preparation and service
- cleaning and disinfection
- hygiene – personal hygiene, staff training

- control systems – stock rotation, pest control, quality control, waste disposal, how cross contamination is avoided
- design of premises – lighting, ventilation, washing facilities, etc.

During inspections EHOs may look at records, take photographs, remove samples.

ACTIVITY

Create a bubble diagram/spider diagram to show the role of the Environmental Health Officer.

KEY POINTS

- The Food Labelling Regulations control what information is on a food label.
- Packaging is essential to protect food products and provide information.
- 'Use by' dates are for high-risk foods. Date and month is shown, after this date the food may not be safe to eat and may be of a poorer quality.
- 'Best before' dates are for low-risk foods. Date, month and year are shown, after this date the food starts to deteriorate in flavour, taste, colour or texture.

KEY TERMS

'USE BY' – the date at which a food must be eaten
'BEST BEFORE' – the date after which the quality of a product may deteriorate

CHAPTER 9

INDUSTRIAL PRODUCTION

By the end of this section you should have developed a knowledge and understanding of:

- CAD/CAM as used in food technology
- commercial food production methods: job/craft; batch production; mass production; continuous flow
- the importance of quality assurance and quality control
- the role of nano-technology in the food industry.

Many manufacturers now use CAD (Computer Aided Design) and CAM (Computer Aided Manufacture) during the designing and manufacture of both the packaging and the food product. Quality assurance and quality control procedures are used in the food industry to set standards which meet consumer demands and expectations.

9.1 COMPUTER AIDED DESIGN (CAD)

Computers can play an important role in collecting and analysing information about the market sector. For example they may be used in:

- desk research – looking at statistics over time to see if the market is growing in size; what products are already available; the value of the market; popular eating trends

- carrying out and analysing data from sensory evaluation tests for appearance, taste, texture, colour, saltiness or spiciness

Figure 9.1 Computers play an important role

help to set the criteria for a successful product

- modelling costs/nutritional analysis/ratio and proportions of ingredients
- designing packaging and labels, advertising.

How can CAD be used in food technology?

Advantages/benefits of using CAD

- Gives greater accuracy, e.g. when working out the nutritional analysis of a product.
- Gives a professional finish, e.g. graphics/art work on food packaging.
- Allows certain tasks to be completed quickly, e.g. speeds up the drawing

process when producing annotated drawings of food products; graphs when presenting results from a questionnaire; graphical work for packaging.

- Colours and graphic effects can be modelled and tried out and the best ones chosen. The design can easily be varied if any of the details change or if special promotional offers are added.
- Modelling of a recipe can be carried out quickly and without actually wasting money trialling the product, e.g. experimenting with different ingredients.
- Designs can be quickly sent by email from the design stage to the manufacturing stage.

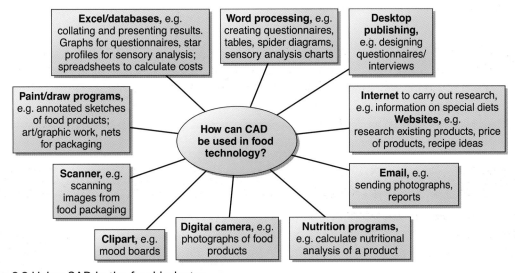

Figure 9.2 Using CAD in the food industry

9.2 COMPUTER AIDED MANUFACTURE (CAM)

Production process systems are becoming increasingly automated and controlled by computers. The whole production line may be fully automated or large sections of the line may be involved.

Automated manufacture is often referred to as CAM (computer-aided manufacture).

Advantages/benefits of using CAM	Examples
Saves time	Repetitive tasks can be carried out quickly, e.g. cutting out several pastry tops rather than one by one.
Standardises production	Process can be repeated with accuracy and precision so a consistent finish is maintained, e.g. consistent thickness of biscuits.
Increases productivity	More products can be made at speed resulting in lower costs, e.g. white sliced bread.
Increases reliability of finished products	All stages of production are controlled and if products are below standard they are automatically rejected, e.g. insufficient maillarding of bread products.
Monitors the production system	Through sensors which detect and record critical control points, e.g. weight, temperature, colour, pH, tolerances, thickness and moisture changes in a product.
Reduces need for storage	A 'just in time' system can be used, i.e. nothing is made in advance and stored. In response to consumer demand and delivered to maintain stocks in the shops.
Increases safety	Workers will not be required to carry out hazardous tasks, e.g. cutting processes.
High standard of packaging can be produced and maintained	Cutting of packaging nets. Printing labelling information on the packaging.
Data handling can deal with the large amount of information	Monitoring of complex production schedules, e.g. HACCP schedule, stock control.

Table 9.1 Advantages of using CAM

Figure 9.3 Preparing dough for bread using computer-controlled equipment

Monitoring the commercial production of food products

Computer sensors monitor pH levels. Acids and alkalis have an effect on the flavour, texture, appearance and nutritional value of food. For example:

- foods with a high acidic level (like fruits) can cause mixtures to curdle, for example if lemon juice is added before a sauce is made the milk would curdle, tomatoes can affect the consistency of a sauce, making it thin

- foods with a low acidic level (like milk) may need to have their acidic level raised to ensure a smooth texture, for example yoghurt.

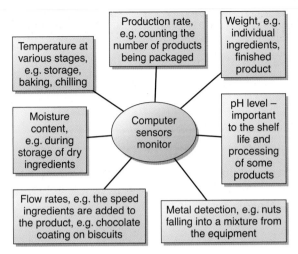

Figure 9.4 How computers control and monitor the commercial production of food products

Some manufacturers are now using computerised systems to assist in the control and monitoring of:

- the sorting and grading of raw materials, e.g. fruit and vegetables
- the weight of the product before packaging
- seals on packaging
- colour and shades of finished products, e.g. degree of brownness of bread products
- decorations and shapes through visual images stored on the computer, e.g. positioning of toppings on cakes
- the bacterial content of products
- stock control of raw ingredients and components.

However, visual checks are still carried out by the workers. Spot checks are carried out at any stage of the production line to check for quality and consistency.

If a food manufacturer decided to buy as much computerised equipment for the factory as possible there would be a number of effects on the workforce:

- Staff would need training in how to operate the computerised equipment.
- Number of people employed would probably be reduced – the machines would do the job(s) of people, particularly lower paid jobs.
- However individual staff costs may be higher because they have a more responsible and skilled job.
- Highly trained computer operatives required.
- Engineers required.
- Problems if the computer system breaks down – staff may not be able to work.
- Jobs available could become monotonous and boring as people are less involved.

Figure 9.5 Baking doughnuts using a computerised temperature-control system

9.3 COMMERCIAL PRODUCTION METHODS

Several production methods are used in the food industry. The method used depends on the food product being produced. When selecting the best methods of production, a food manufacturer would consider the following points:

- The number of food products to be made.
- How often, e.g. every day, weekly?
- Type of equipment available.
- Cost of the final product.
- Number of workers available.
- Level of skill of the workers.
- Money available for investment in new equipment/machinery.

Job/craft production

This is used when one product is made, for instance a wedding or novelty birthday cake.

Figure 9.6 Wedding cake

Benefits

- An individual or unique finished product.
- A high-quality product.

Limitations

- Skilled staff required.
- Can take a long time to manufacture as more processes are carried out by hand rather than machines.
- Can be expensive.

Batch production

This production system is used when small numbers of identical or similar products are made. For example, each day a small bakery may make batches of Chelsea buns, bread rolls and teacakes.

Figure 9.7 Preparing bread using batch production

Benefits

- Small orders can be made.
- The same equipment can be used to make a variety of products.
- Slight adaptations can be made, without incurring too much cost, to meet consumer demand or to create consumer interest.
- Different fillings can be added to fruit pies.

- Different flavourings can be added to biscuits – chocolate, lemon, ginger.
- Different decorations can be used for icing cakes.
- Raw materials and components may be purchased in bulk, therefore reducing the cost
- Only a small number of people are involved.
- Production costs are reduced as more products can be made in the same time it takes to make a 'one-off' product.

Limitations

- Waste can be high if process fails.

Mass production

This production system is used when large numbers of one product are manufactured on an assembly line, for example white sliced loaves, digestive biscuits, potato crisps, sandwiches.

Figure 9.8 A mass-produced product

Benefits

- The manufacturing process is split into tasks and sequenced into an assembly line.

Conveyor belts move the food product from one stage to the next as it is assembled.

- At each stage, specialised equipment or line operators carry out the tasks.
- Orders can be met quickly and efficiently.
- Raw materials and components are purchased in bulk, thereby reducing the cost.
- There is a low ratio of workers to the number of products produced and workers do not have to be highly skilled.
- Parts or all of the production line can be automated.
- Large numbers of a product can be manufactured at a low cost.
- After a large run is finished the production line may be adjusted to make another product.

Limitations

- Maintenance routines and checks must be very thorough and regular to avoid a breakdown which would be very expensive to the company in terms of lost production.
- Initial set-up is expensive as large-scale, specialist equipment is required.
- Many of the tasks carried out by workers can be repetitive and boring.

Continuous-flow production

This production system is computer controlled and extends mass production by producing one specific product continuously, for instance 24 hours a day, seven days a week, every year, in large quantities, for example soft drinks, milk.

Figure 9.9 Olive oil production on a continuous-flow production line

Benefits

- Inexpensive to run once set up.
- High quality product is produced.

- Small workforce is needed.
- A consistent product is produced.
- Orders can be met quickly and efficiently.
- Raw materials and components are purchased in bulk, thereby reducing the cost.

Limitations

- Maintenance routines and checks must be very thorough and regular to avoid a breakdown which would be very expensive to the company in terms of lost production.
- Initial set-up is expensive as large-scale, specialist equipment is required.
- Many of the tasks carried out by workers can be repetitive and boring.

9.4 QUALITY ASSURANCE

The word 'assurance' means 'a level of guarantee' or 'positive declaration'.

Food manufacturers set criteria or specifications for every stage during the designing and manufacturing of food products so that the products are manufactured to agreed standards. The manufacturer then knows that the consumer will be supplied with food products that are safe to eat and of a reliable standard.

We know that when we buy these products we will get safe, good quality products.

Quality assurance checks might include:

- specification checks
- hygiene procedures
- monitoring waste
- sensory analysis.

9.5 QUALITY CONTROL

In the food industry quality control is part of the quality assurance system. It involves checking the standards of a food product at three stages: as it is being designed, during manufacture and at the end of manufacture.

It will also include the critical control points established as part of the HACCP procedure. Quality control checks make sure that the product meets the product specification.

Here is a list of quality control checks made on a batch of biscuits:

- Weighing biscuit ingredients – to obtain the correct consistency.
- Mixing dough to correct consistency – to have an even texture.
- Rolling out the thickness of the dough – to obtain equal depth in the biscuits.
- Cutting dough into accurate portions/portion control on extruder – to obtain equal/exact size/equal shape biscuits.
- Temperature control of the product/use of food probe – to ensure bacteria is controlled/even cooking for colour and crispness.
- Time control during cooking – to ensure even cooking for colour and crispness.
- Colour sensor for cooked biscuits – to guarantee even colour.

- Cooling time – to ensure standard degree of crispness (non soggy).
- Counting into packages – to get correct numbers.
- Sealing packages – to exclude air to keep biscuits crisp.
- Metal detector – to make sure there are no foreign bodies.
- Weighing finished biscuits – for equal products.
- Moisture sensor – to ensure correct degree of crispness.
- Monitoring the rate of production – the quantity/consistency of biscuits produced.
- Alerting to any problems in the system – the quality of the biscuits.
- Checking the number of biscuits made – to re-order the ingredients/stock.

9.6 NANO-TECHNOLOGY

Food experts are always seeking new sources of and novel uses for existing raw materials and ingredients, especially those containing healthy components and ones that will improve the quality of our food. One of the latest trends is nano-technology which is affecting all aspects of technology in a variety of materials. It is working with materials at a microscopic level.

In food science and technology, food is manipulated to one billionth of a meter in scale. Its uses include:

- nano-emulsions which are being used to create double emulsions which improve the texture of sauces
- nano food synthesisers which can create or alter foods molecules
- nano-capsule protection which can deliver a fortifying nutrient to our body which can be slowly released or can release a controlled flavour in a drink
- changes in pH, temperature or the presence of pathogens can be detected by nano-sensors
- nano-bots are microbe-destroying minute robots that can make food safe

QUESTIONS

1. What is meant by the letters CAD and CAM?

2. Give two examples of how CAD is used in the development of a new product.

3. Give two examples of how CAM is used in the development of a new product.

4. State two benefits of using CAD and two benefits of using CAM.

5. Copy and complete Table 9.2 to show how computer sensors can be used to monitor the commercial production of food products.

6. You are asked to produce a batch of 50 cheese and onion pasties. State three ways you could ensure that all the pasties were identical.

7. Food products can be manufactured by different production methods. What points should a food manufacturer consider when selecting the best method of production?

8. Explain what is meant by:
   • Quality Assurance
   • Quality Control.

Computer sensors	Example
Metal detection	
pH level	
Flow rate	
Moisture content	
Temperature	
Weight	
Production rate	

Table 9.2

ACTIVITY

1. Create a visual representation of the different commercial production methods. This could be done by producing a table (see Table 9.3), bubble diagram or mind map, etc. The information you produce should include:

   • The names of the different commercial production methods, their benefits and limitations and at least one example of a product that can be made by each method.

Production method	Benefits	Limitations	Example(s) of food products
Job/Craft			

Table 9.3 Different commercial production methods

2. Copy Table 9.4 and complete to show the control measures you would use to ensure each batch of cheese scones is of an identical standard.

Process for cheese scones	Control measure
Weighing and measuring ingredients	
Rubbing fat into the flour	
Grating cheese	
Rolling out the dough	
Cutting out the scones	
Baking the scones	

Table 9.4 Control measures

3. Look at the following control system for making cake bars in Table 9.5. For each stage of making, a control has been given, so the cake bars can be made to a consistently high standard. In pairs or small groups, discuss the jumbled up statements on page 202 which explain the reason why each control needs to be in place. Decide which statement fits each stage of making and record your answers.

Stage of making	Control	Reason
Preparing self	Wear apron, wash hands etc	
Weigh ingredients	Use electronic scales	
Preparation of cooker	Heat oven to 180 °C/Gas 4	
Preparing Swiss roll tin	Grease the tin	
Creaming margarine and sugar	Electric mixer, full speed for 3½ minutes	
Adding beaten egg	Drop by drop beating well after each addition	
Adding flour	Sieve	
Mixing in flour	Fold in with tablespoon	
Placing in tin	28 cm x 18 cm	
Baking cake	15–20 minutes	
Cutting the bars	14 bars 9 cm 3 4 cm	
Decorating cake bars	Spread on butter cream to edges of bars	

Table 9.5 Control system

Reasons:

a) Correct amount of air is added
b) Ensure high standards of personal hygiene
c) Same thickness of cake
d) Ensure the same appearance each time
e) Ensure same degree of browning and cake is thoroughly cooked
f) Prevent cake sticking to the tin
g) Remove lumps and add air
h) Prevents curdling and a heavy textured cake
i) Achieve identical results each time the cake is made
j) Accurate temperature
k) Prevent air from being knocked out
l) Same size bars each time

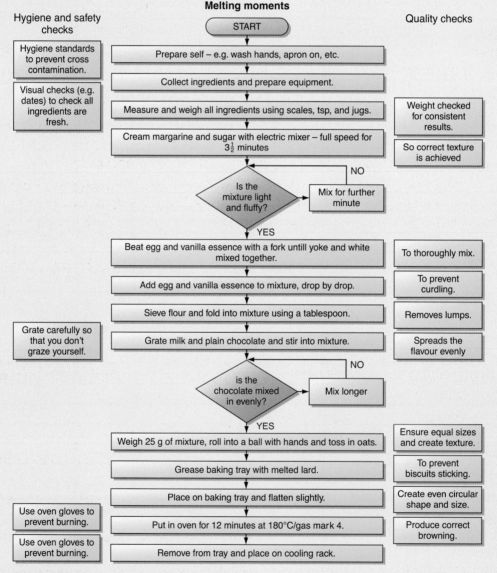

Figure 9.10 Flowchart for melting moments

4. Figure 9.10 on page 202 shows an example of a flowchart for melting moments that includes hygiene, safety and quality checks. Using a product you will be making design a flowchart that includes hygiene, safety and quality checks.

KEY POINTS

- Computers are used in a variety of ways in the food industry.
- Computers are used for designing and manufacturing food products.
- Necessary controls need to be put in place by food manufacturers.
- Job/craft production is used when products are made specifically for one occasion.
- Batch production is used when a specific quantity of a certain product is required.
- Mass production is used when products are made in large quantities.
- Continuous-flow production is used when the same product is made continually, non-stop for 24 hours a day.
- Quality Assurance means 'a level of guarantee' or 'positive declaration'.
- Quality Control is part of the quality assurance system which involves checking the standards of a food product during designing, manufacture and at the end of manufacture. Control checks make sure that the product meets the product specification and is of a quality standard.
- Just in time is a system which means that nothing is made in advance and stored.

KEY TERMS

COMPUTER AIDED DESIGN (CAD) – used for designing during food production, e.g. packaging
COMPUTER AIDED MANUFACTURE (CAM) – using computers to control machinery during food production, e.g. temperatures during baking

Industrial production:
JOB/CRAFT – the production of one product
BATCH – production of a specific amount of a group of similar products at the same time
MASS – producing products in quantity
CONTINUOUS FLOW – computer controlled, producing products 24 hours a day, seven days a week
QUALITY ASSURANCE – a system which lays down procedures for making a safe, quality product
QUALITY CONTROL – a way of checking the quality of a product during or at the end of the production system

PRODUCT ANALYSIS

By the end of this section you should have developed a knowledge and understanding of:

- strategies to determine the suitability of a product for an intended market
- the choice of ingredients and components in a range of products
- the processes used to make products
- evaluation of commercially manufactured food products against moral, cultural, environmental and sustainability issues.

Product analysis consists of looking at all aspects of a product in detail. It is one of the responsibilities of a product development team to carry out product analysis of existing products. Product analysis is carried out at the research stage. The reasons for carrying out product analysis are to investigate how the product is made and the ingredients used. It will help the team to gain ideas for new products, compare differences in brands and to check that their own product meets its specification.

10.1 DETERMINE THE SUITABILITY OF A PRODUCT FOR AN INTENDED MARKET

To be able to decide whether a product is suitable for its intended market you first need to know more about the target market. This is a part of the design process and is usually carried out by questionnaire, interview, consumer profile or survey to determine the identified needs of the target group.

From the analysis of the results the student can list the identified needs.

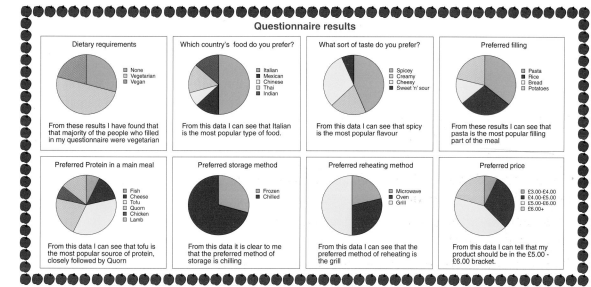

Figure 10.1 A student uses a questionnaire to find out more about the target group

Analysis of Questionnaire

I have collected data by creating a questionnaire and asking members of the public to complete them.

From the results of the questionnaire I can see that my main meal product should be suitable for vegetarians, as the majority of people who filled in my questionnaire were vegetarian and I feel there is definitely a gap in the market for vegetarian main meals.

Also, from my data I have found that the most popular type of cuisine is Italian, closely followed by Indian, Mexican and Thai. This shows me that when I am deciding on recipes I should consider this and choose dishes in the style of this country's cuisine. The flavours that came out most popular are spicy, cheesy and creamy. This is a very good outcome because these flavours compliment the styles of food that came out most popular (i.e. Italian, Indian, Mexican and Thai).

From my results I have also found that most people prefer pasta as the filling part of the meal, although potatoes and rice also scored highly. This is also a very good outcome as these too complement the style of food that came out most popular. The most popular source of protein came out as tofu, closely followed by quorn and cheese. So, when choosing recipes I shall have to take this into account and make sure my recipes contain at least one of the three.

The price bracket that came out most popular was the £5.00-£6.00 bracket. This is a great outcome because it gives me quite a bit of money to work with so I can choose good ingredients.

The preferred storage method came out as chilling and the preferred reheating method as either oven or grill. This means my dish must be suitable for chilling, putting in the oven or the grill.

Identified Needs

- My main meal needs to be suitable for vegetarians.
- My dish should be in an Italian style.
- My recipes should have creamy, cheesy or spicy flavours.
- The filling part of my meal should be pasta, potatoes or rice.
- For the protein part of my meal I should use tofu or quorn.
- The optimum price for my meal is between £5.00 and £6.00.
- My meal should be suitable for chilling.
- My meal should be suitable to be reheated in the grill or oven.
- My main meal must feed two people. (i.e. Have two portions)
- My main meal should be suitable for batch production.

Figure 10.2 The identified needs of the target group

10.2 UNDERSTAND THE CHOICE OF INGREDIENTS AND COMPONENTS IN A RANGE OF PRODUCTS

The product can be evaluated against the identified needs. This may be done by a visit to the supermarket or looking at the packaging, but the best way of doing this is to actually examine and taste test the product. The product must be a similar type of product to what you are intending to design, not merely a product that you know the target group might like to eat!

Guidelines for carrying out product analysis

- Who is the product aimed at and why?

- What is the purpose of the product? When, where, why and how will it be eaten?

- What ingredients, components, additives have been used in the product and why?

- What processes have been used in making it?

- How has it been made safe to eat?

- How does it fit into the Eatwell Plate?

- Does it meet the nutritional needs of the target group?

- How well does it meet the identified needs of the target group?

- How does the product compare with similar ones available?

- Has the manufacturer considered the environment?

- What are the moral, cultural and sustainability issues with the product?

How can you find out the answers?

- Sensory testing – looking at the taste, texture, aroma, appearance, using the opinions of the user group.

- Looking at the packaging. How has it been made safe to eat? Is it chilled/frozen/canned/bottled/ambient? What essential information is included? You will be able to obtain the ingredients list and the nutritional data from here. What is the packaging material used and why has it been used?

- What is the cost of the product? Is it in the correct price range for the user?

- How is the product promoted? Does it have any special claims, such as low in fat? How has it been made to appeal to the target group?

- Is the portion size adequate for the user?

- Use the product, reheat it and before you taste/test it, examine how it has been made (disassemble it). Decide on the processes that have been used.

- Can you work out the carbon footprint of the product? How many miles have the ingredients travelled?

Product Analysis of Root Vegetable Bake

This product was designed for vegetarians but also for people who eat meat, it is from "Designed not just for Vegetarian's" range. I think it is aimed at families because the packaging uses bright colours and shows a picture of the dish to interest buyers.

The root vegetable bake is made up of roasted leeks, parsnips, carrot and celeriac in a Cheddar cheese sauce topped with mash potato with spring onions.

Nutritional Information

Typical Values (cooked as per instructions)	Per 100g
Energy	306 kJ 73 kcal
Protein	2.5g
Carbohydrate of which sugars of which starch	9.6g 2.4g 7.5g
Fat of which saturates mono-unsaturates polyunsaturates	2.7g 1.9g 0.6g 0.1g
Fibre	3.3g
Salt of which sodium	0.2g 0.1g

The Root Vegetable Bake is generally quite nutritious as most of the values are consistent with a recognised healthy amount per 100g. There is little fat (only 2.7g) and sodium (0.1g). Also, there is not too much sugar (2.4g) or saturates (1.9g). There is a lot of fibre in this dish (3.3g); this is because it has a lot of vegetables in it, which are high in fibre. It has under ¾ of an adult recommended daily amount.

I think this meal fulfils the needs of its target group, as it is a good source of vegetables for families. I think it promotes healthy eating because the supermarket have 'The Wheel of Health' system, which clearly shows how healthy a meal is using a colour code system that is easy to understand. Using the 'Wheel of Health' system we can clearly see that as most of the wheel is green this is a particularly healthy dish.

I think that the Root Vegetable Bake is quite a good main meal because it contains a lot of vegetables, which provides lots of fibre, something that many modern diets are lacking. However, it could be made more interesting to the palate by add a meat substitute to vary the flavours. I think this meal is fairly nutritional but it probably needs more protein as there isn't that much and it is an essential part of the diet for growth and repair of the body. On the other hand it is low in fat and salt, which prevents hearth disease and high blood pressure. It is also pretty low in sugar, this means that tooth decay will not occur.

My two criticisms with this product would be the portion size is slightly too large and that it is slightly expensive (£1.99) for a tub of vegetables.

Taste Test

Product Analysis of Cumberland Pie

This product was designed for vegetarians but also for people who eat meat, it is from "Designed not just for Vegetarian's" range. I think it is aimed at families because the packaging uses bright colours and shows a picture of the dish to interest buyers.

The Cumberland Pie is made up of vegetarian mince with carrots, parsnips and green lentils in a rich tomato and red wine sauce with buttery rosemary mash.

Nutritional Information

Typical Values (cooked as per instructions)	Per 100g
Energy	376kJ 90kcal
Protein	2.5g
Carbohydrate of which sugars of which starch	9.6g 1.3g 8.3g
Fat of which saturates mono-unsaturates polyunsaturates	4.6g 2.1g 0.9g 0.9g
Fibre	3.1g
Salt of which sodium	0.5g 0.2g

The Cumberland Pie is quite healthy because it is low in sugar (only 1.3g) and it is also lower in fat (4.6g).

I do not think this meal fulfils the needs of its target group as I feel its flavours would not appeal to children as I think the flavour was too strong and intense for young pallets. I think it promotes healthy eating because the supermarket have 'The Wheel of Health' system, which clearly shows how healthy a meal is using a colour code system that is easy to understand. From the wheel we can clearly see that this meal is not as healthy as the Vegetable Root Bake, but it only has one red segment so isn't particularly unhealthy.

I think the Cumberland Pie is a poor main meal in my opinion, as the flavours do no cater to the whole family, it is too rich and too sweet for a savoury dish. As a dish aimed at the whole family maybe the flavours need to be a little subtler. However, I do think that the amount of fibre in this meal (3.1g) is very impressive as it is 68% of the recommended daily amount for an adult. Finally, I feel the price (£1.59) is quite reasonable.

Test Taste

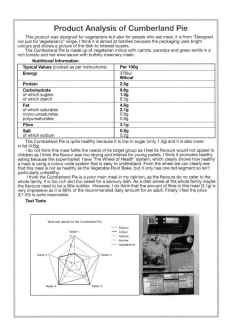

Figure 10.3 Product analysis of a vegetarian product

10.3 UNDERSTAND THE PROCESSES USED TO MAKE THE PRODUCT

By taking a product apart we can see exactly how it has been made. Most products are a variation of an existing product so by using this method it should also give you ideas for new products.

Let's look at an apple pie.

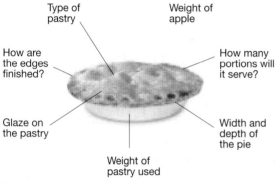

Figure 10.4 Apple pie

- What are the stages in making the pie?
- What is the cost of the pie?
- Has the pie got a base? Why?
- What ingredients have been used in the pastry? Explain why.
- How much sugar has been used in the apple?
- How could the amount of sugar in the apple be reduced?
- How could the quantity of pastry be reduced?
- Have any additives or colourings been used? Why?
- How could the design be improved to meet healthy eating guidelines?
- How much energy has been used in making this product?

10.4 EVALUATE COMMERCIALLY MANUFACTURED FOOD PRODUCTS AGAINST MORAL, CULTURAL, ENVIRONMENTAL AND SUSTAINABILITY ISSUES

When examining a product we should not only consider who is going to eat it and how it has been made but also think about where the ingredients have come from, how the workers were paid and treated and what effect this product will have on the environment. These issues are explained in greater detail in the next chapter, so let's look at our apple pie and consider the moral, cultural, environmental and sustainability issues.

 EXAMINER'S TIPS

You will be examined on moral, cultural, environmental and sustainability issues in Unit A522.

Ingredient	Moral, cultural, environmental and sustainability issues
Pastry	
Flour	Where was the wheat grown? How far has it been transported? How much was the farmer paid for the grain? Where was it ground and packaged? Were pesticides used? Does it need a top and a bottom, could the amount of pastry be reduced? Is it a high-fat/high-sugar product?
Fat	What type of fat has been used? Is it a trans (hydrogenated) fat? Is it morally right to use trans-fats when we know they cause heart disease? Where has it been transported from? If it is a vegetable fat, were pesticides used on the crop? If it is an animal fat, how were they farmed?
Water	If the pastry has been made in the UK we know that it will be clean water. Is it fluoridated?
Filling and topping	
Apple	Are the apples grown in the UK? Not very likely. Where were they grown? How much were the pickers paid? Were pesticides used? How far have they been transported? What is the carbon footprint?
Sugar	Probably from the West Indies. What were the workers paid? What are their living conditions? Do we need so much sugar in a product when there is such a moral problem of obesity in the UK?
Egg glaze	How were the hens reared? Were they free range? Not likely in such a product. What were the hens fed on?
Dish	Does the container need to be foil? Metal uses up the world's resources. Could it have been put in a cardboard container made from either recycled card or from sustainable trees? It is difficult to recycle foil dishes in some areas. Cardboard could easily be recycled. Does it have other layers of packaging? Is it recyclable?
Cooking/ Chilling	How much energy has been used in the ingredients/manufacture/chilling and storage of this product? Has it used fossil fuels?

Table 10.1 Moral, cultural, environmental and sustainability issues for an apple pie

Lattice top to reduce the pastry

Top only reduces pastry

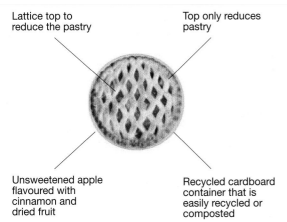

Unsweetened apple flavoured with cinnamon and dried fruit

Recycled cardboard container that is easily recycled or composted

Figure 10.5 An improved lower-fat apple pie

KEY POINT

- Remember that you need to have a target group and know their needs to be able to decide a product's suitability.

ACTIVITY

Carry out a product analysis of a food product. Choose your own or use one of the following:

- cereal bar for child's packed lunch
- fruit flavour yoghurt for an 18 month old
- pasta main course for a teenager
- single portion meal for a senior citizen
- family-sized dessert, e.g. apple pie
- savoury snack for an 'on the go meal'.
- produce a chart similar to the one above to record your findings.

CHAPTER 11

SUSTAINABLE DESIGN

LEARNING OUTCOMES

By the end of this section you should have developed a knowledge and understanding of:

- recycle, reuse, reduce, refuse, rethink and repair in the production of food products.

We need to consider the impact we have upon the world in which we live. We need to increase our use of sustainable resources to ensure that our activities today do not have an adverse impact on others currently, or upon future generations.

During the last century humans have used new and increasingly powerful technology to exploit the earth's resources. As a result supplies of natural resources like coal, oil, minerals and fresh water are likely to run out unless we take action. The world's population is expanding and feeding the world is an increasing problem. Many people are starving whilst others are overeating and throwing away large quantities of food. In order to support sustainable food production, manufacturers must find ways of using more energy-efficient processes. They must reduce the consumption of water, avoid waste and use sustainable resources.

11.1 RECYCLE

The choice of packaging materials

Packaging from glass, metal, card and paper can all be recycled. Some plastics may also be recycled. It is difficult to recycle packaging made from mixed material, for example layers of foil, plastic or card bonded together. Manufacturers should also use materials that are formed from recycled material. It relies on us, the consumer, to make sure that we recycle the packaging that we have.

Packaging and the environment

Many people are concerned about the environment. Food packaging can cause a number of environmental problems because:

- it uses up natural resources, e.g. oil, trees, metal ore
- it can cause air, land or water pollution
- it cannot always be recycled and is not biodegradable. It has to be disposed of in landfill sites.

Consumers can reduce environmental impact by:

- buying re-usable containers, e.g. bags, jars, egg cartons
- reusing carrier bags, e.g. plastic or thick paper
- taking waste packaging to recycling centres, e.g. glass, cans, paper
- buying minimum packaging, e.g. single-wrapped rather than double-wrapped products
- selecting biodegradable materials wherever possible.

Figure 11.1 Consumers can sort their waste for recycling

Manufacturers can minimise the environmental impact of waste by:

- reducing the amount of packaging
- using paper or card which has come from sustainable forests

- avoiding harmful processes, such as bleaching wood pulp with chemicals
- using materials which the consumer can recycle
- printing symbols on the packaging which inform consumers, e.g. recycling logos, plastic identification symbols, anti-litter symbols
- providing information about the packaging materials.

ACTIVITY

Create a leaflet or fact sheet on the environmental problems caused by food packaging and how waste can be reduced by both the manufacturer and the consumer. The leaflet/fact sheet should contain images as well as text.

Recycling of tins, plastic card and paper

Most people associate recycling with packaging.

- We wash out tins and bottles ready to be collected or to take to a recycling centre.
- More than half of food packaging is plastic. This is made from a non-renewable source and is the most difficult to recycle.
- There are mixed materials used in packaging such as Tetra-pak. These are difficult to recycle because a mixture of different materials is used.
- The average family gets through 4 glass jars or bottles, 13 cans, 3 plastic bottles and 5 kg of paper each week.

Figure 11.2 Many Local Authorities provide households with recycling systems

ACTIVITY

In one of your practical lessons wash and save all the packaging that is used by your class. In the next lesson look at the packaging and consider all the sustainability issues. Decide what could be recycled or reused. Could less packaging be used?

▶ Composting

If raw food waste cannot be reused for another product it can be composted to produce useful fertiliser for a garden. Like any recipe, your compost relies on the right ingredients to make it work.

Things you can compost include:

- vegetable peelings
- fruit waste
- teabags
- plant prunings
- grass cuttings
- crushed eggshells – to add useful minerals.

These are considered 'Greens'. Greens are quick to rot and they provide important nitrogen and moisture.

Other things you can compost include:

- cardboard egg boxes
- scrunched up paper
- fallen leaves.

These are considered 'Browns' and are slower to rot. They provide fibre and carbon and also allow important air pockets to form in the mixture.

Certain things should never be placed in your bin. No cooked vegetables, no meat, no dairy products, no diseased plants, and definitely no dog excrement or cat litter.

Figure 11.3 Adding a tea bag to a kitchen composting bin

▶ 11.2 REUSE

▶ Products that can be reused for either the same purpose or as a new product

Britain throws away £20 billion worth of unused food every year – enough to lift 150 million people out of starvation. When food waste cannot be reused it ends up in landfill sites, it rots and produces methane, which is a powerful greenhouse gas. Raw waste can be composted but it is not so easy to reuse leftover foods.

In food technology it is difficult to reuse foods apart from reusing leftover food and reusing food containers.

▶ Reuse of leftover ingredients to make other food products

According to government figures we each waste about £8 worth of food each week. There are hygiene issues with using leftover food but, as long as normal food safety rules are followed, it is perfectly safe to use leftovers in creative and innovative ways.

Traditionally chicken or turkey broth was made with chicken or turkey carcasses. Shepherd's pie was made from minced leftover lamb and cottage pie from minced beef. Bread and butter pudding was made from stale bread and trifle from stale cake. The original concept of a burger was minced leftover beef, mixed with an onion and held together with egg, but they were called rissoles!

Suggestions for reusing leftovers

- Mix pasta with leftover sauce, add a few fresh vegetables to make a pasta salad.
- Use leftover rice with salad dressing and some beans/nuts/vegetables for a salad.
- Leftover rice can be stir fried with meat or vegetables but must be used quickly, stored below 5 °C and must be heated to over 72 °C to prevent food poisoning from bacillus cereus.
- Make frittata or a hash from leftover potatoes.
- Salad vegetables can be turned into a salsa.
- Cheese can be grated and used for topping jacket potatoes or pasta bake.
- Use unused vegetables to make soups.

Figure 11.4 Trifle can be a useful way of using leftovers

Food safety rules for using leftovers

- Store leftover food in plastic tubs or in covered bowls.
- Make sure that your refrigerator is set at below 8 °C.
- Do not overcrowd your refrigerator.
- Most foods will need to be used within 24 hours.
- Take particular care with high-risk foods.

ACTIVITY

Analyse a celebration meal (e.g. Christmas or Diwali) and research how you could use the leftover foods.

Produce a leaflet of recipes and ideas for leftover food.

▶ Buy products with little or no packaging

Plastic packaging and carrier bags are made from oil, although occasionally they are made from recycled plastics. They can take up to 500 years to decay in a landfill site.

We could use paper and card but they are much heavier and therefore use more fuel to transport them to the shop and they break easily when they become wet. For shopping we could use a reusable bag, made from organically sourced fair-traded hemp or cotton, but what can we do about the actual packaging on food products?

We could choose to shop at a local market stall, farmer's shop or local small business where the products may be sold without packaging. We can choose to buy 'loose' fruit and vegetables rather than pre-packed. Do bananas really need to be wrapped in plastic?

ACTIVITY

Make two lists of foods and ingredients. The first list of ones that could be sold without any packaging and the second a list where packaging is essential. Discuss your lists with a partner and then put an action plan together to send to a supermarket giving advice on how they could reduce food packaging.

11.3 REDUCE

▶ Reduce the effects on health by using balanced recipes, low in fat, salt and sugar

The National Health Service costs millions of pounds each year and many of the people using it are there because of a poor diet. This is not because they are lacking in food but because they are eating too much of the wrong foods. By following the advice of the Eatwell Plate and adapting recipes to reduce fat, salt and sugar we can reduce heart disease, strokes, diabetes and obesity in the UK (see Chapter 2).

ACTIVITY

Create a summary of the information given in the Eatwell Plate which would be suitable for a class of primary school children.

▶ Reduction in the use of processed foods

Processed foods require a lot of energy to produce them. Each stage of the process has an impact upon the environment: growing the raw materials used in the product, the transporting of ingredients, manufacturing the product, transportation to the supermarket, the supermarket energy used to maintain the condition of the product and finally the cooking of the product at home, all will contribute to the product's carbon footprint.

Carbon footprint is the amount of carbon emissions produced during the growing, processing and distribution of our food.

Processed foods are often high in fats, salt and sugar. They have at least two layers of packaging, using more resources. Portion sizes of processed foods have increased, for example a packet of crisps is now 35 g instead of 25 g. Instant mashed potato may be convenient to use but the potatoes have to be washed, peeled, chopped, cooked, freeze dried and packaged by machines.

ACTIVITY

Select three different processed products and carry out an analysis of each one to show the processes involved in their manufacture. What is the effect of these products on the environment?

▶ Reduce energy in methods of cooking

A lot of energy is used in the cooking of food. One of the biggest users of energy in the home is the kettle. How many times do you boil the kettle and then leave it to cool again? How often do you fill the kettle just for one cup of coffee? The energy used to boil a kettle would light a room for a whole evening.

Some suggestions for reducing energy use:

- Never put the oven on for just one food product. Plan the whole meal using the oven.
- Use a steamer with several vegetables cooking at once.
- Use a pressure cooker to cook stews in 20 minutes or whole meals at once.
- Use a microwave to quickly cook products.
- Turn the heat down and use a lid on the pans.
- Stir fry as a quick method of cooking.

- Use hand skills of chopping, grating, shredding, whisking instead of using electrical equipment.
- Try to make 'one pan' recipes, e.g. risotto.

ACTIVITY

Make a list of recommendations to a family of ways that that they could reduce their energy use in the kitchen.

▶ Eco footprint

More people are stopping to consider the impact that our food has on the environment.

Food miles

The distance food travels from field to plate, is a way of indicating the environmental impact of the food we eat. Half the vegetables and 95 per cent of the fruit eaten in the UK comes from beyond our shores. Food is transported across the world because we want to buy foods out of season. Asparagus is only in season for May and June but we want to buy it all year. It comes from Italy or Spain for a few months and the rest of the year it comes from Peru!

Planes are powered by fossil fuel oil. When the oil is burnt it gives off carbon dioxide gas emissions which contribute hugely to global warming. You can offset this by planting trees to absorb the CO_2 given off. This is called 'carbon offsetting'. The carbon offset cost of trees for a return flight to New York is £13.50 but the trees take 25 years to absorb the carbon dioxide.

If we reduced the amount of packaging used in products it may actually reduce costs and save energy in terms of fuel and transportation.

What can we do? Buy local! This means supporting local growers. It's much better for the environment if you grow and/or buy organic produce.

Figure 11.5 Transportation by aeroplane increases the effect on the environment

ACTIVITY

Look at the ingredients in a ready meal and work out the food miles in the product.

We can grow apples in the UK. Have a look in your local supermarket and see where the fruit is imported from. Record on a map where all the fruit has come from.

Ways of reducing waste food

The average family throws away £600 worth of food every year. In our busy lifestyles we shop without planning meals. Our lifestyles have changed and we tend to shop weekly buying foods but this often creates a lot of unused wasted food.

Manufacturers can avoid waste by selling by-products, for example whey from milk is sold to baby food manufacturers.

We can try to reduce food waste by using leftover foods in creative and innovative ways.

Figure 11.6 Reduce food waste by preserving

Reduce the use of pesticides

Most farming relies heavily on artificial chemical fertilisers and pesticides. Around 350 pesticides are permitted, and it is estimated that 4.5 billion litres of them are used annually. While there are government rules about accepted levels of pesticide residues in our food, there can be concerns about their long-term effect on us and they can harm the environment too, for example chemicals in pesticides leach into rivers and pollute the water.

Organic agriculture is carried out to a set of legally defined standards. Producers then pay to have their produce monitored and certified by one of several organic organisations, of which the Bristol-based Soil Association is by far the largest in the UK.

Organic farming strictly limits the use of artificial chemical fertilisers or pesticides. Antibiotics for animals are kept to an absolute minimum. Instead it emphasises farming methods such as crop rotation to keep the soil healthy and natural pest-control systems. Genetically modified crops are forbidden. Organic bodies also demand more space for animals and higher welfare standards.

In Brazil thousands of children pick oranges to be made into concentrate, which is then processed into juice. They are often exposed to high levels of pesticide and may be paid as little as 13 p an hour (www.sustain.co.uk).

QUESTIONS

1. Copy and complete Table 11.1 to show how the leftover foods could be used.

Leftover food	Recipe idea	Other ingredients needed
Cold chicken		
Pack of carrots		
Half a sandwich cake		
200g Cheddar cheese		
4 plums		
2 slices of cooked ham		

Table 11.1 Using leftovers

2. List rules to ensure that leftover food is safe to eat.

3. Make a list of the ways that a family could reduce the waste food that they have, for instance plan meals, check store cupboard and shop for what they need.

11.4 REFUSE

Issues related to sustainable design in packaging

The quality of food packaging can indicate the target market for the product. The packaging often reflects the social group that the manufacturer has targeted to buy the product. The social group may be families, or a couple who both work professionally, for example.

The aesthetic implications of the packaging relate to the way the packaging is designed and how it looks. Some supermarkets are designing very simple packages and labels for their budget products, such as canned

tomatoes and beans. By saving money on the packaging design, the product becomes cheaper to buy. The cost of products which have elaborate packaging, such as Easter eggs, will be higher than something packed simply. You are paying for the packaging which decorates and protects the product.

Food is the largest single factor affecting our eco footprint. Packaging, processing and transport use huge amounts of energy and discarded packaging creates massive waste. Throw-away drinks containers have become very popular. Stop and think. Where do these end up? Usually in landfill or as litter! This is a waste of materials and even if they were recycled the process would take up energy and cause pollution.

On average a UK person throws away each year:

- 450 kg of waste
- 149 kg of paper and card (that is 570 magazines!)
- 90 kg of organic material (2000 banana skins!)
- 50 kg plastic (900 fizzy drink bottles!)
- 32 kg metal (6320 baked bean tins!)

▶ Refuse high fat, salt and sugar foods

If people ate a balanced diet and followed the advice of the Eatwell Plate they would be less likely to get heart disease, diabetes, osteoporosis, diverticulosis and some cancers.

The first step is to ensure that you eat at least five portions of fruit and vegetables a day and to refuse to buy high fat/salt/sugar foods. Make sure you have enough fibre, vitamins and minerals.

Processed foods usually contain more salt, sugar and fat and, together with red meat and dairy products, have a high impact on the planet. Increased portion size of processed foods is also likely to lead to even more wastage of food.

ACTIVITY

Carry out a product analysis on portion sizes of ready meals.

Investigate how much rice and pasta you need to cook for one portion.

QUESTIONS

1. Discuss the reasons why we buy so much processed foods.

2. List the reasons why people don't cook at home as much as they used to.

3. Explain why processed foods have a bigger environmental impact than fresh produce.

ACTIVITY

Working in groups, look at the packaging on a variety of food products, such as:

- Microwave meal
- Can of Coke
- Easter egg/box of chocolates
- Pack of fresh fruit
- Ready-to-cook pizza
- Pack of fresh cakes.

You could choose your own selection of food products.

Discuss how you could refuse to have the packaging but still buy the product.

What materials are used? How much of the packaging can be recycled? How?

11.5 RETHINK

▶ Rethink the average UK high-fat diet

Despite efforts by the UK government to encourage us to rethink our diet it seems to be having very little effect on the growing numbers of overweight or obese people or those with diet-related medical conditions. The problems of the high-fat diet have been explained in Chapter 2. Use that information when doing the following activities and questions.

QUESTIONS

1. List the actions that food manufacturers have taken to help people choose lower-fat products.

2. Choose a recipe for a meat casserole. Explain how the recipe can be adapted to a lower-fat version.

3. Explain the problems of having a high-fat diet.

ACTIVITY

In groups in your class, discuss what measures you would take if you were the Minister for Health responsible for reducing the UK high-fat diet.

Rethink your diet. Produce a leaflet for a GP surgery giving advice and suggestions.

▶ Examine the impact of food products on health

How often do you think about what you are eating? 'We are what we eat' is a very true statement. Everything that you eat will have some impact on your body and your health.

Throughout this book you have read about nutrients, foods and food products and their effect on you. To rethink about the impact of food products on health you are going to look at two different diets in the Activity below.

ACTIVITY

Jack is 2 years old

Breakfast
Cereal with milk
Tea

Mid morning
Milk

Figure 11.7 Jack

Lunch
Cheese sandwich
Yoghurt
Orange squash

Family Meal
Lentil soup
Fish fingers, peas, potatoes
Banana custard
Glass of milk

Bedtime
Glass of milk

Javed is 17 years old
Javed is in training for an important swimming race.
He is not overweight.

Figure 11.8 Javed

Breakfast
Rice Krispies
Bacon sandwich (white bread)
Toast and jam
Cup of tea

Mid morning
Coffee and choc biscuits

Lunch
Cornish pasty, chips
Coke

Tea
Orange squash and chocolate bar

Evening meal
Spaghetti bolognese
Apple crumble
Coffee

Evening
Coke and crisps

JACK

1. Why do Jack's parents/carers give him milk throughout the day?
2. What other protein foods occur in Jack's diet?
3. Why is it important for Jack to have protein?
4. Which foods in Jack's diet provide carbohydrates?
5. Are there any crunchy foods in Jack's diet to develop his teeth?
6. Can you see any nutrients that may be missing from Jack's diet?
7. How does Jack's diet compare with the Eatwell Plate?
8. List the foods that you would change in the diet.
9. Suggest improvements to Jack's diet.

JAVED

1. List the carbohydrate foods in Javed's diet.
2. What do you think about the amount of carbohydrate he is having?
3. Why is Javed concerned about a high carbohydrate intake?
4. Do you think Javed is having enough vitamin C?
5. Is this important? Why?
6. Young people need calcium as they are still growing and building up bones. Is Javed having enough calcium?
7. How does Javed's diet compare with the Eatwell Plate?
8. List the foods in Javed's diet that you would change.
9. What recommendations would you make to Javed's diet to improve its balance?

ACTIVITY

You could now carry out a similar activity with your own diet. Write down what you eat and drink in a typical day and than consider what the long-term effects of your diet may be.

▶ Rethink the use of healthy ingredients in creative designs

There is a wide range of fruits and vegetables available to use in recipes as well as many different pulses, nuts, and cereal grains. In your coursework you are encouraged to be creative and innovative by adapting recipes and using different ingredients. Many of these ingredients will not only improve the nutritional content but also the taste, texture, colour and aroma of a product.

ACTIVITY

Scones are a low-fat product but they tend to be rather dry and boring. Adapt the following recipe to produce four new creative designs using ingredients recommended by the Eatwell Plate. Choose one of the designs and cook them.

Basic Scone Recipe

200 g self-raising flour
1 level tsp baking powder
50 g margarine
125 ml milk
Additional ingredients of your choice, about 50–75 g

Method:

- Pre heat the oven to 220 °c/gas no 7.
- Sieve the flour and baking powder into a mixing bowl.
- Rub the margarine into the flour with your fingertips.
- Now add any additional ingredients.
- Add the milk and mix together to form a soft dough with a knife.
- Put the dough on a slightly floured worksurface and knead gently.
- Roll out using your hands to a circle about 2 cm thick.
- Cut out into shapes using cutters or templates.
- Place on a greased baking sheet. Glaze with milk or anything else of your choice.
- Bake for 10 minutes. Cool on a rack.

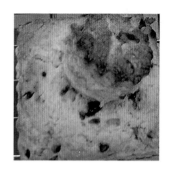

Figure 11.9 Ideas produced by some pupils

11.6 REPAIR

The function of nutrients in repairing and maintaining a healthy body

In Chapter 2 you learned all about the functions of nutrients and how important they are in maintaining a healthy body. You should now be able to understand how important it is for ourselves and society that we act responsibly when we choose our food.

The following activities will reinforce your knowledge and understanding of nutrients and their role.

KEY TERM

CARBON FOOTPRINT – the amount of carbon emissions produced in the growing, processing and distribution of our food

QUESTIONS

1. Nutritional needs vary at different stages of life.

Discuss what the nutritional needs of the following people are and give examples of how these needs can be met.

- A pregnant woman
- An elderly person
- A toddler (nine months to two years' old)
- A Vegan.

ACTIVITY

Produce a chart listing all the important nutrients and their role in keeping your body healthy.

CHAPTER 12

CONTROLLED ASSESSMENT UNIT A521 – INTRODUCTION TO DESIGNING AND MAKING

Controlled assessment forms a very important part of GCSE Food Technology as it accounts for 60 per cent of your final grade. If you are studying the Full Course GCSE you will need to produce two pieces of controlled assessment work:

- *Unit A521 – Introduction to Designing and Making*
  - *– 30% of the total GCSE marks (short course 60%)*
  - *– 20 hours controlled assessment*
- *Unit A523 – Making Quality Products*
  - *– 30% of the total GCSE marks*
  - *– 20 hours controlled assessment*

For the Short Course GCSE you will need to produce only the controlled assessment for Unit A521. Unit A523 is discussed in detail in Chapter 14.

12.1 GCSE CONTROLLED ASSESSMENT

The whole controlled assessment, including the final product for each unit, must not exceed 20 hours of work and should be undertaken under formal teacher supervision. Some of your work may be undertaken outside school under limited supervision, for example research work, taste/testing of products.

You will need to record your work throughout the whole process to produce a detailed portfolio. You should structure your work to follow the assessment criteria and present your work in section number order. Quality of work is more important than quantity.

Your work should be focused and appropriate ensuring that you include sufficient evidence to enable accurate assessments to be made.

The evidence you present for assessment must be submitted on paper or in electronic format. If submitted on paper you can use either A3 or A4 size paper. Sheets should be securely bound.

Electronic folios should be produced using PowerPoint. If you are putting sound and video clips into your folio it is important to remember to save the final copy using 'pack and go' before it is submitted to the examination board.

You must use appropriate ICT to help you with the work. This might include CAD/CAM, control programmes, data analysis and ICT based resources for research and design relevant to your task.

You should make your own judgements and decisions. Your teacher will advise, support and assist you. Sufficient work must be carried out under the direct supervision of your teacher for the whole of your work to be verified.

Throughout the controlled assessment you must remember that you will be expected to sign a declaration saying that the work is your own original work.

The completed portfolios will be marked by your teacher and moderated by OCR using the Assessment Criteria for this Unit.

Your projects will be marked against the following assessment objectives:

Assessment objectives		Controlled assessment Unit A521 Marks	Controlled assessment Unit A523 Marks
AO1	Recall, select and communicate knowledge and understanding in design and technology	16	
AO2	Apply knowledge, understanding and skills in designing and making products	37	52
AO3	Analysis and evaluate products	7	8
Total marks		60	60

Table 12.1 Assessment objectives for Units A521 and A523

Characteristics of successful portfolios

- Organising yourself and managing your portfolio is the single most important ingredient for success.
- Set yourself clear targets.
- If working on paper keep all your work in order in a folder. Be systematic in how you save files on the computer and how you transfer them between different computers. If you are producing an electronic folio using PowerPoint you must ensure that you save work regularly and keep a back-up copy of any files.
- Use your initiative.

- Take responsibility for keeping your portfolio on track.
- When carrying out tasks for the portfolio ask yourself:
  - Is this the best that it could be?
  - Have I thoroughly checked that I have covered all of the aspects that I need to?
- Train yourself not to do the minimum or to just meet the minimum standard to satisfy your teacher.
- Be self-critical and always ask yourself 'How can I improve my work further?'.
- Present your work clearly and concisely. Use a range of communication techniques, such as text, photographs, digital images, drawings, graphs.

- Relate all your work to your chosen task and product.

We will now look in detail at the work that you need to present for assessment Unit A521 controlled assessment:

- The assessment criteria – with the marks.

- What you need to do – the requirement for each section of the project.

- Using ICT – suggestions where/how ICT can be used.

- Examples – of students' coursework showing the type and quality of work you should aim to produce.

12.2 CONTROLLED ASSESSMENT UNIT A521 – INTRODUCTION TO DESIGNING AND MAKING

For this piece of controlled assessment you will be expected to design and make a creative and innovative food product. You must select one of the published products/themes set by OCR. Once selected, you then need to identify a starting point that is associated with the theme.

You will then be required to research, investigate and select an area of current dietary advice before designing a number of creative and innovative ideas which show consideration of your design specification.

Trialling and testing of ideas will allow you to demonstrate your ability to plan, carry out a range of practical skills and evaluate before arriving at a final solution. You will be expected to critically evaluate existing products and your own final product.

Now let's get started

In order to skilfully design, model, make and test your final product you need to undertake the following processes.

Select a product/theme from the OCR published list and identify a starting point associated with your chosen product/theme. The list of product/themes will be reviewed by OCR every two years, so it is important that the product/theme you choose is from the current OCR Specification. Your teachers will be able to give you details of the current product/themes.

Remember all the work you produce must relate to your chosen product/theme and starting point.

You must develop a new product which meets an identified aspect of current healthy eating guidelines, for example:

- reduce intake of fat
- reduce intake of sugar
- reduce intake of salt
- increase intake of fibre.

Product/Theme	Outline/Starting point
Celebrations	A product suitable for a special occasion and an identified target group
Special diets	A product for a chosen special diet
Luxury products	A luxury product which will appeal to an identified target group
Ready meal	A ready meal for an identified target group
Food products from around the world	A product from a chosen country which will appeal to an identified target group
Staple foods	A product based on a chosen staple food and an identified target group
Protein foods	A product based on a protein food/foods which will appeal to an identified target group
'Eating on the go'	A product that can be 'eaten on the go' for an identified target group
'Filling the energy gap'	A product that will fill the 'energy gap' which will appeal to an identified target group
'Filling the energy gap'	A product that can be 'eaten outside the home' which will appeal to an identified target group

Table 12.2 OCR themes for examination in 2010

Assessment criteria and marks

Cultural understanding

	Cultural understanding	Marks
Basic ability requires constant support and help	Identifies using one or two simple examples of how cultural issues have influenced the range of food products available today	0–1
	Identifies using one or two examples how wise choice of food products can promote healthy lifestyles	
Demonstrates ability, some help & guidance given	Identifies using examples of how cultural issues have influenced the range of food products available today	2–3
	Identifies using examples how wise choice of food products can promote healthy lifestyles	
Works competently with independence	Identifies using appropriate examples of how cultural issues have influenced the range of food products available today	4–5
	Identifies and compares using examples how wise choice of food products can promote healthy lifestyles	

Table 12.3 Cultural understanding

Through research using the internet (ICT-based research), textbooks, food magazines, etc. you are required to identify and record:

- how changes in society, including cultural issues have influenced the range of food products available today

- how wise choice of food products can promote healthy lifestyles, e.g. in terms of intake of fat, sugar, salt and fibre.

Initial research

To begin with you need to collect and present information on how changes in society have influenced the products available today and how wise food choices can help promote healthy lifestyles. Students tend to collect and present too much information at this early stage. Only collect information that is *relevant*.

Look at Figure 12.1 which shows the information presented by a student regarding current dietary advice. Read the examiner's comments below so you can see the standard you should be aiming for. It is not necessary to give specific detailed medical information about the dangers of eating certain foods.

Examiner's comments
Good points

- A lot of information has obviously been researched by the student but this has been summarised well.

- The summary is in the student's own words and is not a direct copy from books or other sources.

- Only the main facts have been presented.

- The student has considered up-to-date information on how wise choice of foods can promote healthy lifestyles.

Areas for improvement

- The student could have stated all sources of this information, e.g. research findings from doctors.

Promoting Healthy Lifestyles

There are many reasons why people eat or wish to eat healthy foods. These include:

- For your own general wellbeing
- To look better
- To increase calcium content in body which benefits bones and teeth
- To lose weight
- To improve general energy
- To keep fit
- To feel better

Food experts can now prove that having a poor diet can have serious effects on your health, whether it affects our health now or in the long term.

The links between diet and health continue to be researched. It has now been shown that obesity is linked to energy intake; heart disease to total fat intake and possibly total food intake; dental care to sugar intake; many diseases of the large bowel to dietary fibre intake and possibly high blood pressure; and stroke to salt intake.

Doctors are worried about the number of children/teenagers who are overweight and who eat a lot of fatty and sugary food. These children/teenagers may look perfectly all right now but doctors know that in 10 years' or 20 years' time they will probably suffer from many problems.

The government has identified eight guidelines for a healthy diet.

- Enjoy your food
- Eat a variety of different foods
- Eat the right amount to be a healthy weight
- Eat foods rich in starch and fibre
- Don't eat too much fat
- Don't eat sugary foods too often
- Look after the vitamins and minerals in your food
- If you drink alcohol, keep within sensible limits

To help us to follow these guidelines the Foods Standards Agency has produced the Eatwell Plate.

The Eatwell Plate is based on the 5 food groups.

- Bread, rice, potatoes, pasta and other starchy foods
- Fruit and vegetables
- Milk and dairy foods
- Meat, fish, eggs, beans and other non-dairy sources of protein
- Foods and drinks high in fat and/or sugar

This is a diagram of the Eatwell Plate which is divided up to show the proportions of groups of foods that a person should eat. It encourages people to choose different foods from the first four groups every day, to ensure they remain healthy. Foods from the fifth group, those high in fat and/or sugar, are not essential to a healthy diet.

Do not be misled by the plate. It is not necessary to eat all these foods in one meal. If the balance is achieved over a day and a variety of foods is chosen, people will be healthy and consume the range of nutrients their body needs.

Figure 12.1 How wise food choices can help promote healthy lifestyles

Creativity

	Creativity	Marks
Basic ability requires constant support and help	Makes simple/limited links between principles of good design and technological knowledge Existing products identified with some evaluation	0–1
Demon-strates ability, some help & guidance given	Identifies associations linking principles of good design and technological knowledge Existing products identified considering some of the needs of the intended user	2–3
Works competently with indep-endence	Identifies complex associations linking principles of good design and technological knowledge Existing products identified and fully evaluated against the needs of the intended user	4–5

Table 12.4 Creativity

Step 1

- Through investigation, for example a questionnaire/interviews, you are expected to identify your target group, the qualities required for the design of a creative, innovative food product for that group and research associated with your area of current dietary advice, for example:

  - lower in fat – no more than 5 g per 100 g portion

  - low in sugar – no more than 5 g per 100 g portion

  - low in salt – no more than 0.3 g per 100 g portion or no more than 0.1 g sodium per 100 g portion

  - high in fibre – at least 6 g per portion.

  - Salt is also called sodium chloride. Salt = 2.5 x sodium. When you work out how much salt is in a recipe, multiply the sodium by 2.5. Sodium is sometimes measured in milligrams (mg). There a 1,000 mg in 1 g so 600 mg = 0.6 g.

- You can use ICT to design the questionnaire and to present your findings

- You are then required to arrive at your chosen design brief, e.g. Design and make a lower-in-fat cook-chill ready meal aimed at teenagers.

Your research will involve you obtaining information from consumers through a questionnaire and/or interviews to arrive at a design brief. The aim of this research is to find out the qualities consumers would like to see in a creative, innovative food product, who the target group for your product is and the area of current dietary advice that your portfolio will focus on.

Your questionnaire and/or interview needs to be designed so it helps you extract specific information from people. The questions need to be clear, easy to understand and answer. It should also be easy for you to collate the results. You might also use this method of research to generate possible ideas for products. The questionnaire should be given to 12 people but you should only include one sample of a completed questionnaire in your project. You should produce your collated results as graphs, tally charts, etc, before analysing them and drawing conclusions.

Figure 12.2 shows a questionnaire from a student who chose the theme 'Luxury Products', with the chosen product being a dessert. The student's presentation of results through graphs and written analysis for a number of the questions are shown in Figure 12.3.

Examiner's Comments on Figure 12.2

Good Points:

- A clear introduction that sets the scene and focuses respondents on the theme so thoughts are clear.
- Questions are short and concise encouraging respondents to think about their responses.
- The range of questions asked allows the student to collect the information required.
- Use of closed and open-ended questions. Closed – can be a very quick way of finding out specific information and results are collated easily. Open-ended – can produce a wide variety of responses, give some interesting results and could give valuable information to the way forward or an idea not previously thought about.

Areas for improvement:

- Question 2 needs to be phrased a little more clearly to indicate the type of response required.
- Question 4 is limited in terms of possible responses.
- There needs to be a question asking which target group the product should be aimed at.

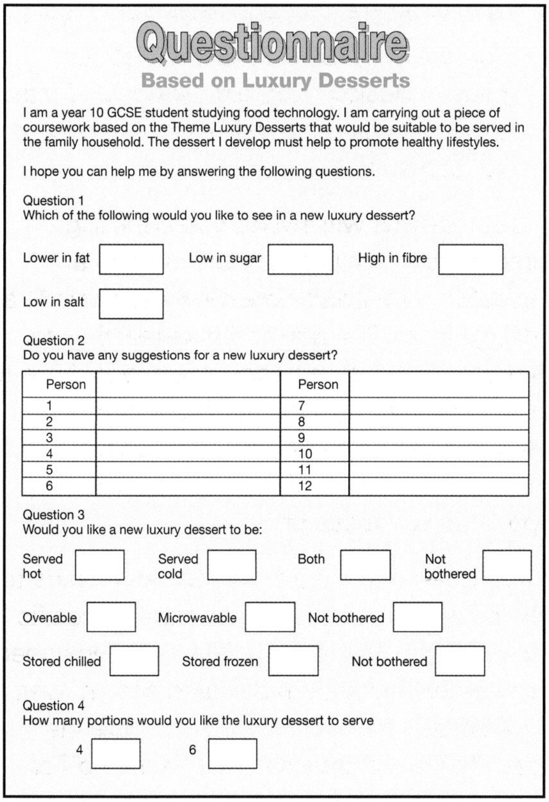

Questionnaire

Based on Luxury Desserts

I am a year 10 GCSE student studying food technology. I am carrying out a piece of coursework based on the Theme Luxury Desserts that would be suitable to be served in the family household. The dessert I develop must help to promote healthy lifestyles.

I hope you can help me by answering the following questions.

Question 1
Which of the following would you like to see in a new luxury dessert?

Lower in fat ☐ Low in sugar ☐ High in fibre ☐

Low in salt ☐

Question 2
Do you have any suggestions for a new luxury dessert?

Person		Person	
1		7	
2		8	
3		9	
4		10	
5		11	
6		12	

Question 3
Would you like a new luxury dessert to be:

Served hot ☐ Served cold ☐ Both ☐ Not bothered ☐

Ovenable ☐ Microwavable ☐ Not bothered ☐

Stored chilled ☐ Stored frozen ☐ Not bothered ☐

Question 4
How many portions would you like the luxury dessert to serve

4 ☐ 6 ☐

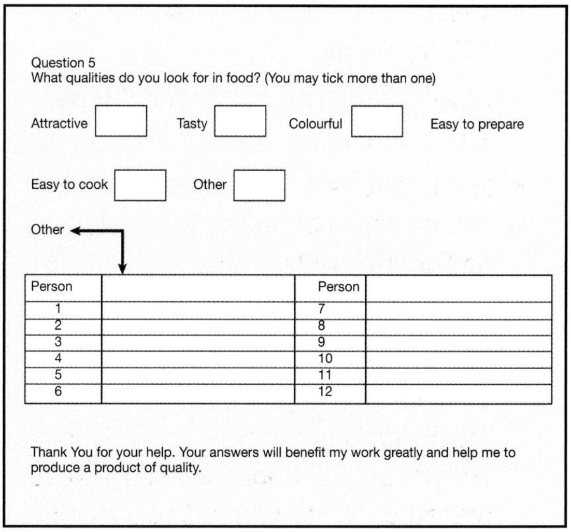

Question 5
What qualities do you look for in food? (You may tick more than one)

Attractive ☐ Tasty ☐ Colourful ☐ Easy to prepare

Easy to cook ☐ Other ☐

Other

Person		Person	
1		7	
2		8	
3		9	
4		10	
5		11	
6		12	

Thank You for your help. Your answers will benefit my work greatly and help me to produce a product of quality.

Figure 12.2 Carrying out initial research through a questionnaire

Graphs based on Questionaire results

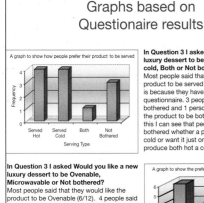

A graph to show how people prefer their product to be served

In Question 3 I asked Would you like a new luxury dessert to be served hot, served cold, Both or Not bothered?
Most people said that they would like the product to be served Hot (4) or Cold (4). This is because they have equal tallies on the questionnaire. 3 people said they weren't bothered and 1 person said they would like the product to be both hot and cold. From this I can see that people either aren't bothered whether a product is served hot or cold or want it just once so I may have to produce both hot a cold option.

In Question 3 I asked Would you like a new luxury dessert to be Ovenable, Microwavable or Not bothered?
Most people said that they would like the product to be Ovenable (6/12). 4 people said they would like a new product to be microwavable and the other 2 said they were not bothered how it needed to be cooked. This shows that the new product will need to be ovenable.

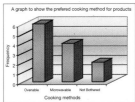

A graph to show the prefered cooking method for products

In Question 3 I also asked Would you like a new luxury dessert to be stored Chilled, Frozen or Not bothered?
Most people said that they would like e product to be Chilled (8) rather than being frozen (4). 2 people said that they were not bothered whether the product was chilled or frozen.

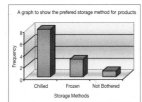

A graph to show the prefered storage method for products

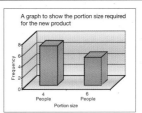

A graph to show the portion size required for the new product

In Question 4 I asked Would you like a new luxury dessert to serve 6 or 4 people?
Most people said that they would like the product to serve 4 people (6) rather than 6 (4).

In Question 5 I asked What qualities do you look for in food products?
Tasty (12) and attractive (10) came up as the most popular quality wanted in a product. Colourful and easy to prepare also came up in quite a lot as a required quality.

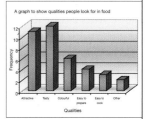

A graph to show qualities people look for in food

Examiner's comments

- The student has clearly analysed each graph and come to conclusions.
- ICT has been used effectively to present the results.
- All work is presented concisely.

Figure 12.3 Analysing the results of a questionnaire

Through this initial research the student arrived at the following design brief:

Design and make a lower-in-fat luxury dessert suitable to be served in a family household.

Step 2

- Using at least one method of research, such as the internet (ICT-based research), textbooks, leaflets, etc., you are required to identify and record data to help you design a creative innovative product. The data should be relevant to your design brief.

- You should then carry out further research relevant to your design brief. You need to ask yourself what additional information is needed. You should use at least one method of research, for example the internet, textbooks, and the information presented should be relevant, summarised so it is concise and in your own words.

For example:

- ways of reducing fat content in products
- what a diabetic can and cannot eat
- the products already available for your chosen culture
- the range of products suitable to be included in a packed lunch box
- functions of ingredients.

Step 3

- Using one method of research, such as supermarket survey, the internet (ICT research), packaging (ICT scanning), tasting sessions, etc., you are required to identify four appropriate existing products. You should critically evaluate how these meet the identified qualities required for a creative innovative product. Findings could be presented in a chart with a conclusion. One further product should be evaluated in detail.

Your final stage is to evaluate some existing products so you can see what products are already available and consider how they meet your identified needs. Carrying out this research may also give you some ideas for the designing stage of your project.

Figure 12.4 shows how one student has evaluated a range of existing desserts against the needs identified in her questionnaire. Four products have been evaluated by using a chart, then one of the products has been evaluated in more depth.

Evaluation of existing products

Name of product	Dessert	Lower in sugar no more than 5g/ 100g	Aimed at 5-19 year olds	Sold chilled	4+ portions	Attractive /10	Colourful /10	Easy to prepare and cook /10	Tasty /10	Good portion size /10	£3-£4 pounds
Heinz weight watchers Tiramisu	Yes	No (27.8)	Yes	No (Frozen)	No (2 in a box)	8	6	6	8	8	Unknown
Somerfield's sticky toffee pudding	Yes	No (45.0)	Yes	No (Frozen)	Yes (serves 4)	7	8	6	9	6	Unknown
Weight watchers toffee chocolate dessert	Yes	No (27.1)	No	No (Frozen)	No (2 in a box)	7	7	7	8	8	No (£1.29)
Weight watchers Raspberry trifle	Yes	No (13.7)	Yes	No (Frozen)	No (2 in a box)	8	7	8	6	8	Unknown

Conclusion

Looking at the four products I could only find the price for one of the products I evaluated I have looked at every supermarket website (Sainsbury's, Somerfield's, Morrison's, Tesco and Netto) and still didn't manage to find the price of each product. I have therefore written. The weight watchers toffee chocolate dessert was under price identified by my target group. Looking at the 4 products I found that only 1 scored 3 yes's. So I decided to add up the marks for Attractive, Colourful, Easy to prepare and cook, tasty and good portion size. The result, was that Weight watchers raspberry trifle and Weight watchers chocolate toffee dessert both scored the same and they both scored 7/10 for colourfulness Heinz weight watchers tiramisu met the least required needs. None of the existing products were sold chilled and only 1/4 of them had 4 or more portions. If I look at all the results it is clear there is room in the market for a new lower in sugar desset which is aimed at teenagers as not one product that I evaluated met all the teenagers identified needs.

Detailed Evaluation   Weight watchers toffee chocolate dessert

The weight watchers toffee chocolate dessert is a dessert. The sugar content per 100g is 27.1g so it is not lower in sugar and the required sugar amount is 5g per 100g. I do not think it is aimed at 5-19 year olds because it is a dietary product which normally adults start diets to lose weight and not children or teenagers. but I think the product itself and the ingredients it contains would be aimed at 5-19 year olds this is because it contains chocolate and toffee which is what children like and teenagers to eat however the product is more marketable as a dietary product because if teenagers go on diets then they will want to buy 'weight watchers' product. The product is not chilled but stored frozen so this does not meet my identified needs. In a box there are only 2 portions and my target group require 4+. So again another identified need has not been met. The attractiveness of the product is high because it catches the eye. Colourfulness and tasty both score high because the ingredients will taste really nice together and the colour of the product is good the product is a nice shade of brown. It is a good portion size because it is the right size for a dessert and it is easy to prepare and cook because you only have to defrost the product. The price of the product is £1.29 which is well below the £4 suggested.

Figure 12.4 Evaluating existing products

Examiner's Comments

- Existing products have been fully evaluated against the identified needs of the user

- Appropriate products i.e. desserts, have been chosen to evaluate

- The required number of products have been evaluated i.e. four in the chart and one in detail. The student could have selected a different product from the four already evaluated in the chart to evaluate in detail

- The results from the chart have been analysed in a detailed conclusion showing a thorough understanding of the work

- There is evidence of a suitable product being evaluated in detail.

Designing

Designing		Marks
Basic ability requires constant support and help	Using results from research and a brief produce a simple specification for the product	
	Record design ideas using simple techniques	
	Apply simple trialling procedures	
	Make some decisions about the ingredients and equipment for the final product	0–4
Demonstrates ability, some help & guidance given	Using results from research and a brief produces a suitable specification for the product	
	Record creative design ideas through appropriate techniques	
	Apply trialling procedures	
	Make decisions about ingredients and equipment and any changes that need to be made to the final product	5–10
Works competently with independence	Using results from research and a brief produces a detailed specification for the product	
	Record creative and innovative design ideas using appropriate presentation techniques	
	Apply detailed trialling procedures	
	Make reasoned decisions about ingredients and equipment and any changes that need to be made to the final product	11–14

Table 12.5 **Designing**

Step 1

- Using results from your research and your design brief you are expected to develop a design specification for a creative innovative product.

Whenever a new product is made the designer has to produce a specification. At this stage it is called a design specification as the criteria used are general points and not specific to one product.

To produce your design specification for this portfolio you must look back at your design brief, the needs identified from your questionnaire and any other relevant research. The identified needs from your questionnaire are particularly important and the examiner will be looking to ensure that you have included these when you design your specification.

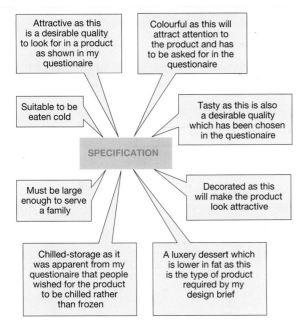

Attractive as this is a desirable quality to look for in a product as shown in my questionaire

Colourful as this will attract attention to the product and has to be asked for in the questionaire

Suitable to be eaten cold

Tasty as this is also a desirable quality which has been chosen in the questionaire

SPECIFICATION

Must be large enough to serve a family

Decorated as this will make the product look attractive

Chilled-storage as it was apparent from my questionaire that people wished for the product to be chilled rather than frozen

A luxery dessert which is lower in fat as this is the type of product required by my design brief

Figure 12.5 Example of a detailed design specification written for the design brief *Design and make a lower-in-fat luxury dessert suitable to be served in a family household*

Step 2

- Using existing recipes, you are required to select four products for trialling that allow you to demonstrate a range of practical skills appropriate to your brief. For example, peeling, chopping, grating, meat preparation, shaping, rolling, sauce making (roux, blended, all-in-one), kneading, piping, skills used in the different methods of cake, biscuit and pastry making. For each of the three products, you are expected to produce a creative and innovative idea by using appropriate presentation techniques which show consideration of your design specification (ICT graphical drawings).

- Show evidence of testing by three tasters, e.g. tasting charts, star profiles.

- Evaluate each product against the design specification.

- Discuss any improvements that need to be made to the product.

You need to select four appropriate products for trialling that allow you to demonstrate a range of practical skills. To gain ideas you could:

- look back at your research to see if people suggested any ideas for suitable products

- look in magazines, leaflets, etc.

- look in recipe books to see if there are any appropriate recipes

- look on the internet for suitable recipes etc.

You could list the different ideas that you find to give you time to think and make decisions as to which products you will trial. Remember to make a note of where you find the recipe(s) so you can quickly find the recipe again should you want to use it for trialling.

There are many different ways of presenting your design ideas. You could use labelled diagrams/drawings, text, etc. For each product to be trialled you need to:

- list the ingredients you will use

- explain clearly the modifications/adaptations you are making to the recipe to produce creative and innovative ideas that meet your design brief. Give reasons for these modifications/adaptations.

- list the practical skills you will use

- analyse the recipe, according to the nutritional focus of your design brief (ICT nutritional analysis programme

- make each product and provide photographic evidence (ICT use of digital camera)

- show evidence of testing by three tasters, e.g. tasting charts, star profiles

- evaluate the product against each point in your design specification
- discuss any improvements that could be made to the product, taking into account users' views.

You then need to choose the trialled ideas that will be your final product and record this decision.

The stages shown in red will be awarded marks from the making section of the assessment criteria during your designing work.

Look at Figure 12.6 and then read the examiner's comments. This design idea relates to a design brief for a high-fibre ready-cook chill meal suitable for busy professionals.

Examiner's comments

Good points:

- An existing recipe is used as the basis for the design idea.
- All ingredients are listed with quantities.
- Adaptations to the original recipe are given and explained.
- Nutritional analysis is evident in relation to the dietary focus – high fibre.
- Ideas are presented concisely and clearly.
- Photographic evidence is evident.
- Three tasters with results displayed in a tasting chart.

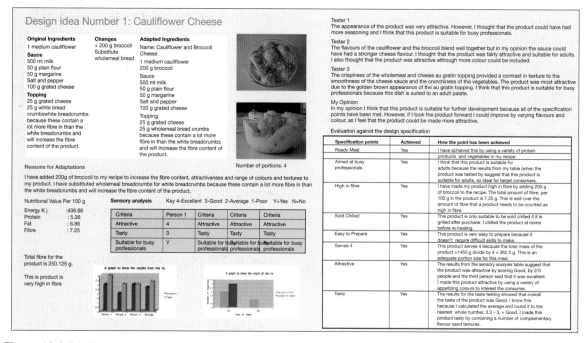

Figure 12.6 Trialling a design idea for a high-fibre product aimed at busy professionals

- Improvements have been suggested by tasters and the student.
- Evaluation is against the design specification. Comments show some consideration of tasters' opinions.

Areas for improvement:

- The student could have been more creative with his idea.
- To increase fibre other vegetables, ingredients could have been used which are higher in fibre than broccoli.
- Practical skills have not been listed.
- Evaluation against the design specification could have included more detailed evidence from testers as this would have reflected more detailed conclusions.
- Suggestions for improvements to the product could have been more specific.

Step 3

- You are required to choose one of your trialled ideas for the final product.

Record your decision.

You are required to show evidence for the planning of your final product by:

- giving reasoned decisions for any changes that you need to make to your product showing consideration to the comments given when your product was originally trialled
- giving reasoned decisions for the choice of your final ingredients and equipment.

You need to state which design idea you have chosen to be your final product. Look back at the product when it was originally trialled to see whether you need to make any changes

before making your final product. Look at the comments made by tasters, your own opinions and the nutritional analysis in terms of your nutritional focus. You need to then state the changes you are going to make with reasons.

Any suggestions you make regarding modifying the nutritional content will be awarded to the making section of the assessment criteria.

You then need to list your final ingredients/components giving reasons for choice and applying relevant nutritional data. Marks for comments on nutritional data will be awarded to the making section of the assessment criteria.

List the equipment you will use explaining what job each piece of equipment will be used for.

Making

- Carry out nutritional analysis of your product with reference to your design brief (ICT nutritional analysis program).
- Produce a plan for the making of your final product, e.g. flowchart.

You need to analyse your final recipe, according to the nutritional focus of your design brief (ICT nutritional analysis program).

A detailed flowchart should show an effective order of the sequences required for making your final product.

Figure 12.7 shows an example of a detailed flowchart written for the design brief *Design and make a lower-in-fat Italian product aimed at teenagers.*

You should then make your final product and provide photographic evidence of the result (ICT use of digital camera).

	Making	Marks
Basic ability requires constant support and help	Organise activities Select and use appropriate ingredients Select and use appropriate equipment Work safely and hygienically Prepare, shape, form, mix, assemble and finish food products Products will exhibit a reasonable standard of outcome (photographic evidence)	0–6
	Apply limited nutritional knowledge	0–1
	Produce a simple flowchart for the final product	0–1
Demonstrates ability, some help & guidance given	Organise activities Select and use appropriate ingredients Select and use appropriate equipment Work safely and hygienically Work effectively to prepare, shape, form, mix, assemble and finish food products Products will exhibit a good standard of outcome (photographic evidence)	7–13
	Apply nutritional knowledge to suggest a possible modification to design ideas	2–3
	Produce a flowchart that includes all key stages for the final product	2–3
Works competently with independence	Organise activities Select and use appropriate ingredients Select and use appropriate equipment Work safely and hygienically Work skilfully to prepare, shape, form, mix, assemble and finish food products Products will exhibit a high-quality outcome (photographic evidence)	14–20
	Apply detailed nutritional knowledge to suggest possible modifications to design ideas	4
	Produce a detailed flowchart that specifies an effective order of sequences for the final product	4

Table 12.6 **Making**

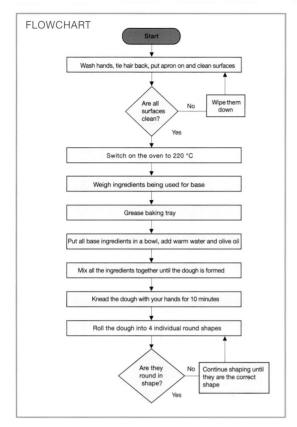

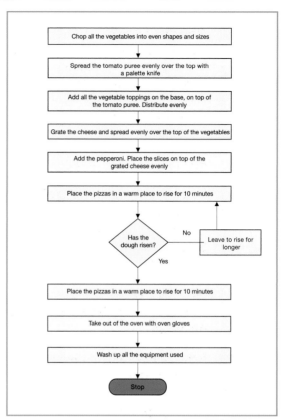

Figure 12.7 Flowchart for a pizza

Evaluation

	Evaluation	Marks
Basic ability requires constant support and help	• Evaluation through superficial testing • There will be little or no use of specialist terms. • Information may be ambiguous or disorganised • Errors of spelling, punctuation or grammar may be intrusive	0–2
Demonstrates ability, some help & guidance given	• Evaluation with reference to the specification through relevant testing leading to a possible improvement • There will be some use of specialist terms, although these may not always be used appropriately • The information will be presented for the most part in a structured format • There may be occasional errors in spelling, punctuation and or grammar	3–5
Works competently with independence	• Critical evaluation related to the specification through detailed testing with meaningful conclusions leading to suggestions for possible improvements • Specialist terms will be used appropriately and correctly • The information will be presented in a structured format • The candidate can demonstrate the accurate use of spelling, punctuation and grammar	6–8

Table 12.7 Evaluation

You are expected to:

- show evidence of testing by five tasters, e.g. tasting chart, star profile
- critically evaluate your final product against your design specification and your design brief and suggest modifications to improve your product.

Evaluation is all about making judgements. Your comments need to show how successful you have been in terms of your design specification and your design brief. Comments from testers can support your views and they can be given as evidence when you offer conclusions for your work. It is a good idea to ask your testers how the product can be improved as this will help you suggest further modifications.

Figure 12.8 shows an example of a testing chart completed by five people for the design

brief *Design and make a lower-in-fat luxury dessert suitable to be served in a family household.*

An evaluation of the final product can be seen in Figure 12.9.

Examiner's comments

Good points:

- The student has evaluated against her design specification in detail and has given evidence from her testers to give conclusions.
- All points in her specification have been evaluated.
- The evaluation does show evidence of a critical analysis as she has recognised some weakness in her work.

Areas for improvement:

- Some points have been identified for improvements to the product but more detail could have been given here. For example the product did not score full marks on tasty so this is an area that suggestions for improvement could have been made.

Tasting and testing for the final product

I have chosen 5 people to taste my final product.

Specification	Person 1	Person 2	Person 3	Person 4	Person 5	Average
Low in sugar	5	5	5	5	5	5
Luxury dessert	5	5	5	5	5	5
Attractive	5	5	5	5	5	5
Colourful	5	5	5	5	4	4.8
Tasty	5	5	5	5	5	5
Good portion size	5	5	5	5	5	5
Decorated	5	5	5	5	5	5
Suitable to be served in a family home	5	5	5	5	5	5

Key 1 = Poor 2 = Satisfactory 3 = Good 4 = Very good 5 = Excellent

Comments
Person 1 The product looked attractive to the eye and I believe it would appropriate for a family.
Person 2 I liked the different flavours of the cheesecake.
Person 3 I think that the base was a bit too chocolaty but otherwise I found the product fine.
Person 4 I found the product very successful on all the specification points.
Person 5 I found the colour off the cheesecake a little off putting but otherwise fine.

Photograph of the product

Did you find the colour of the decoration attractive? (please tick appropriate box)

Yes ▢   No ▢

Was the chocolate a nice flavour for the base (please tick appropriate box)

Yes ▢   No ▢

Figure 12.8 Tasting and testing the final product

Evaluation

Looking back at my design brief which was **Design and make a lower-in-fat luxury dessert suitable to be served in a family household** the aim now is to see whether I have been successful.

Evaluation against my Design Specification
The first specification point **suitable to be served in a family household**, the five tasters rated this point 4.2 on average (5, 4, 4, 4, and 5). This was good marks and I was pleased with this. As my product was tasted by my family this shows that it would be suitable for the whole family as everybody said they enjoyed it.
The second point was **lower in fat**. It was obvious to both the testers and me that the fat content was very low indeed for the type of product and that is why my product was rated highly at 4.8/5 on average (5, 5, 5, 5 and 4). The fat content of my final product was 4.98g per 100g. I made my cheesecake low in fat by using low fat cheese and low fat yoghurt. I also removed the oats from the base, added raisins and cherries to the base and added extra fruit for a topping to bulk out the ingredients which then lowered the fat content further.
The next point my product must be is **suitable to be eaten cold** so obviously my product meets this point well because a cheesecake has to be served cold gaining 5/5 on average (5, 5, 5, 5 and 5).
Another thing my product should be is **tasty**. This was given 4.2/5 on average which is pretty good but could be better. To make the cheesecake tasty I added plenty of lemon, extra ingredients to the base and added a fruit topping.
The next point is that the product should be **attractive and colourful**. In the table I can see that the testers all gave the product 4 out of 5 giving the product an average of 4. I believe that the product was very colourful because of the fruit topping. I should have asked the testers how I could have improved this score as this is one are that would need to be improved. It would have been better to split these two points in my tasting chart then I would have known where the improvements needed to be made.
Decorated is the next possible point to compare my product against. I found that this got an average of 4.8 which is very good. I think this is down to the chunks of strawberry and orange used to decorate the top of the cheesecakes.
Can be chilled is a specification point that got full marks 5/5 because it must be chilled to stay fresh. Finally all my testers thought that the cheesecake was large enough to serve 4 portions.

Figure 12.9 Evaluating the final product

CHAPTER 13

UNIT A522 – SUSTAINABLE DESIGN

By the end of this section you should have developed a knowledge and understanding of:

- the 6Rs – recycle, reuse, reduce, refuse, rethink and repair in relation to food technology
- social issues
- moral issues
- cultural issues
- environmental issues
- design issues.

13.1 INTRODUCTION TO SUSTAINABLE DESIGN

This unit of the GCSE course aims to develop your knowledge and understanding of sustainability, environmental concerns, cultural, moral and social issues. You will work through this unit in Food Technology.

You will look at how design and technology have evolved through analysing food products from the past and the present. You will need to consider how future designs and products will impact on the world in which we live.

By looking at food trends you will gain an awareness and understanding of developments and innovations in the design, manufacture, labelling and packaging of food products and the impact that these have on the environment, society and the economy.

Moral, cultural, economic, environmental and sustainability issues are important in food technology.

Through this unit you will develop a knowledge and understanding of:

- what we mean by the 6Rs in relation to food products
- the social issues governing the trends in food consumption
- the moral issues concerning food production
- the impact of cultural issues on food products
- how to select ingredients/materials that are both suitable and sustainable
- current issues affecting the design of new products.

Also see Chapter 11 for more detailed information on sustainable design.

The assessment of this unit is through an externally set and marked examination:

- The paper will consist of questions that focus on sustainable design.
- This assessment unit can be taken in either the January or June examination session.
- The unit can be retaken once, with the best result used.
- It represents 20 per cent of a full GCSE qualification or 10 per cent of a Short Course qualification.
- The maximum mark for the unit is 60.
- The duration of the examination is 1 hour and the paper is divided into two sections.

Section A consists of 15 short-answer questions. They will be a mixture of multiple choice, one-word answers and true or false questions. The section will carry 15 marks in total. It is expected that you will spend 15 minutes on this section

Exemplar question:

Which of the following is **not** a renewable energy resource?

a. water

b. coal

c. wind

d. solar power

Section B consists of three questions requiring answers that may involve sketching, annotation, short answers and more extended writing which will require you to relate your knowledge and understanding of the 6 Rs and product analysis to the design of food products. Each question will be marked out of 15 marks. It is expected you will spend 45 minutes on this section. One of the questions marked with an asterisk (*) will also be marked for the quality of written communication.

Exemplar question:

- Products become 'obsolete' after a few years. Discuss the difference between fashion and planned obsolescence.

Key skills to achieve high marks in this unit are:

- think, with an 'open' mind about design and be aware of current dietary advice
- recall, select, use and communicate your knowledge and understanding of sustainability concepts and issues within food technology
- develop innovation and flair in the design of food products. Be able to produce high-quality designs using detailed annotation and sketches
- seek out and use information from chefs, existing food products and manufacturers
- analyse and evaluate design and production skills and techniques in existing products
- understand ingredients and components in food products
- consider how past and present design technology affects society
- develop an understanding of the wider effects of sustainability, society, the economy and the environment on the development of food products.

13.2 THE 6 RS

RECYCLE	How can it do the job better? Is it energy efficient? Has it been designed for disassembly?
REUSE	Which parts can I use again? Has it another valuable use without processing it?
REDUCE	How easy is it to take apart? How can the parts be used again? How much energy to reprocess parts?
REFUSE	Which parts can be replaced? Which parts are going to fail? How easy is it to replace parts?
RETHINK	Which parts are not needed? Do we need as much material? Can we simplify the product?
REPAIR	Is it really necessary? Is it going to last? Is it fair trade? Is it unfashionable to be trendy and too costly to be stylish?

Table 13.1 The 6 Rs

Recycle

Recycling is what we do with the objects we use in our daily lives when we have finished with them. Recycling is taking apart an existing product that is no longer required and reprocessing the material for use in a new product. The process of recycling does however require energy for reprocessing and transportation.

Figure 13.1 Recycling logo

Why recycle?

Everything we dispose of goes somewhere, although once the container or bag of rubbish is out of our hands and out of our houses we forget it instantly. Our consumer lifestyle is rapidly filling up landfill sites all over the world. As this happens our concerns for the environment grows. When designing and making a new product designers and manufacturers need to consider how their product can be recycled at the end of its life cycle.

ACTIVITY

There are many different recycling logos. Using the internet and existing products, record the different logos you have found and say what types of products they are used on.

The three main types of recycling are as follows.

Primary recycling

This is the secondhand use of products, for example:

- using a plastic carrier bag as a bin liner in your peddle bin
- ice cream tubs or margarine cartons used to store dry ingredients
- glass jars reused for storage or homemade jams and pickles
- re using carrier bags for shopping
- eating leftover food – this can be classed as recycling as well as reusing.

Figure 13.2 Re-use of a carrier bag

Secondary or physical recycling

This is the process in which waste materials are recycled into different types of products. Some products can be left to biodegrade before being regenerated into something else, for example raw vegetable waste can be composted. Foods that can be composted are:

- raw vegetable and fruit waste
- egg shells
- cardboard.

See Chapter 11 for more detail.

Packaging used for food is often difficult to recycle, however biodegradable packaging such as 'potatopak' has been developed.

When manufacturers are packaging food products they need to consider:

- the type of packaging material used
- where the materials come from
- how the packaging can be disposed of and the effects this might have on the environment.

ACTIVITY

Look at a range of products and complete a chart like the one in Table 13.2.

Product	Packaging material	Can the material be recycled?	What could it be recycled into?
Chocolate bar	Paper Foil	Yes	Recycled paper, e.g. writing paper Metal product

Table 13.2 Recycling possibilities

Tertiary or chemical recycling

Products are broken down and reformulated, for example:

- Plastic bottles can be recycled into fibres and then respun into polyester to make fleece fabric used for coats and blankets.
- Composting could be classed as this as the vegetables are broken down into matter that can then be put back on the garden.

Most if not all things can be recycled in some way. Recyclable materials include glass, paper, metals, plastics and food waste.

Figure 13.3 Recycling – plastic, metal, glass and paper

Food manufacturers have to consider carefully the materials they choose to package food products in. Table 13.3 shows the advantages and disadvantages of different food packaging materials. Further information can also be found in Chapter 7.

Some manufacturers are reusing or recycling food packaging and making them into new products.

Figure 13.4 Shopping bag made from recycled drink cartons

QUESTIONS

1. What does the term recycling mean?
2. List three products that can be recycled.
3. Name a material made from recycled products.

KEY TERM

RECYCLE – to reuse a product

Packaging material	Benefits/Advantages	Limitations/Disadvantages
Glass	Recyclable Can be made from recycled glass Can be moulded in a variety of shapes Can be reused in the home to store other products Contents can be seen Withstands high temperatures Strong Cheap to produce	Easily broken Heavy
Metals including foil and cans	Recyclable Strong Withstands high temperatures Lightweight Easy to store Variety of different shapes produced	Cannot see the food Cannot be used in the microwave
Plastic	Some are biodegradable (these plastics can be expensive) Cheap to produce Can be moulded into a variety of shapes Available in different thickness Can be used in the microwave Easy to print on Lightweight and waterproof Most do not react with foods Can be transparent or coloured Can be heat resistant	Can be difficult to dispose of Made initially from oil – a non-sustainable source A lot of plastic is still not recyclable
Paper/card	Recyclable Biodegradable Can be made from recycled material Cheap to produce Can come from sustainable sources Available in different thickness /weights Easy to print on Can be laminated Lightweight Variety of shapes	Can tear easily Not waterproof unless it is laminated Easily crushed

Table 13.3 Advantages and disadvantages of packaging materials

▶ Reuse

This mean taking an existing product that has become waste and using the material (food) for another product without further processing.

- Products can be reused for either the same purpose or designed into a new product. This will reduce waste and encourage the conservation of our materials and resources.

- Food products and ingredients can be used in the home but because of food safety and regulations this cannot be done on a large scale.

It is estimated that 6.7 million tonnes of food waste is produced each year in the UK. Most of this food could have been eaten if we had planned more efficiently.

Figure 13.5 How surplus tomatoes can be used

 ACTIVITY

Suggest how these leftover foods could be used in a new dishes:

- Mashed potato
- Cold chicken
- Cold pasta
- Stale bread.

Make one of these dishes and evaluate how successful you have been in using the leftover food.

Figure 13.6 Shepherd's pie made using leftover potato

Reduce

This means to minimise the amounts of materials (food and packaging) and energy which is used in the lifecycle of the product.

Life cycle of a product

A new product progresses through a variety of stages from conception of idea to its decline where it might be discontinued or disposed of. You must consider the impact of a product on the environment and its impact on society as a whole. The main stages involved are:

- The raw materials – where do they come from, are they sustainable, how are they harvested, made?
- The production process – how is the product made, does it require further processing at home?
- Transport and distribution – you need to consider what, how, where and the cost?
- Uses – what is the intended use of the product? How will it be used by the consumer? What is the effect of the product on diet and health?

- Can any of the parts of the product be reused or recycled?
- Preparation and cooking – what is needed and is it environmentally friendly?
- Disposal – the waste from manufacturing or the product itself. Ask yourself the question: what is the effect on the environment?

KEY TERM

LIFE CYCLE – the stages a new product goes through from conception to eventual decomposition

Eco footprint

This is the term used to refer to the measurement of our actions on the environment. You as a designer must consider the effect of your product on the environment from the first stages of your design ideas through to the final making and eventual disposal or recycling of your product. Your eco footprint involves showing that you have designed the product with the environment in mind and have tried to minimise the damage caused by the various stages throughout your product's life cycle. Further information can be found in Chapter 11.

Figure 13.7 Carbon footprint logo

ACTIVITY

Investigate the different symbols which may be found on products to show eco footprints.

Built-in obsolescence

This is where the product has been designed to last a set period of time. The built-in obsolescence in food products is their use by or best before dates.

Energy

The consumption of non-renewable energy resources such as coal and oil are causing an energy crisis. These resources will eventually run out. Using non-renewable resources adds to the pollution problem as products made from oil often take a long time to break down in the environment. Transportation of products is a high user of oil and petrol – both are refined fossil fuels.

Green energy is obtained from alternative energy sources which are considered environmentally friendly and non-polluting.

Figure 13.8 Wind turbines

It is energy generated from natural sources:

- wind power
- solar power
- geothermal
- hydro power
- tidal/wave.

When preparing and cooking foods we need to consider how we can reduce our energy costs. You need to think about:

- the methods of cooking used
- the length of the cooking processes
- where the products have come from and how much energy was used to get them to the plate?

Waste

Waste management is a growing problem, from chemicals that get into the water system, to paper and card used in packaging. Switching off our computers or not leaving the television on standby can help us to reduce the energy wasted. Reusing carrier bags or buying locally made products all helps to reduce material waste and bring about a more eco friendly footprint. Manufacturers now have to follow guidelines on how to get rid of their waste (effluent). Research into effective management of pollution, energy and other material waste is ongoing. You need to be aware of current changes within these areas.

QUESTIONS

1. Explain how methods of transportation can harm the environment.

2. Discuss how a family can reduce their energy consumption in the preparation of meals.

3. Suggest ways a family can reduce the carbon footprint of the foods they buy.

EXAMINER'S TIPS

These are open-ended questions and will require you in your answer to discuss relevant points in the context of your chosen specialist subject/material area. Use of specialist terms and factual information used appropriately will allow you to score at the higher mark level.

Also see Chapter 15, page 282, for help with answering 'discuss' questions.

❯ Refuse

This means not accepting a product if:

- you don't need it
- it's environmentally or socially unsustainable.

Issues relating to sustainable design

Processing, manufacturing, packaging and transport of our products use huge amounts of energy and can create lots of waste. You need to look at the sustainability of a product from the:

- environmental impact
- social viewpoint.

How is the product made and can we ensure that no or little harm is done to the environment by this method of manufacture?

You need to consider whether the workers have good working conditions and have been paid a fair wage. Sometimes a choice between the performance of the product required and the impact on the environment by its manufacture has to be considered and debated. Organisations such as Traidcraft use only ethically produced ingredients, which helps both the producers and manufacturers in developing countries. Through Traidcraft, workers get paid a fair price for their produce and work. You need to be aware of the moral implications of Fairtrade and can help by buying fairly traded goods.

Figure 13.9 Tea picker

ACTIVITY

Look on the Fairtrade website and produce a leaflet which encourages people to buy ethically produced ingredients.

Materials we should refuse to use

Why should you refuse to use some products? The answer can be for a variety of reasons:

- It may be because the product is made unnecessarily from a man-made source instead of a natural one, e.g. plastic carrier bags.
- It might be because of the pesticides and chemicals used in the production, e.g. crops

- What about the manufacturing process itself – has the product been made under safety regulations?
- What about the rights of the workers and the conditions they have been working in?
- Think about the conditions that the animals are kept in, e.g. battery hens.
- Packaging and transport distances and costs. Think of the food miles.
- It might not be good for you, e.g. high fat , salt and sugar content.

You should think about these issues before you accept a product and above all do not buy it if you do not need it.

▶ Rethink

You need to rethink about your lifestyle, the way in which you buy products and the energy required to use them. Society is constantly evolving and changing and you can evaluate how you could make a difference.

How it is possible to approach design problems differently?

- Use seasonal foods. Make jam from blackberries in the autumn.
- Buy local produce.
- Encourage your family to grow some of their own foods. You can grow strawberries or tomatoes in a plant pot.
- Buy British fresh produce. Since the 1950s there has been a massive decrease in orchards in the UK. Apples from South Africa have travelled 5000 miles.
- Using an existing product that has become waste for another purpose without processing it. What can you design, what could be designed?

- How can we use foods which are low in fat in creative and interesting ways?

- When choosing foods, how can we be encouraged to think about the impact they will have on health?

ACTIVITY

1. Design and make a product using seasonal foods.

2. Produce monthly posters of seasonal foods with recipes.

3. In groups, discuss what makes you want to buy a food product.

4. Discuss and consider what you have bought recently and why. Did you really need it?

▶ Repair

We live in a throwaway society, where it is quicker and easier to throw it away rather than repair it. You have looked at built-in obsolescence earlier in this chapter, whereby manufacturers encourage consumers to repurchase rather than repair.

- We eat food to repair our body. We need to rethink whether we are eating the best foods for repair or whether we are actually doing more harm. Look in Chapter 2 for information on the repair of your body.

- Products that can be repaired. When was the last time your family took any kitchen equipment to be repaired? Could they get it repaired?

- Unwanted electrical equipment is the fastest growing waste area. How many pieces of electrical or non-electrical kitchen equipment has your family got hidden away at the back of a cupboard?

The need to change the attitude to this is enormous. How can you do this?

ACTIVITY

Choose ten different pieces of kitchen electrical equipment. Put them in order of priority of use.

Choose two that you couldn't do without. Choose four that you could easily do without.

13.3 PRODUCT ANALYSIS AND THE DESIGN OF PRODUCTS

▶ Social issues

We live in a global society. You need to be aware of the ways this can affect the designing of products. Designing a food product to be eaten by a range of different cultures and nationalities means that they will all have different specific needs. Society

today has become multicultural and diverse, some products may be designed for a specific section of society while others may be universal across all. You will need to think about the following:

- Social development: we need to assess consumer needs when designing new food products.

Figure 13.10 Logo depicting global unity

- In our society, there are many different trends in food consumption and new products are designed to meet the changing needs.

- Issues associated with economic development and employment – where foods come from, costs of components and manufacturing including labour and the transportation of the finished product.

- Values of society – what foods do we eat? Where do we eat? What influences our choice of foods?

- How do we present important information to the consumers on nutrition, safety, food and hygiene so that it can be understood by everyone?

- Many labels are used on food products to inform you and to help you make decisions about whether to purchase a product. Some of these labels are for safety reasons, for instance the coeliac sign for people who are allergic to gluten; others are to help you make informed choices, such as suitable for vegetarians, or are linked to how a product has been

produced, for example local milk or organic products. Others are for safety reasons, for example the lion mark on eggs to show that the eggs have come from salmonella-free hens, or the number of stars on a freezer.

ACTIVITY

Produce a display of the different signs you will find on foods and equipment – classify them under the following headings:

- Food safety

- Nutritional symbols

- Allowing consumers to make informed choices.

You will also need to be aware and think about the trends in food consumption. There is a lot of publicity about our eating habits and there is great concern that many people are not eating foods which will help them to be healthy. See Chapter 2 for detailed information on requirements.

ACTIVITY

Using the internet or reports from newspapers:

1. What are the current eating trends of the UK population?

2. What recommendations are being made on how we should change our diets?

▶ Moral Issues

Moral issues are concerned with the way in which products are manufactured and the way in which they affect the safety, comfort and well-being of people who make them and those who come into contact with the products. Many companies now try to follow a code of practice and ensure that products are made in good conditions without exploiting workers.

In food technology moral issues affect the following areas:

Safety within the food preparation area

- Has the food worker been provided with all the correct training?

- Have they been shown how to prepare, cook, serve and store food safely so that the consumers will not be harmed?

- Does all the equipment work correctly so that foods are stored at the correct temperature?

Safety of food products/safe shelf life

- All foods are date stamped with either a best before date or a use by date.

- It is against the law to sell food products which are past their use by date.

- The temperatures of cold storage units in shops and food manufacturers have to be checked regularly and records kept.

QUESTIONS

1. Which types of foods have a best before date? Name five products.

2. Which types of foods have a use by date? Name five products.

3. What are the important temperatures which manufacturers have to adhere to for:
   - chilled storage?
   - freezing?

▶ Fairtrade products and their effect on the conditions of the workers

Figure 13.11 FAIRTRADE Mark

The Fairtrade Foundation is the independent non-profit organisation that licenses use of the 'Fairtrade Mark' on products in the UK, which meet internationally agreed Fairtrade standards set by Fairtrade Labelling Organisations International (FLO). The Foundation was established in 1992. See www.fairtrade.org.uk for more information.

Advantages to consumers of buying Fairtrade are:

- There is now a huge range of products with the FAIRTRADE Mark available.

- Fairtrade standards have been developed to do something positive to help the ever-growing number of people in the developing countries living in poverty.

- Farmers receive a fair and stable price for their goods. That covers the cost of sustainable production.
- Workers get a safe and healthy working environment.
- Producers get an extra sum called the Fairtrade premium to invest in community development projects.

Figure 13.12 Fairtrade rice farmer in India (Traidcraft photo)

Over the past few years consumer awareness of Fairtrade products has grown enormously and is increasing every year. As consumers you can make choices whether to buy or refuse a product. By choosing to purchase Fairtrade products you are saying that the welfare of the producers in developing countries is important to you.

ACTIVITY

Look in the supermarket or your local shops and make a list of the products they are selling which have the FAIRTRADE Mark on them.

The Ethical Trading Initiative (ETI) is a group of companies which promote good, safe working conditions for their employees. This means that the employees have basic labour rights and that they also take care to protect the environment in the packaging and transporting of their products. There are an increasing number of companies which will source their ingredients from producers who care for their employees and the environment.

GM Food production

Some consumers are very concerned about genetically produced products.

Scientists are now able to use genetic engineering in a number of ways in food production, for example:

- to help plants resist disease or insect infestation
- to produce fruits with better flavour or that will have a longer shelf life
- to produce crops that will cope better with the different climate conditions.

All foods which have been genetically modified have been carefully checked for safety. Some consumers will not want to eat GM foods for a variety of reasons. These can include:

- they believe that the natural ecology of plants and animals is destroyed
- the welfare of the animals may be affected.

As a consumer you need to consider the advantages and disadvantages of using genetic modification in the production of foods.

More information relating to GM food can be found in Chapter 2.

Intensive/factory farming

Some people choose to refuse to buy foods which are intensively farmed or factory farmed. This is because they:

- don't like the way the animals are being treated
- don't like how they are being fed.

However, for some consumers, food produced by these methods provides relatively cheap sources of important nutrients such as protein which are expensive to buy.

Free-range production of foods

There are many varieties of free-range products available for sale in shops and supermarkets. These are linked to poultry products – the description 'free-range' is only for poultry. The poultry must be allowed to have access to the open air, and there are rules about the amount of space the poultry must have and the types of shelter provided. Other animals such as pigs are often described as 'free-range' or 'outdoor reared,' but these terms are not legally defined. The other type of labelling often seen on food products is organic and there are a wide variety of both meat and vegetable products produced organically.

The use of additives in food products

Additives are used to extend the shelf life of food, improve colour and to improve the consistency of foods. Some consumers choose not to purchase foods containing additives, particularly colourings, because they think they can affect health and in some cases behaviour in children.

Further information can be found in Chapter 4.

ACTIVITY

1. List the groups of additives and their function in food products.

2. List all the benefits to the manufacturer of using food additives.

3. List reasons why a consumer may not buy food products containing additives.

▶ Cultural issues

Many cultures have important traditions that form part of their identity. How do products affect the quality of lives within different cultures? The use and maintenance of traditional skills and cultural knowledge can have an impact on the foods we eat.

- Look at the different foods available for you to purchase in the shops – where do they originate from?

- How have these products influenced new products?

Figure 13.13 Organic sheep

- In some cases different people's cultures and beliefs will affect the foods they can eat and how some foods are prepared.

Many consumers are choosing to buy products locally and from farmers markets. You need to consider what the advantages of these are:

- supporting local industry
- eating foods which are in season
- foods have not travelled a great distance – therefore eco footprint may be lower
- helping to sustain local varieties of foods, e.g. types of apples
- often organic produce is sold – some consumers consider that these are better for them.

KEY POINT

- Culture is about the way that people behave and relate to one another. It is about the way that people live, work and spend their leisure time. It is about people's beliefs and aspirations.

▶ Environmental issues

In a modern, fast-changing society, where products are continually being changed, it is important that you keep up to date with issues related to food technology. You will need to address the following key areas.

Understand and be able to select ingredients and materials that are both suitable and sustainable. You will need to be aware of the following:

- The disposal and recycling of materials.
- The appropriate methods of producing and

manufacturing of food products. Think about where the products have come from, how they have been produced and if they are being eaten in season.

- Preparing ingredients economically, allowing waste to be kept to a minimum. When there is leftover food, consider how this can be used in other products.
- When packaging foods consider the impact the packaging will have on the environment.
- The pollution and waste from manufacturing can be high and ways to reduce this are continually being investigated. A successful example of this is Cornerways Nursery, which grows tomatoes. It recycles heat and carbon dioxide from British Sugar's refinery which is close by; this makes it a very green greenhouse.
- The need to dispose of redundant products and their packaging in a safe and environmentally friendly way. The use of labelling for specific packaging is helpful to the consumer when buying products.

You will need to ensure that you are aware of and keep up to date with these in relation to your specialist area.

ACTIVITY

1. Produce a chart to show when different foods are in season.

2. Prepare a dish to illustrate ingredients which are in season at the moment.

3. Produce a recipe leaflet a supermarket could use to promote local seasonal produce.

Carbon footprint

This is a measure of the impact human activities have on the environment in terms of the amount of greenhouse gasses produced through the outlet of carbon dioxide. This is all having an impact on global warming.

The carbon footprint is not just about how far food has travelled, it is about all or any of the following which are involved in the production of a food product:

- fuel for the machines that harvest the crops
- the fuel and energy used in the manufacturing process, including the packaging
- the transportation of the foods
- the storage of the food product
- the energy required to dispose of the packaging.

Figure 13.14 shows the carbon foot print symbol which is on some products showing the carbon emissions in grams. This has been developed by the Carbon Trust to help consumers make informed choices www.carbontrust.co.uk.

There are a variety of ways you can reduce your carbon footprint:

- buy fresh local produce
- cook fresh meals
- use local seasonal ingredients
- cut down on your consumption of meat – more energy is used to raise animals than to grow vegetables.

Reforestation is the term used to describe the restocking of existing forests and woodlands. The advantage of this method is that the areas restocked can provide the ecosystem with resource benefits to soak up some of the negative effects of carbon dioxide.

Design issues

Identify how good design and product choice improves the quality of life

You will need to relate this to how different food products lead to an improved quality of life. You need to think about the following:

- foods you choose to purchase
- the way you cook them.

When buying products they can be can be expensive, so you need to ensure it will benefit you in some way. Food products are often packed giving you a lot of information so that you can make an informed choice about purchasing the product.

Look at the way that food manufacturers respond to changing styles, taste, technological advances and environmental pressures

Think about the types of products available to purchase, look at:

- the different speciality ranges .e.g. 'healthy options', 'free-range', 'organic', etc.
- how products are sold – the way they have been preserved and packaged
- what is added to products to improve them – use of additives, fortification

- how manufacturers are responding to consumers wanting more environmentally friendly products; this needs to be considered from the start of production to the growing of the foods, to the disposal of the packaging and waste materials.

ACTIVITY

Investigate the different symbols found on packaging of food which:

- tell you how to dispose of the product

- inform you it has come from a sustainable or recyclable source.

QUESTIONS

1. What sort of information is put on food products to help you make an informed choice about whether to buy a product or not?

2. Discuss the way food manufacturers have responded to:
   (a) consumers' changing lifestyles
   (b) environmental pressures.

Eco design and the impact of globalisation on ingredients and food products

When designing new products it is important to consider the whole of the production process from design to the finished product, its use of materials and energy. Eco design is the process of designing a product considering all the ecological and environmental issues and trying to minimise the damage caused to the environment by the product's life cycle.

A designer must think through the following main stages if the product is to be successful and acceptable as eco-designed:

- product planning
- product development
- design process
- suitability for the purpose and the intended user
- safety – with particular reference to manufacture and storage of foods
- technical issues and requirements – linked to production, safety and nutritional issues
- quality of the finished product.

The globalisation of food products

Today you can buy food products in a supermarket which represents the global market. Sixty years ago there was much less choice of foods available to the consumer. The creation of food products is no longer just a local or regional activity; it is produced all over the world and transported to where it is needed.

Many large companies will pay farmers to grow products just for them and can give a valuable income and jobs to a previous poor area; however, some will take advantage of low labour wages.

Recently, there has been a trend to encourage manufacturers and consumers to source ingredients from local and regional suppliers to help to reduce the eco footprint.

13.4 SUMMARY

Many areas in this chapter are also covered in specific subject detail in other chapters. Where possible these have been cross referenced for you. Sustainable design is a world issue and a constantly changing one. You should want the world to be a great, sustainable place to live in, one that is for you, your friends and relatives and for future generations.

A sustainable way of producing food products can have an impact and positive effect on everyone. As a designer you need to remember and consider the social, economic and environmental implications of your decisions.

Useful websites which will help you keep up to date with issues included in this section of the specification include:

www.nutrition.org.uk
www.food.gov.uk
www.carbontrust.co.uk
www.fairtrade.org.uk
www.recyclenow.com
www.soilassociation.org
www.foodlink.org.uk
http://www.eatwell.gov.uk/healthissues

EXAMINER'S TIPS

To help you prepare and revise for this examination here are some useful tips. There are also some useful tips in Chapter 15.

- Read the question carefully and highlight or underline the key words. Marks are frequently lost in exams through not answering the question that has been asked.

- When a question asks you to 'list', 'state' or 'name' this usually indicates a one-word or short sentence is acceptable.

- Words such as 'justify', 'analyse', 'describe' or 'explain' in the question require a more detailed, structured answer which should not take the form of a list or a series of points. An example of how to score 2 marks on an explain question is shown in Figure 13.5. You must make statement and then back it up with a reason.

> The sale of Fairtrade products has increased.
> Explain two reasons consumers are choosing these products.
>
> 1. Consumers know that the producer will get a fair price for the product and this will help them to have an improved lifestyle. [1 mark] [1 mark]
> 2. There has been increased media attention paid to poor working conditions of workers and therefore they are prominently displayed in supermarkets encouraging consumers to purchase them. [1 mark] [1 mark]

Figure 13.14 Candidate's response to an 'explain' question

- Use specialist vocabulary and terminology where appropriate. Avoid terms such as healthy, cheap, quick, easy.
- Answer all of the questions. If you feel you cannot answer a part of a question leave it and go back to it later.
- Look at how many marks are available for each section of the question. This indicates how much detail is needed in the answer.
- Practise using past examination questions; this will help you interpret the questions and gain confidence.

CHAPTER 14

CONTROLLED ASSESSMENT UNIT A523 – MAKING QUALITY PRODUCTS

In your second portfolio you will be expected to develop further the skills and abilities gained while undertaking the Controlled Assessment for Unit A521 in order to design and make a creative and innovative product from a theme set by OCR. You must choose a completely different theme from the theme you studied in Unit A521. The type of product you select needs to be challenging but realistic in terms of the resources and time you have available.

You should consider your own needs/ requirements or those of an identified user group and the situation in which the product should be used.

You will be required to consider the focus of the design before developing a design specification. You need to demonstrate your ability to plan, develop creative, original ideas and carry out a range of practical activities.

You will be expected to critically evaluate your ideas against the design specification to identify with reasons, the chosen design proposal for product development. As a result of product development you will be expected to give reasoned decisions for the ingredients and equipment required for the production of your final product which will be tested and critically evaluated against a product specification.

Now let's get started

In order to skilfully design, model, make and test your final product you need to undertake the following processes.

Select a theme from the OCR published list. Themes are reviewed every two years. Refer to the current GCSE food specification for an up-to-date list. Your teacher will be able to advise you about this.

The list for examination in 2010 includes:

A new product that:

- increases the intake of fruit and/or vegetables
- meets the nutritional needs of a specified age group
- is suitable for a person on a limited budget
- is suitable for a person with a special dietary requirement
- reflects an identified country from around the world
- is suitable for a celebration
- is suitable for inclusion in a packed lunch
- is suitable for the luxury market
- incorporates an alternative protein food

- increases the use of locally grown/seasonal foods
- increases the range of desserts
- increases the range of baked products
- increases the range of snack products.

Remember all the work you produce must relate to your chosen theme and the chosen theme must be completely different to the theme you selected for Controlled Assessment Unit A521.

Assessment criteria and marks

Designing

	Designing	Marks
Basic ability requires constant support and help	Produces a simple specification for the chosen design brief	0–1
	Record design ideas using a limited range of strategies	
	Present a cursory evaluation with unsupported choice of design proposal	
	Apply simple trialling procedures	0–5
Demonstrates ability, some help & guidance given	Produces a suitable design specification for the chosen design brief	2–3
	Record creative design ideas and communicate these by using appropriate strategies	
	Select design proposal by clear evaluation	
	Apply trialling procedures	6–8
Works competently with independence	Produces a detailed specification for the chosen design brief	4
	Record creative and innovative design ideas and communicate these in detail using appropriate strategies	
	Select design proposal chosen as a result of detailed evaluation	
	Apply detailed trialling procedures. Record creative and innovative design ideas using appropriate presentation techniques	10–12

Table 14.1 Designing

Step 1

- You are required to consider the focus of your design brief and produce a design specification for your creative and innovative product.

How you approach this portfolio to arrive at your design brief will depend on the theme you chose and the direction you wish your portfolio to take. Some of the listed themes require you to make a decision at the beginning of your work, for example to chose a culture or an identified celebration.

Some themes could be left open or a decision could be made on the type of product at this stage, for example a cake product could be chosen as a focus for the baked product theme as developing a new cake product will allow you to demonstrate a wide range of practical skills and use different ingredients. Or you could have your focus for the design brief as a baked product so you could trial a cake, a biscuit and a bread product, etc. It is important that your design brief and design specification allows you to demonstrate a wide range of practical skills when you carry out your practical work.

Once you have decided on your theme and design brief you will need to analyse them carefully so you can arrive at a design specification. You could present

your ideas as spider diagram, brainstorms, charts, simple notes, etc.

Your analysis needs to make your own interpretation of the brief quite clear. There is no right or wrong answer but you do need to identify a target group so your practical ideas can be tested and evaluated.

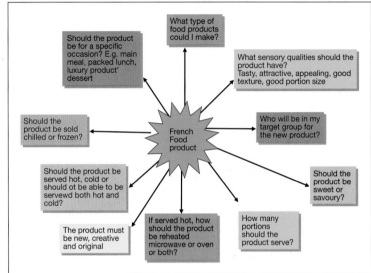

Figure 14.1 Analysing a design brief based on a new French food product

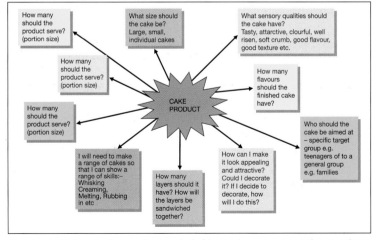

Figure 14.2 Analysing a design brief based on a new cake product

Figures 14.1 and 14.2 give examples of analysing design briefs. Both examples show how you can quickly pick out the important points so that you can develop a suitable design specification.

Using your analysis you should then develop your design specification which must include a target group.

Step 2

- You need to show evidence of forward planning – produce a week-by-week plan
- Using existing recipes, you are required to select four products for trialling that allow you to demonstrate a range of practical skills appropriate to your brief. For example, peeling, chopping, grating, meat preparation, shaping, rolling, sauce making (roux, blended, all-in-one), kneading, piping,

Date	Work carried out at school	Work carried out at home
Wednesday 7th November	Complete plan of action. Write out ingredients for chocolate cookies. Say how the recipe will be adapted. Design evaluation sheet and tasting and testing chart for all 4 products.	Complete the designing of the tasting and testing chart.
Friday 9th November	Make chocolate cookies.	Test and taste and start evaluation against specification.
Wednesday 14th November	Write out ingredients for milk chocolate cake and ginger biscuits. Say how each recipe will be adapted. Complete the evaluation of the chocolate cookies.	
Friday 16th November	Make milk chocolate cake.	Test and taste and evaluate against specification.
Wednesday 26th September	Make ginger biscuits. Write out the ingredients for Swiss roll and say how the recipe will be adapted.	Test and taste and evaluate against the specification.
Friday 23rd November	Make the Swiss roll.	Test and taste and start the evaluation against the specification.
Wednesday 28th November	Complete the evaluation of the Swiss roll. Chose the product I will take forward for product development and start to explain why I have chosen it as my final design proposal.	
Friday 30th November	Explain why I have rejected the other 3 ideas I trialled.	Complete any unfinished work.

Table 14.2 A detailed plan of action

skills used in the different methods of cake, biscuit and pastry making. For each of the four products, you are expected to produce a creative and innovative idea by using appropriate presentation techniques which show consideration of your design specification

- Show evidence of testing by three tasters, e.g. tasting charts, star profiles.
- Evaluate each product against your design specification
- You are then required to choose one of your ideas to take forward to product development and explain why the idea has been chosen and why other ideas have been rejected.

Marks from the making section will be awarded for making the products and forward planning.

You need to select four appropriate products for trialling that allow you to demonstrate a range of practical skills. To gain ideas you could:

- look in magazines, leaflets, etc.
- look in recipe books to see if there are any appropriate recipes
- look on the internet for suitable recipes, etc.

You could list the different ideas that you find to give you time to think and make decisions as to which products you will trial. Remember to make a note of where you find the recipe(s) so you can quickly find the recipe again should you want to use it for trialling.

You will need to show evidence of forward planning by producing a week-by-week/lesson-by-lesson plan.

Table 14.2 shows an example of a detailed plan of action written for the design brief *Design and make a baked product aimed at teenagers.*

There are many different ways of presenting your design ideas. You could use labelled diagrams/drawings, text etc. For each product to be trialled you need to:

- list the ingredients you will use
- explain clearly the modifications/adaptations you are making to the recipe to produce creative and innovative ideas. Give reasons for these modifications/adaptations
- carry out nutritional analysis if this is relevant to your brief or specification (ICT nutritional analysis programme
- make each product and provide photographic evidence (ICT use of digital camera)
- show evidence of testing by three tasters, e.g. tasting charts, star profiles
- evaluate the product against each point in your design specification
- discuss any improvements that could be made to the product, taking into account users' views.

Figure 14.3 shows the student's evaluation against the design specification for a cake bar. The evaluation is detailed and all points in her specification have been evaluated. She has used results from testers as evidence when evaluating. The design idea is creative and innovative.

Once you have trialled your four products you will then have to decide which product you will take forward for product development. You need to clearly explain why you have chosen

Product 2- Choc chip cake bar Evaluation

Taste test results

Specification point	Aimed at teenagers	Filled	Filled	Aimed at teenagers	Aimed at teenagers	Filled	Filled	Aimed at teenagers	Filled	Filled	Aimed at teenagers	Luxury/snack product
Number of votes (out of 12)	12	12	12	12	12	12	12	12	12	12	12	12

Evaluation

For my second product, I have adapted the recipe for a creamed cake in to chocolate flavour so that it fits in with my specification. It contains chocolate chips, which most but not all of the people I asked thought was a sufficient filling for the product. It gained full marks for being aimed at teenagers, decorated, chocolate flavour, topped, rectangle shape, tasty, attractive and soft textured. I believe the product is suitable for teenagers because it is very chocolaty, which is a very popular flavour among teenagers. It was topped and decorated using melted chocolate, which I first covered it with milk chocolate then piped white and dark chocolate on top and created a marbled. I think this has made the product very attractive. It contains milk and white chocolate chips which most people but not all thought was a sufficient filling for my product with 9 out of 12 votes. Only 5 teenagers considered the product small size, and only 7 thought it was suitable to be sold as 2 per packet, which suggests that people thought that the product should be sold separately at the size it was made but smaller if it is to be sold as more than 1. Most thought the product was a luxury/snack product. I believe this was because the product was decorated using a marbled effect and three different coloured chocolates, creating a luxurious finish. The small size and easy to eat rectangle shape make this product a snack. All teenagers thought my product was soft textured, which means that if I made a cake product as my final, I would make it creamed.

Figure 14.3 Evaluating a trialled idea against the design specification

Final Design Proposal

My final product will be product 4, the toffee and smarties cookies based on the all in one method chocolate and cherry cookie recipe. I have chosen this product because I believe there are no existing products like this on the current market, so it will fill a gap and will not have to compete with other similar biscuits. I believe this because it is sold as an individual snack product, which is unusual for a biscuit, and it is crunchy which makes a different texture to the usual soft texture of a cookie. The product was taste tested by three teenagers, who said that they would buy this product if it was improved by such things as the decoration because the specification requires the product to be decorated, and I failed to achieve that point with only one agreeing that it is sufficiently decorated. I will try different decoration techniques such as piping and drizzling. Two teenagers also commented that they would like the product to be larger in size to make it a little bit more luxury, which would also help achieve the specification points. However, overall the cookies did well in the taste test, showing that people liked then, which could mean that the product would sell well when developed. The cookies recipe meets other specification points of being tasty caramel and chocolate flavour created by using toffee and smarties, circle shape and attractive.

I decided against further developing product 1, the raspberry filled short crust pastries based on the Cornish pasties recipe because although there are not many similar products on the market, people said they wouldn't buy it if it was developed further. I think this is because many teenagers thought it was aimed at an older audience as it was decorated very simply with piped glace icing and also because they did not like the raspberry filling very much. It didn't meet my specification for aimed at teenagers or decorated. It also didn't do well for the specification point 'Small/ Medium size'. I think these points weren't achieved because it isn't big enough. Although it was filled and fruit flavour, people did not enjoy the raspberry filling very much. It was the correct rectangle shape and contained 2 per packet but did not achieve very highly on the crucial points; tasty, attractive and luxury/snack product.

I decided against further developing product 2, Choc chip cake bar based on a muffin recipe using the creamed method because less than half the people I questioned thought it achieved 'small size', and because the bar is quite chunky, it would be difficult to fulfil this specified point. Not everyone thought the chocolate chips were a sufficient filling, or that it was suitable to be sold as two per packet. Most importantly, not all of the questioned people thought the product was a luxury/snack product. Therefore, I will not be developing this product because it did not do well when compared to the specification.

I decided against further developing product 3, Chocolate butter cream filled cake bar based on a chocolate roll using the whisked method because it did not meet all of its specification points such as small size. Not everyone who tasted the product thought it was aimed at teenagers as some thought it would be more suitably aimed at an older audience of adults. It didn't get full marks on 2 in a packet because some people thought it was too big for a two per packet snack, like in product 2 above. It gained almost full votes on luxury/snack product but some teenagers commented that it was too luxurious to be a snack product. The biggest problem with this product is that it did not achieve top votes for soft texture because the whisked method recipe I used does not create a sufficiently soft texture for my specification.

Figure 14.4 Final design proposal for a baked product

this product and why you have rejected the other three ideas. This is sometimes known as the final design proposal.

Figure 14.4 shows the final design proposal from a student working on the design brief

Design and make a baked product suitable for teenagers. The student has clearly explained in detail the reasons for choice of the final idea and why the other three ideas were rejected.

Making

Making	Marks
Basic ability requires constant support and help	
Trialling/product development/final product Organise activities Select and use appropriate ingredients Select and use appropriate equipment Work safely and hygienically Prepare, shape, form, mix, assemble and finish food products Products will exhibit a reasonable standard of outcome (photographic evidence) Apply simple trialling procedures during product development	0–9
Final Product Information Make some decisions about ingredients and equipment Produce a simple Product Specification	0–2
Produce a simple forward plan for the trialling of design ideas Produce a simple flowchart for the final product	0–2
Demonstrates ability, some help & guidance given	
Trialling/Product Development/Final Product Organise activities. Select and use appropriate ingredients Select and use appropriate equipment Work safely and hygienically Work effectively to prepare, shape, form, mix, assemble and finish food products Products will exhibit a good standard of outcome (photographic evidence) Apply trialling procedures to suggest possible modifications during product development	10–17
Final Product Information Make decisions about ingredients and equipment Produce a Product Specification	3–4
Produce a forward plan for the trialling of design ideas Produce a flowchart that includes all key stages for the final product	3–4

Table 14.1 **Making**

Making	Marks
Trialling/Product Development/Final Product Organise activities Select and use appropriate ingredients. Select and use appropriate equipment	
Work safely and hygienically	
Work skilfully to prepare, shape, form, mix, assemble and finish food products	
Products will exhibit a high quality outcome (photographic evidence)	
Apply detailed trialling procedures to suggest possible modifications during product development	18–24
Final Product Information Make reasoned decisions about ingredients and equipment Produce a detailed Product Specification	5–6
Produce a detailed forward plan for the trialling of design ideas Produce a detailed flowchart that specifies an effective order of sequences for the final product	5–6

Works competently with independence

Table 14.3 continued

Step 1

You are required to carry out two developments and make the final product (ICT use of digital camera). For each development you are expected to:

- apply trialling procedures – during product development

- list ingredients, cost ingredients (ICT spreadsheet) and give reasoned decisions for the changes you make to the product showing consideration to the comments given when the product was originally trialled and to the comments made by testers during development work.

- Show evidence of testing by five tasters, for example tasting charts, star profiles and carry out nutritional analysis if this is relevant to your brief or specification (ICT nutritional analysis program).

Development work is all about changing, testing or modifying all or part of your product until a desired outcome (your final product) will meet your product specification. Development gives you the opportunity to try out changes and evaluation enables you to make appropriate decisions. Simple notes, charts or diagrams with comments are adequate ways of recording your results.

There are many ways that you could develop a product. For example, changing the taste, texture, finishing technique, size, shape, how it is assembled etc. The key is that the product must be developed according to users' needs so you must consider their views as you develop your product.

Your starting point, therefore, for this section of your project is to look back at the work you completed when the chosen product was originally trialled. Look at your evaluation and your tasting chart to see where changes/improvements can be made. Using this information you need to plan for your first development which should then be made and tested by five possible users. Evaluation of this work should then lead to further development. By looking at comments given by your testers this should lead to further

modifications/changes which should be reflected in your second development.

Evaluation of your second development along with consideration of any comments from testers should then lead to the planning of your final product. By working in this way you are developing your product according to users' views.

Figure 14.5 shows the work carried out during the second development of a product, by a student working on the design brief *Design and make a low in sugar pastry product aimed at everybody.*

Development2:
Custard Filled Éclairs

Improvements:
Could the product be improved in any way? Please be specific.
Person 1- No improvements Person 2- No improvements Person 3- No improvements
Person 4- No improvements Person 5- Presented a little bit neater

Successful Changes
The adaptations to the recipe were successful. The only improvement I got was to present the éclairs a bit neater. When considering my final product this can easily be adapted as I can spend more time putting the éclairs together so that they look more attractive.

Ingredients

	Cost		Cost
67g Plain flour	£0.07	Pink Icing- 50g Icing Sugar Few drops red food dye	£0.10 £0.13
50g Margarine	£0.08	75g Strawberries	£0.63
125ml Water		Custard Filling:	
1/8 Teaspoon Salt	£0.01	2 medium eggs	£0.40
¼ Teaspoon Canderel	£0.02	¼ teaspoon vanilla essence	£0.02
¼ Teaspoon Vanilla Essence	£0.02	300ml milk	£0.26
2 Medium Eggs	£0.40	2 tablespoons corn flour	£0.15
125ml Whipping Cream	£0.60	4 tablespoons canderel	£0.18
Chocolate Icing- 50g Icing sugar 1 tablespoon Cocoa	£0.10 £0.05		

Nutritional Value:

	Typical Value	
	Per 100g	Per Serving
Energy	778 KJ	420KJ
	186 kcal	100kcal
Protein	6.16g	3.33g
Carbohydrate	17.9g	9.66g
of which sugars	3.58g	1.93g
Fat	10.5g	5.66g
of which saturates	3.75g	2.03g
Fibre (NSP)	0.58g	0.31g
Sodium	0.2g	0.11g

Adaptations to Recipe:
For development 2 I will be changing the filling from cream to a custard based filling. I will still be adding strawberries into the centre of the éclairs with the custard. I will also still be using chocolate icing to drizzle

Total Cost: £2.92
Cost per Serving:
£0.24
Recipe serves up to: 12
Cost per Packaging: £0.96

Evaluation

Overall the development of the product worked well, all the changes I made were successful and I met almost all of my specification points.

The taste testers seemed to prefer the éclairs more once I had made changes as I received full marks for each criteria point apart from one, which was the tastiness of the product. 4/5 of the taste testers gave me full marks apart from one, but I can easily improve this, as when I asked if there could be any improvements two of the taste testers said that the pastry could be crispier. The other taste testers said that they would not improve anything. When I first made the product the improvements were to; make a bigger portion size; add more cream; add another flavour. I did change them by adding another ingredient which was the strawberries, I didn't add more cream as I changed the filling to custard, but due to the sugar content I did not make the portion size bigger, but they were still a success.

Reasons for changes:
I have decided to change the cream to custard in development two because in development one when I asked the taste testers what they thought of the éclairs I got full marks apart from one person witch gave me 3 out of 4 for the taste so I decided to change the filling to see if this way they were more tastier. I also cooked the pastry for longer because when I asked the taste testers to specify on any improvements two said that they would prefer the pastry a bit crispier.

The product met all the specification points and the sugar content was reduced per 100g. The only criteria the product did not meet was whether the product could be served hot or cold, but by the choice of consumer they could be served with hot chocolate sauce, but this would increase the sugar content. I tested whether the product could be sold frozen by putting them in the freezer over night then defrosting them the next day, this did work and the strawberries also defrosted.

Taste Testing   Key: 1-Poor 2-Average 3-Good 4-Excellent

	1	2	3	4	5	Total/20	Average
Colourful	4	4	4	4	4	20	4
Attractive	4	4	4	4	3	19	3.8
Tasty	4	4	4	4	4	20	4
Suitable	4	4	4	4	4	20	4

I think that the improved product worked very well, and as a result of the taste testers it shows that the product is suitable for everyone, as I asked 5 different people of an age range to test the product. Also I am aiming to make a healthier product which I have achieved as the sugar content per 100g is only 3.58g and also by changing the filling the éclairs are healthier as they now contain less fat.

Figure 14.5 Product development for a low-in-sugar pastry product

The student has listed and costed the ingredients, shown evidence of the adaptations she will make and because her design brief is for a low-sugar product she has carried out nutritional analysis of the product by using a computer program.

The evaluation of the product clearly indicates that the student has developed her product according to users' views. She has considered her testers suggestions for improvement from her first development when she carried out this second development and will consider her testers suggestions for further development when she makes her final product. There is evidence of testing by five tasters (tasting chart). Reference is also made to the sugar content of the product.

Step 2

You are required to show evidence for the planning of the final product by:

- giving reasoned decisions for the choice of your final ingredients and equipment
- costing the ingredients (ICT spreadsheet)
- carrying out nutritional analysis if relevant to your brief or design specification (ICT nutritional analysis program).

The ability to understand scientific principles and their application to food production is an essential part of development work. When you give reasons for the choice of your final ingredients you are really giving the function of each ingredient for your particular product.

For example a particular ingredient could give:

- crunchiness to a product or perhaps give a fruity flavour; a particular ingredient may increase the fibre or lower the fat content of the product; using yeast in bread making

allows the bread to rise and gluten free flour is used for a coeliac as they have an intolerance to gluten.

You are also required to give reasoned decisions for the equipment you will use to make your final product. This will involve you listing the pieces of equipment and stating the job that each piece will be used for.

Figure 14.6 is an example of a student's work showing her decisions for the ingredients required to make her final product – melting moments.

Final product ingredients Melting moments			
Ingredient	Weight	Cost	Why?
Margarine	105g	12p	Adds colour and flavour. Also creates texture.
Caster sugar	70g	11p	Sweetens the mixture adds flavour. Helps to hold air in like a raising agent
Egg	½ medium	4p	Adds colour and flavour to mixture. Also helps to bind the ingredients.
Self raising flour	150g	10p	Forms the main structure of the biscuit.
Oats	40g	8p	Adds texture to the outside of the biscuit.
Vanilla essence	1 tsp	5p	Adds flavour and helps to bind.
Milk chocolate (grated)	10g	8p	Adds the chocolate flavour to the biscuit.
Plain chocolate(grated)	10g	9p	Develops a strong chocolate flavour.
Milk chocolate	15g	16p	Used to marble and adds to the chocolate flavour.
White chocolate	30g	18p	Used to decorate and adds to the chocolate flavour.

Cost to make 12 = £1.01
Cost per pack of 6 = 50p
Cost per biscuit = 8p

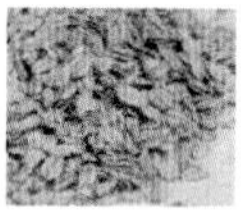

Figure 14.6 Reasons for the choice of ingredients for the final product

Figure 14.7 shows reasoned decisions for the equipment she will use to make the biscuits. If your design brief or design specification includes reference to an aspect of nutrition you need to carry out a nutritional analysis of

Final product equipment	
Melting moments	
Equipment	**Why?**
Baking tray	To put the biscuits on in oven.
Pastry brush	To brush melted lard onto the baking tray.
Weighing scales	To measure out the ingredients accurately.
Mixing bowl	To mix all ingredients in.
Electric mixer	Cream the margarine and sugar with.
Wooden spoon	To mix flour into the mixture.
Grater	Grate the milk and Plain chocolate to go into the mixture.
Plastic jug	Beat the egg and vanilla essence in.
Fork	Beat the egg and vanilla with.
Teaspoon x3	Measure vanilla essence Stir white chocolate whilst in microwave. Stir milk chocolate whilst in microwave.
Plate	To put oats on for biscuits to be tossed in.
Oven	To cook the biscuits.
Cooling rack	To cool the biscuits after being in the oven.
Small bowls x2	Melt the white and milk chocolate in for decorating.
Microwave	To melt the milk and white chocolate used to decorate.
Palette knife	Used to get the biscuits off the baking tray.
Skewer	Marble milk and white chocolate with on top of the biscuits.
Pan stand	Protect the work surface from the hot baking tray.
Drizzling bag	Used to drizzle the white chocolate onto the milk chocolate before marbling.

Figure 14.7 Reasons for the choice of equipment for the final product

your final product. This analysis only needs to concentrate on the area of nutrition that is relevant. For example if you design specification states, high fibre, you only need to analyse the fibre content of your final product to find out if your final product is high in fibre.

Step 3

- Produce a product specification.
- Produce a plan for the making of your final product, for example flow chart.

You are required to make and provide photographic evidence of your final product (ICT use of digital camera).

When you have carried out all your product development work and made your decisions for the final product you will need to produce a product specification. A product specification does not cover very general points like the design specification. Instead, it describes very specific characteristics which a product must have. At this stage it would be too general to say 'It must be tasty'. Instead you would need to say:

- It must be tasty. The product filling will have:
  - sausage
  - two flavours of cheese
  - bacon
  - carrot.

The product specification should conclude with a labelled sketch/drawing of the final product.

Figures 14.8 and 14.9 show two very detailed product specifications. Both students have used ICT to present a labelled drawing of their product.

You need to design a detailed flowchart. This should show an effective order of the sequences required to make your final product.

You should then make your final product and provide photographic evidence of the result (ICT use of digital camera).

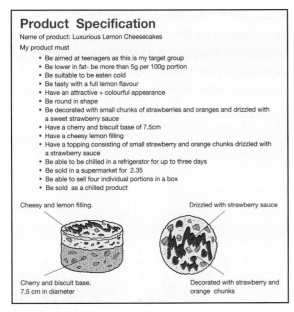

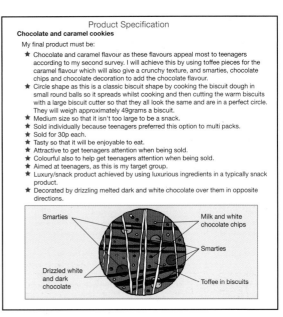

Figure 14.8 Product specification for luxurious lemon cheesecakes

Figure 14.9 Product specification for chocolate and caramel cookies

Evaluation

	Evaluation	Marks
Basic ability requires constant support and help	• Evaluation through superficial testing • There will be little or no use of specialist terms • Information may be ambiguous or disorganised • Errors of spelling, punctuation and grammar maybe intrusive	0–2
Demon-strates ability, some help & guidance given	• Give an evaluation of the final product with reference to the Product Specification • Show superficial testing and reflect how to improve the product • There will be some specialist terms, although these may not always be used appropriately • The information will be presented for the most part in a structured format • There may be occasional errors in spelling, punctuation and grammar	3–5
Works competently with indep-endence	• Critically evaluate the final product against the Product Specification • Undertake detailed testing, present meaningful conclusions leading to proposals for modifications to improve the product • Specialist terms will be used appropriately and correctly • The information will be presented in a structured format • The candidate can demonstrate the accurate use of spelling, punctuation and grammar	6–8

Table 12.4 Evaluation

You are expected to:

- show evidence of testing by five tasters, e.g. tasting chart, star profile
- critically evaluate your final product against your product specification and your design brief and suggest modifications to improve your product.

Your comments need to show how successful you have been in terms of your product specification and your design brief.

Comments from testers can support your views and they can be given as evidence when you offer conclusions for your work. It is a good idea to ask your testers how the product can be improved as this will help you suggest further modifications.

Evaluation-Tasting and testing

I asked these 5 people to fill in a tasting chart for my product.

Specification Point	Tester 1	Tester 2	Tester 3	Tester 4	Tester5	Average
Suitable for adults	5	5	4	4	5	4.6
Meaty	5	4	5	5	5	4.8
Tasty	5	5	5	5	4	4.8
Attractive	5	4	5	5	5	4.8
Square shaped	5	5	5	5	5	5
Small	3	4	5	4	4	4
Crisp texture	5	5	4	5	5	4.8
Suitable for 1 person	5	5	5	4	5	4.8

Key   1-Very poor 2-Poor 3-Good 4-Very good 5-Excellent

I also asked the 5 people three other questions

Question 1 How could the product be improved?
Question 2 Would you buy my product?

Two people said my product could be improved. Person 1 said "To add more cheese to add flavour". Person 2 said "Make smaller so can be used for a packed lunch".

4 people said they would buy my product. Person 2 said "I would consider buying your product if more products were in a pack".

Evaluation against the product specification

My product specification states that my product had to be suitable for adults. I have met this point by making my product a simple square shape instead of a fancy shape that would attract children. Three out of the five testers that I asked gave this point 5 out of 5 but two people gave this point 4 out of 5. This gave me an average of 4.6, this shows that I can still improve my product further. Meaty was the next point on my specification, I have met this point by adding sausage meat and bacon to the filling. When I tested this product with my target audience I found that four out of the five testers said that it was excellent and one person gave it very good.
My product specification indicated that my product must be of a square shape. I have met this point on my specification completely as I used a square template to make the product and all of my testers gave my jalousie five out of five.
Tasty is the next point on my specification. I attempted to make it tasty by adding sausage, bacon, 2 different cheeses and a carrot to the filling. I met this point of my specification because four out of the five testers gave the jalousies five out of five. One tester gave this product four out of five so this tester thinks that this can be improved if I was to make this product again.
Attractive was the next point on my specification again four of the testers from my target audience said that this was excellent, but one person gave it very good. To make my product attractive I made sure that they were all the same size and I glazed the pastry with egg before I cooked it so that it turned golden brown after it was cooked. Even though one person said that this point could be improved a little I would not need to improve this aspect of the product because the majority of people are happy with the attractiveness of the product.
My product had to have a crisp texture, I feel that I have met this point because I cooked the product until it was golden brown, I made sure that my product did not burn. I did not test this point with my testers as I felt that I had already met this point of my specification.
Each Jalousie had to be suitable for one person, again I did not test this point with my testers because I feel that each person is different so it would not be an accurate result, but I do feel I have achieved this point as they can be sold as individual portions.
The next point on my specification is that the jalousies had to be able to be reheated if the buyer wanted the jalousie as a warm snack or as part of a meal. After reheating in the oven they were still found to be of a very good standard so reheating did not change the flavour, texture or finish of the Jalousie.
The final point in my specification was for the product to cost £3.40. I asked my testers if they thought £3.40 was a fair price for 4 jalousies, 4 testers said yes and I said they were unsure about this.

Improvements

I found that 3 out of the 5 people I asked did not think that my products could be improved, however as 2 people thought that it could be improved I would have to take this into account if I was making this product again. One person suggested adding more cheese to add more flavour another suggested making them smaller so they could be used in a packed lunch.
Of the 5 people I asked if they would buy the product 4 people said they would and 1 person said that they would consider buying them if there were more jalousies in the pack. This was the same tester who suggested that the jalousies should be smaller.

Suitable for adults might be another area for improvement as this point only scored full marks from 3 testers. As people enjoy different flavours I could perhaps consider having a range of fillings in the Jalousies. This would give a selection for each adult to choose from. The cost could be reduced by using a cheaper cheese rather than Danish Blue or by putting slightly less filling in the jalousies as one of my testers was unsure about the price. I would need to experiment with these ideas though because changing the filling might alter the final product in terms of flavour.

Figure 14.10 Testing and evaluating the final product

Figure 14.10 shows how one student has evaluated her final pastry product and the comments given by an examiner.

Examiner's Comments

Good Points:

- Five tasters have tested the final product. A tasting chart is evident.

- The student has evaluated against her product specification in detail and has given evidence from her testers to give conclusions

- The evaluation does show evidence of a critical analysis as she has recognised some weakness in her work.

Areas for Improvement:

- The student has not evaluated against all points in her product specification. Points omitted are:

  - 10cm by 10cm in size.
  - Sold and stored chilled.

- Able to be eaten hot or cold as a snack or part of a meal, if this product is part of a meal it

- Could be served with potatoes and vegetables.

- Assembled by using a square of flaky pastry filled with a mixture of sausage meat.

- Chopped bacon, grated carrots and two cheeses. Covered with another layer of flaky pastry and then sealed.

- Finished with two slits in the top of each Jalousie with the edges knocked up.

- The student has not mentioned her design brief.

CHAPTER 15

UNIT A524 – TECHNICAL ASPECTS OF DESIGNING AND MAKING

The unit A524 examination is a 1 hour 15 minutes examination worth 20 per cent of your GCSE marks. It is externally marked.

The paper consists of five questions that focus on the technical aspects of designing and making in food technology.

Section A
Section A consists of three questions based on aspects of working with ingredients, tools and equipment.

Section B
Section B has two questions on the design of food products with particular emphasis on sustainability and how products meet people's needs. One of these questions will be design based.

The questions are each worth 12 marks, giving a total of 60 marks. Each question starts with easy parts and they get progressively more difficult. One of the questions will be marked with an asterisk (*). In this question the 'quality of your written communication' will also be assessed.

▌ Introduction to the Unit A524 assessment

How can I achieve my best in the Unit A524 examination?

Examination success depends on a variety of factors:

- Your folder/book throughout the whole course should be kept in an organised way so that you can use it for revision. This includes all notes, handouts, research, tests and homework. Use section dividers and use the chapters from the book as a guideline. Make sure that you know the key points from each topic that you study. You could keep a separate notebook for revision and list the key points throughout the course.

- Revision is very important. There are many ways that you can make this more interesting. There are some suggestions in this chapter.

- Take every opportunity to practise examination papers. This will develop your examination technique.

- Make sure that you understand the words that are used in examination papers.

Figure 15.1 Make revision notes as you go along

How can I remember the key facts?

After you have covered a topic in lessons make a summary of the facts. A useful way of doing this is to a make a few points under the following headings:

Topic.................

Points I MUST KNOW	(*2–3 Vital facts that are really important*)
Points I SHOULD KNOW	(*4–5 additional pieces of key information*)
Points I COULD KNOW	(*extra information to help your understanding*)

Example of must/should/could notes on dietary fibre

Key facts I must know

- Dietary fibre is found mainly in cereal foods, beans, lentils, fruit and vegetables.

- Dietary fibre can not be broken down by human digestive enzymes.
- Dietary fibre helps to prevent constipation and lower blood cholesterol and glucose levels.

Facts I should know

- In the UK most people do not eat enough fibre (the average intake is 12 g per day). The recommended intake for adults is currently 18 g per day.
- A low fibre intake is associated with constipation and some gut diseases such as diverticulitis and bowel cancer.
- Foods and food products that contain 6 g fibre per 100 g or 100 ml may be labelled as a 'high-fibre' food.

Facts I could know

- There are two types of fibre: insoluble and soluble.
- Soluble fibre is found in oats, fruit, vegetables and pulses (beans, lentils and chickpeas).
- Insoluble fibre is found in wholegrain cereals and wholemeal bread.

▶ Revision techniques

Charts

A simple method is to put your facts into charts. It is much easier to remember visual information.

The Nutrients chart shown here as Table 15.1 would be a good way of recording your information in the first place.

Brace maps

On a brace map you can record key information. (See Figure 15.2)

ACTIVITY

Use a brace map to record a revision guide to a topic. You could work in groups and choose a topic such as preservation. Each one of you could cover a different aspect and then you could share your results.

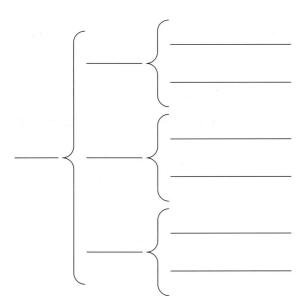

Figure 15.2 Brace map for revision

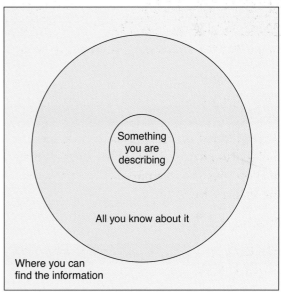

Figure 15.3 Circle map

Circle maps

Write the topic in the middle and then put all the information you know around the outside. Some candidates find it more useful to put the very important points at 12 o'clock, 3 o'clock, 6 o'clock and 9 o'clock, and then fill in the rest.

This is sometimes a good way of planning exam answers as well!

ACTIVITY

Use a circle map to write a revision of special dietary needs.

Bubble map

Some topics have information that is all important. In this case a bubble map is useful.

Name	Function	Source	Deficiency
Carbohydrates:			
Starch	Energy. Extra is stored as fat.	Cereals (wheat and rice), root vegetables (potatoes), Pulses (peas, beans, lentils) Nuts	Lack of energy.
Sugar	Energy but not essential.	Sweet fruit, honey, sugar, treacle	
Dietary fibre	Helps to pass faeces easily.	Fruit, vegetables or wholegrain cereals.	Constipation, haemorrhoids (piles), diverticulosis
Protein:			
Many different types e.g. • **Gluten** • **Collagen** • **Albumin**	Growth and repair.	Animal – High Biological Value (HBV) e.g. meat. Plant foods – Low Biological Value (LBV) e.g. cereal, pulses	Body tissue repair affected. Stunted growth.
Fats:			
Vegetable Fats (oils) **Animal Fats**	Energy Protection of organs Warmth Provides fat-soluble vitamins A, D, E and K and essential fatty acids (EFAs)	Seeds (sunflower), Olives, Soya Bean, Nuts Lard, Butter, Cheese, Cream, Oily Fish (salmon)	Reduced energy intake can lead to weight loss. Vitamin deficiency problems
Vitamins:			
A (retinol / carotene)	Aids night vision. Forms cells of the skin and internal linings of the body.	**Retinol**: Liver, eggs, butter, fish oils **Carotene**: yellow and orange fruits or veg e.g. carrots, tomatoes, mangoes	Dry skin. Impaired vision and in severe cases blindness.
D (calciferol)	Aids the absorption of calcium to ensure strong teeth and bones.	Margarine and low fat spreads (fortified), fatty fish, eggs. Produced under skin by the action of sunlight.	Can cause rickets (bow-legs).

Table 15.1 The Nutrients chart

Name	Function	Source	Deficiency
B (thiamin, niacin, riboflavin)	Release energy.	Cereals, wheatgerm, yeast, meat, fish, eggs, dairy products, pulses.	Beri beri, sore or cracked lips, pellagra
Folic acid	Correct formation of foetus in pregnant women to prevent spina bifida.	Green veg, sprouts and potatoes.	Anaemia. May lead to spinabifida in the unborn. Required to form red blood cells.
C (ascorbic acid)	Helps absorb iron. Protects against infection. Formation of connective tissue.	Citrus fruits e.g. oranges, lemons. Strawberries, blackcurrants, tomatoes, green veg, red and green peppers.	Slow healing wounds. Poor skin condition. Scurvy.
Minerals:			
Iron	Helps transport oxygen. Is an important part of haemoglobin (the oxygen carrying molecule in red blood cells).	Liver, kidney, corned beef, cocoa, plain chocolate, watercress, white bread, curry powder, dried fruits and pulses.	Anaemia.
Calcium	Gives hardness and strength to bones and teeth.	Milk, cheese, white bread (fortified), bones of canned fish e.g. salmon. Can also be found in hard water and green vegetables.	Osteoporosis (bone weakness). Children's teeth do not form correctly.
Sodium (salt)	Maintains extra-cellular fluids in the body.	Found naturally in most fish. Added to most manufactured foods.	Muscle cramp.
Fluoride	Combines with tooth enamel to protect teeth.	Fluoride may be added to water in some places and to toothpaste.	Can lead to tooth decay / dental caries.
Phosphorus	Aids the formation of bones and teeth.	Cereal products, nuts, meat, bananas and fish.	Unknown in most humans.
Water:			
Water	Blood and for all body secretions digestive juices. Assist in the removal of waste and regulates body temperature	Drinks Moist foods	Dehydration No one can survive for more than a few days without water.

Table 15.1 continued

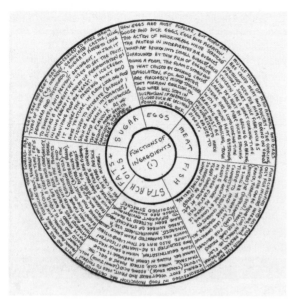

Figure 15.4 A student's revision of functions of ingredients

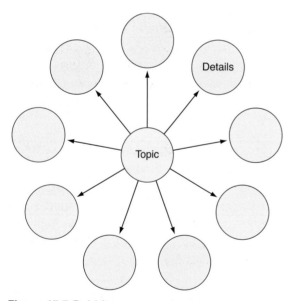

Figure 15.5 Bubble map

ACTIVITY

Use a bubble map to do revision notes on food contamination.

▶ Understanding the terms used on an examination paper

The language that is used in an examination paper is very important and many candidates lose valuable marks because they have not done what they were asked to do.

State

This is a simple instruction and will be worth only 1 mark. It is the very rare occasion where a one-word answer may be accepted but it depends on the question.

Example:

1. State the name of the equipment that is used in the food industry to check the temperature of chilled foods.
   Answer:
   Food probe   (1 mark)

2. State four control checks when preparing and cooking bread.
   Answer:
   Weighing the ingredients
     accurately   (1 mark)
   Checking the temperature of the
     water   (1 mark)
   Dividing the dough into even
     pieces   (1 mark)
   Hot enough oven, gas mark 7   (1 mark)

You can see from this that to get the marks you need to make a full statement because you cannot give a control check in one word.

Reasons

The question requiring reasons usually start with the word 'give' or 'state'. On early parts in the question it is often a one-sentence answer. As you progress through the question you should justify and give examples for what you are saying.

Example:

1. Give two reasons why cereal bars have become more popular.
   Answer:
   They are a quick replacement for breakfast. (1 mark) Children like them because they are made from their favourite cereals. (1 mark)

Give

Give is used as an introduction to a question usually with a 'reason' or a 'way'.

Example:

1. Give two ways manufacturers consider environmental issues when designing and making packaging.
   Answer:
   By reducing the amount of packaging that they use on their products. (1 mark) They could use paper or card for packaging that has come from sustainable forests. (1 mark)

Examples

If you are asked to give more than one example in an answer they need to be different.

A poor example of this is:

1. Give two ways that a manufacturer could promote their product.
   On television   (1 mark)
   Adverts   (0 marks)
   These are both the same so can get only 1 mark.
   A correct answer for the second example would have been:
   Giving away taster samples in a supermarket. (1 mark)

Another poor example is:

2. Give two ways that dried fruit could be used to reduce the sugar in a recipe.
   Cakes   (0 marks)
   Biscuits   (0 marks)
   This answer is not specific enough and therefore does not get any marks.
   Correct answer would have been:
   You could put sultanas with apple in a crumble.   (1 mark)
   Dried apricots could sweeten cereal bars.   (1 mark)

Explain

This must be a full sentence that includes a *reason* or *justification* and an *example* if it helps.

Example

1. Computers are often used in batch production.
   Explain how computer aided design (CAD) can improve the quality of the packaging.
   An answer worth 2 marks would be:
   Attractive labelling can be produced (1 mark) therefore helping to sell the product. (1 mark)

2. Explain two nutritional benefits of eating a variety of fruits and vegetables each day.
   An answer worth 2 marks would be:
   Fruits and vegetables do not contain any fat (1 mark), therefore if people eat more fruit and vegetables this will help reduce their fat intake. (1 mark)
   An alternative response would be:
   Fruits and vegetables contain vitamin C (1 mark) which protects the body against infection (1 mark) and prevents scurvy.

Function

This is asking you to explain the function (job) that a ingredient or tool performs. It is a more difficult part of a question and therefore needs a detailed answer.

Example

1. Manufacturers often add preservatives and emulsifiers to products.
   Explain one function of preservatives and one function of emulsifiers in food products.
   Answer:
   Preservatives – they help to keep food safe for a longer shelf life (1 mark) *because they protect the food against the growth of micro organisms.* (1 mark) *Emulsifiers – are used to help substances that contain oil and water mix together.* (1 mark) *These would normally separate, for example mayonnaise.* (1 mark)

Evaluate

You should write from two points of view, for example the consumer and the manufacturer or the supermarket and the manufacturer. You will have had experience in evaluating in other parts of the course and need to remember these skills when completing exam questions. You could use the Double Bubble map shown in Figure 15.6 to practise answering evaluate questions.

Answers should be well organised and clearly presented. Example:
A 14-year-old boy's packed lunch consisted of:

    Cheese sandwiches on white bread
    Packet of crisps
    Chocolate Bar
    Apple
    Can of Coke

Evaluate the packed lunch.
Answer:

Good points
Cheese contains calcium and protein although it is high in fat.

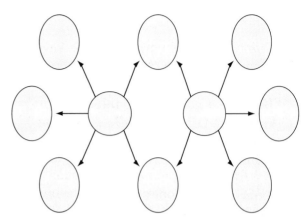

Figure 15.6 Double Bubble map for evaluation and disadvantage/advantage questions

White bread contains some fibre but there would have been more if it had been wholemeal bread.
The apple is providing some vitamin C and some fibre.

Poor points
Lunch is high in fat from crisps and chocolate bar.
It is high in salt from the crisps.
High sugar content due to the chocolate bar and the Coke.
Low in fibre apart from the apple.

Conclusion
Remove the crisps and replace with an unsalted snack or vegetable such as salad.
Change white bread for wholemeal.
Replace Coke with fruit juice or water.
Do not include the chocolate bar or replace with a fruit-based cake (muffins).

A candidate will gain high marks in this question if they have recognised most of the healthy eating issues and have made sound comments to improve the menu.

Specification

In an exam paper you should not be writing detailed sentences when responding to a specification question. However, you cannot write a specification with single words. You need to be specific and exact, not vague and general.

You have written both a design specification in Unit A521 and a product specification in Unit A523 of your controlled assessments. You will not be awarded a mark for repeating what is in the design brief. For example, if your brief was to 'Design and make a snack product for a teenager', no marks would be awarded for stating:

- Must appeal to teenagers

- Must be a snack.

You must think about the needs of a teenager. So you could include:

- Must be hand-held size

- Must be able to be eaten 'on the go'

- Must contribute to 5 a day

- Must be able to be eaten without cutlery

- Must be low in fat/low in salt.

QUESTIONS

Give four specification points for the following design briefs:

1. a cereal bar for primary-aged children

2. a meal for one for the elderly

3. a cake suitable for 8 year olds

4. a lunch pot salad suitable for office workers.

Benefits and limitations

This is similar to advantages and disadvantages. You need to make sure you do not just say opposites.

Example:

1. Give two benefits to a manufacturer of using repetitive flow production.
   Efficient and faster than other methods. (1 mark)
   Produces high-quality products. (1 mark)
2. Give two limitations to a manufacturer of using repetitive flow production.
   It is initially expensive to set up. (1 mark)
   If it breaks down all the production stops. (1 mark)
   This candidate has given four different points for 4 marks.

ACTIVITY

List the benefits and limitations of:

Freezing
Chilling
Drying
Canning
Using pre-manufactured components
Buying local produce

Describe

If you were in an English examination and you were asked to describe you would plan and carefully think out what you were going to write. Too often candidates put one- or two-word answers for a describe question.

Example:

1. Describe how freezing increases the shelf life of vegetables. [2]

Possible answers could include:

Cold temperature slows down the speed at which bacteria multiply but does not destroy the bacteria. (1 mark)

Bacteria need warmth to multiply. A freezer does not provide warmth. (1 mark)

Water becomes unavailable for the bacteria to reproduce as it forms ice crystals. (1 mark)

Chemical changes in the food are slowed down because of the cold temperature. (1 mark)

Candidates did not get any marks for saying: stops vegetables going off!

Discuss

When you are asked to 'discuss', you must give well-reasoned points and explanations, adding examples will often help to show the examiner what you are thinking.

One-word answers are not acceptable. Look at the number of marks awarded to identify how much to write.

You need to practise these types of questions and these are the most difficult.

There are usually 6 marks for this part of the question. You need to include about three points, explain them and use examples to show that you understand.

Table 15.2 is a good grid to practise with.

Example:

There has been increasing publicity about the health of the UK population.

Food manufacturers often respond to nutritional guidance and current trends. Discuss how food manufacturers have responded to this publicity.

There would be 6 marks available for this type of question. It would have an asterisk(*) next to it to show that it will be marked for the quality of written communication. This is called banded marking. The answer grid for this question is shown in Table 15.3.

 QUESTIONS

1. Discuss the implications of Health and Safety legislation to both the manufacturer and the consumer. (6 marks)

2. Discuss the implications to the consumer of buying cook-chill products. (6 marks)

3. Discuss the implications of the use of additives in food products. (6 marks)

Statement	Explanation/discussion	Example if possible

Table 15.2 Practice grid

Discussion points	Explanation	Example/Evidence
Adapting of traditional foods to comply with current nutritional thinking	Reduction of fats, salt, sugars in foods for health reasons	Health reasons clearly linked to the reduction, e.g. fat and links to obesity/ heart disease, sugar linked to obesity/issues with teeth Salt linked to high blood pressures/heart disease
Production of foods which are linked to healthier options	Consumer preference has led to a demand for these products	Targeted at certain groups of people, e.g. weight watchers, children's lunch boxes
Clearer nutritional labelling	So consumers can make informed choices easily Some supermarkets think this is confusing Not all supermarkets are using the same methods	Information clearly shown on the front of products – as % of RDA, how many portions of fruit and veg it contributes to May use a traffic light system – red consume in moderation, green good for you
Products developed in relation to 'new' diets	Products developed to complement the latest trends – this may be linked to general nutrition or specific diets	GI index – indicated on the front of packets
Increased amount of organic foods available	People are choosing to purchase these foods because they feel they are better for them	Not used fertilisers on them, free from genetic modification

Table 15.3 Table used by examiners for discussion answer

Answering design questions

You will have to answer a design-based question within the examination so will need to practise your design work. The most important part of a design question is explaining how you have met the design specification. Lots of candidates leave it to the examiner to work it out for themselves and so they get very few marks.
Example:
A manufacturer wants to develop a new pastry product. The design specification is shown in Figure 15.7.

Use sketches and notes to design a product which will meet the design need.

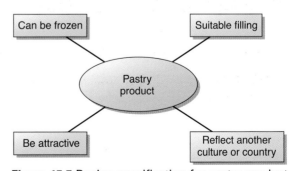

Figure 15.7 Design specification for pastry product

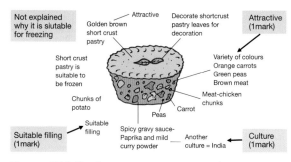

Figure 15.8 Student response to question

Your drawing should be clear and precise and the annotation should explain how the design meets the specification.

 QUESTIONS

Produce designs to meet the following specifications:

1. Dessert – layered/high fibre/low sugar/variety of textures. [4]

2. Pasta product – appeal to children/economical/contribute to 5 a day/low fat [4]

3. Casserole product – luxury/filling/have a rich sauce/source of iron [4]

How can I achieve my best in the examination?

Many candidates do not achieve their best in the examination for a variety of reasons, even though they know the correct answers.
Here are a few guidelines to help you get those valuable marks:

- Read the instructions on the front of the paper.

- Read each question carefully and highlight the key parts of each question. Lots of candidates answer what they think the question is about instead of the actual question.

For example, on a question about hygiene when taste testing food, many candidates just put hygiene rules. Nothing to do with tasting!

- Look to see how many marks are allocated to the parts of the question.

- It is rare to have a question that requires a one word answer. The examiner will have allowed the number of lines they think is needed for you to answer the question to gain the marks.

- Make sure you give an answer to the question and not just reword the question.

A good example of this is:

How can you improve the colour?

Answer:

Use different colours. (0 marks)

How can you improve the flavour?

Answer:

Use different flavours. (0 marks)

Correct answer would be:

Improve the colour by adding chopped green peppers and yellow sweetcorn.

Improve the flavour by adding mixed herbs.

- There is a list of frequently used words in answers that will not get you any marks because they are not qualified or explained. Examples of these are: Healthier; quicker; longer; faster; because it's healthy; cheaper; easier

- Finally when you have completed your examination you must always read and check your answers. Check to see where you think the examiner is going to be able to award marks to you. If you cannot see a correct answer then the examiner certainly will not!

INDEX

Entries for illustrations (figures and tables) are in italics, e.g. *8*. Entries for essential information (key points and key terms) are in bold, e.g. **30**